Internet Policy and Economics

Second Edition

William H. Lehr • Lorenzo Maria Pupillo
Editors

Internet Policy and Economics

Challenges and Perspectives

Second Edition

Springer

Editors
William H. Lehr
Massachusetts Institute of Technology
Cambridge, MA
USA

Lorenzo Maria Pupillo
Telecom Italia
Rome
Italy
and
CITI
Columbia University
New York, NY
USA

ISBN 978-1-4419-0037-1 e-ISBN 978-1-4419-0038-8
DOI 10.1007/978-1-4419-0038-8
Springer Dordrecht Heidelberg London New York

Library of Congress Control Number: 2009926041

The first edition of this book was published as *Cyber Policy and Economics in an Internet Age*, Copyright © 2002 by Kluwer Academic Publishers

Printed on acid-free paper

Springer is part of Springer Science+Business Media (www.springer.com)

Contents

Part I
Introduction

Chapter 1
Internet Policy: A Mix of Old and New Challenges

William H. Lehr and Lorenzo Maria Pupillo

Introduction

The Internet is now widely regarded as essential infrastructure for our global economy and society. It is in our homes and businesses. We use it to communicate and socialize, for research, and as a platform for E-commerce. In the late 1990s, much was predicted about what the Internet has become at present; but now, we have actual experience living with the Internet as a critical component of our everyday lives. Although the Internet has already had profound effects, there is much we have yet to realize.

The present volume represents a third installment in a collaborative effort to highlight the all-encompassing, multidisciplinary implications of the Internet for public policy. The first installment was conceived in 1998, when we initiated plans to organize an international conference among academic, industry, and government officials to discuss the growing policy agenda posed by the Internet. The conference was hosted by the European Commission in Brussels in 1999 and brought together a diverse mix of perspectives on what the pressing policy issues would be confronting the Internet. All of the concerns identified remain with us today, including how to address the Digital Divide, how to modify intellectual property laws to accommodate the new realities of the Internet, what to do about Internet governance and name-space management, and how to evolve broadcast and telecommunications regulatory frameworks for a converged world.

Participants at the conference were enthusiastic and also somewhat daunted by the range and breadth of policy concerns impacted. Not only was the Internet going to force the wholesale reform of communications policy, it was also going to impact consumer protection, business, tax, and international trade policies. To help raise awareness of the scope of issues for a wider audience than those lucky enough to attend the conference in Brussels, we decided to prepare a volume of Internet policy essays that would capture the diversity of challenges confronting the Internet future. The second installment in this collaborative effort was the volume of essays,

---

W.H. Lehr (✉) and L.M. Pupillo
Research Associate, Computer Science and Artificial Intelligence Laboratory (CSAIL), Massachusetts Institute of Technology, Cambridge, MA, USA
e-mail: wlehr@mit.edu

W.H. Lehr and L.M. Pupillo (eds.), *Internet Policy and Economics*,
DOI 10.1007/978-1-4419-0038-8_1,

entitled *Cyberpolicy and Economics in an Internet Age* (Kluwer, 2002). The authors were all leading scholars or industry/government policymakers renowned for their path-breaking work in Internet economics and policy studies, representing a diverse array of backgrounds from law to economics, from communication studies to engineering. The contributions were, for the most part, specially prepared for inclusion in the volume with the idea that they should provide a sophisticated, yet accessible, view into an important current Internet policy question.

Since the previous book was completed, a lot has changed. The tragedy of 9/11 has heightened concerns about global terrorism and national security. The Internet has been used by terrorists to plot and publicize their acts, whereas security officials have used it to track and monitor threats. E-commerce, E-Government, and Internet penetration have all continued to expand, whereas the population of experienced Internet users has continued to mature with additional years of usage behind them.

The Internet itself has changed substantially also. It is now a broadband Internet with the majority of users in many countries accessing the Internet over always-on, multimegabit per second bandwidth pipes. Broadband access makes it feasible to deliver much richer multimedia experiences. The transition to Web 2.0 facilitates more interactive web services. The upgrading of mobile networks to 3G services and WiFi becoming increasingly commonplace are helping to make the Internet mobile, further increasing its ubiquity. The beginning transition to post-PC devices such as tablets, smart phones, GPS navigators, and robot toys herald a new range of Internet-enabled appliances.

These expanded capabilities have allowed us to benefit from further enhancements in Internet-based services and have encouraged us to become even more dependent on the Internet in our everyday lives. These improvements have helped social networking, virtual reality, and multiplayer gaming takeoff.

At the same time, new challenges have emerged. Distributed-Denial-of-Service, SPAM, and malware of many sorts have shown how the same openness that has helped the Internet grow can also be an Achille's Heel that shows its vulnerability. The growth of cybercrime, identity theft, and assaults on personal privacy have also become more common and loom larger. We also see new policy language being used to reframe old questions as we consider whether universal service ought to apply to broadband and once again examine open access regulation in the guise of net neutrality rules for the Internet or NextGeneration network regulation for fiber-to-the-home infrastructure.

In collecting the 12 essays for the present volume, in recognition of how much has changed and how much as stayed the same, we are reprinting several of the papers from the 2002 book that remain current,[1] are offering updates or new papers from scholars who were involved in the earlier efforts,[2] as well as new papers from several scholars who are new to this project.[3]

The essays have been grouped thematically into four parts. The first on Policy Challenges examines some of the key issues confronting communication policy-makers in the converged world. The second on the Development Challenge focuses on perspectives toward the Internet from the developing world. The third on the Privacy Challenge looks at the implications of the Internet for personal privacy. The fourth and final part focuses on Economic Challenges posed by the Internet.

In the following sections, we briefly review the essays included in this volume.

The Policy Challenge

In "Regulating Telecoms in Europe: Present and Future," Professor Cave, an economist, provides a summary and review of the European regulatory framework for communication services that was adopted in 2003. Professor Cave finds many admirable characteristics in the new framework, noting its firm grounding in competition analysis and law, and recognition of the industry convergence that has resulted from technical innovations and market growth. Such convergence points to the challenges of legacy silo-based regulatory frameworks and the need to move toward more symmetric treatment or "technically neutral" regulation of access platforms. The outcome of this is a three-step process: market definition, market power assessment, and remedies. A market must first be shown to be subject to significant market power before becoming eligible for the imposition of ex ante regulatory interventions. Thus, the system defaults to the standard of competition law.

The European Commission initially defined 18 markets in the first step. National regulatory authorities, acting under the directives, then began inquiries into whether there is significant market power in each of the markets. The genius of this approach is that it provided a trajectory to help manage national regulatory authorities toward a common, converged vision of more liberalized and integrated European communication services markets.

While Professor Cave generally approves of the framework and the direction of European communication policy, he also notes some of the weaknesses that have become apparent in the years since the new regime was adopted. These do not challenge the basic structure of the framework, but rather the difficulties of implementation and transitioning to a new model in a more integrated European community. First, the regulatory process for determining whether there is significant market power have been overly prolonged and costly, and second, have seldom delivered the hoped for benefit of further market liberalization. National regulatory agencies have too seldom taken advantage of the European framework to reduce regulatory barriers to competition. Professor Cave challenges policymakers to adopt more focused remedies that are explicitly designed to promote competition, and with its success, further deregulation. He notes with approval the 2007 revision to the framework, reducing the number of markets to be examined for market power (and hence to be considered candidates for ex ante controls).

In the next contribution in this part, "Infrastructure Commons in Economic Perspective," Professor Frischmann, a legal scholar, examines the net neutrality debate from the perspective of a commons. He notes that the Internet is increasingly viewed as basic critical infrastructure and considers what this means for our economy and society.

As basic infrastructure, the Internet supports the production and consumption of both market and nonmarket goods. These latter include social and public goods, the provision of which is difficult to support in a market economy. Professor Frischmann concludes that open access regulations may represent a political fix to the difficult challenge of supporting via subsidies or otherwise the creation of social and public goods that otherwise might be underprovided by unregulated markets.

Professor Frischmann notes that to properly engage these questions, it is necessary to broaden the discussion of net neutrality to consider the larger economic context of the Internet as a "mixed commercial, public, and social infrastructure." Most of the prior discussion of this issue has focused too narrowly on the regulatory economics of last-mile broadband access carriers. When viewed more appropriately as basic infrastructure, there is much more support for a strong government role than if the Internet is viewed simply as just another market that may suffer from competitive deficiencies in need of regulatory remediation. Moreover, when viewed as an infrastructure "commons," there is a strong tradition of open access regulation. Professor Frischmann makes the case for why the Internet should be viewed as commons infrastructure that is especially important in the creation of nonmarket social and public goods.

In the final contribution, "Dumbing Down the Net: A Further Look at Net Neutrality," Professors Jamison and Hauge, two economists, examine the net neutrality debate regarding the need for new regulatory controls to limit the ability of broadband access providers to offer quality-differentiated services for different uses, users, and content accessed via their networks. On one side of the debate, those supporting strong net neutrality controls argue that last-mile broadband access services are basic infrastructure and it is inappropriate for such services to offer discriminatory services. The pro-net neutrality advocates argue that additional controls are needed to protect innovation and content diversity at the edge (e.g., by content providers and end-users), and to protect against access providers trying to leverage any market power they may have in an effort to capture additional profits from content providers or end-users. On the other side of the debate, are those who believe that the offering of discriminatory services (basic and higher priced/higher quality premium services) are a welfare enhancing and commonly employed practice in many robustly competitive industry contexts. In summarizing the debate, the authors comment on the lack of rigorous analysis in much of the debate thus far. Their paper seeks to address this gap by presenting the results of a theoretical model that explicitly examines the decision by an access provider to offer premium services. As their title suggests, the authors' results are more supportive of those who oppose new net neutrality regulations. Their model shows why it is reasonable to expect the offering of premium services to be welfare enhancing: to be consistent with increased edge-innovation (content diversity), lower prices overall, and competition.

The chapter is noteworthy in its attempt to move beyond rhetoric toward the use of basic economic theory and formal modeling to sharpen the discussion of this important issue. As they note in citing the prevalence of premium offerings in many market contexts unrelated to the Internet, the fact that premium services are consistent with welfare enhancements is hardly surprising. While their analyses is not beyond critique and alternative theoretical presentations (with different results) are certainly feasible, Jamison and Hauge have raised the standard for those who would argue in favor of strong net neutrality regulations, putting them on notice to provide a sounder foundation for assertions that differentiated broadband services need to be limited by regulation.

The Development Challenge

In the first contribution in this part, "Three Digital Divides," Professor Noam, an economist and lawyer, discusses the current debate over the digital divide and cautions policymakers against focusing too narrowly on connectivity. Professor Noam reminds us that the real issue will not be whether everyone has access to the Internet but rather how the benefits of such access are distributed across and within the populations of nations. While assuring universal Internet access poses a more complex and, perhaps, more difficult problem to solve than assuring universal telephone access, the most difficult divide to close is likely to be the E-commerce gap. The connectivity delivered by resolving the challenges of assuring global universal access to telephones and the Internet – the first two divides – will likely exacerbate the E-commerce gap separating rich and poor, North and South. This is because the underlying economics will likely favor scale and scope economies and first-mover advantages for the more technically advanced rich nations of the North. One likely response to a widening E-commerce gap will be a reaction against the free trade policies that have played such a strong role in promoting economic growth over the last several decades. Professor Noam points to the legacy of Spain and Portugal in the sixteenth and seventeenth centuries as a cautionary tale. They grew wealthy and powerful on the basis of leadership in the arts and techniques of seafaring trade, but then the forces of reaction blocked the adoption of the next generation of technology and global economic leadership was ceded to the industrial north. To help avert the anticipated reaction to a widening E-commerce divide, Professor Noam recommends a number of proactive policies that might be adopted by Internet-developing countries to assure that the information highways that are created offer two-way opportunities for growth.

In the second essay entitled "IPR and the Developing World," Dr. Pupillo examines the challenge of Intellectual Property Rights (IPR) management (e.g., copyrights) in light of the growth of the Internet from the perspective of developing economies. He notes the importance of such rules for the international flow of digital media content and commerce. Internet technologies create new opportunities for markets and services and pose new challenges for digital rights management. This suggests the need for reforming IPR rules and frameworks, and business models to take account of such changes. Dr. Pupillo suggests a more flexible approach toward a copyright that is needed to appropriately support the new opportunities, especially emerging markets in developing countries. Historically, developing countries have adopted copyright frameworks based on their cultural heritage/relationship with more developed markets.

Dr. Pupillo notes the conflicting needs of developing countries to support strong copyright protection to support content creation and commerce, while seeking weaker copyright protection to facilitate closing the Digital Divide.

Dr. Pupillo provides a useful overview of the many IPR issues that confront global policymakers. In addition to copyright policy, these include specialized initiatives to address such issues as database protection, computer software, patentability of business models, and reverse engineering. The policy space here is rich and complex, and how these various policies are resolved will have important implications for our global Information economy and the evolution of E-commerce on the Internet.

The Privacy Challenge

The first essay by Professor Varian "Economic Aspects of Personal Privacy" provides an elegant economic framework for considering the privacy issue. Considering privacy as an economic good over which we can assign property rights provides a basis for evaluating conflicting privacy claims. Firms need to know a lot about an individual in order to provide the individual with customized service. Individuals who want such customized service may also want the firm to have the information. In most cases, the mere possession of information (what is collected) is not in itself a problem, rather the problem arises through the potential misuse of information. Therefore, it may make more sense to focus on allocating property rights or defining privacy rules in terms of how the information is used instead of whether someone has a right to own the information. If we imagine establishing a property right over the right to use privacy information, we can then use economics to evaluate alternative mechanisms for allocating this right. Whether this right should be assigned to firms or to individuals may depend on the costs of alternative allocation mechanisms (e.g., Who is in a better position to control access? How are enforcement costs affected?). Moreover, we might imagine markets in different types of privacy property rights that could leave everyone better off. Individuals may place quite different valuations on their personal information and many may be quite happy to share their personal information if they are appropriately compensated (e.g., to get free content, you need to register). One point this analysis makes clear is that public policies that focus too narrowly on trying to restrict the collection or limit the possession of personal information are not able to address such complexities and are likely to be inefficient.

In the second and third essays, Professor Strossen, a legal scholar, significantly updates her earlier paper on "Cybercrimes v. Cyberliberties." In the original paper, Professor Strossen expands the discussion beyond privacy to the broader question of civil rights in cyberspace. She focuses on the twofold question of whether rights of free expression may be criminalized in an online world, thereby abrogating basic liberties, and second, whether the need to prosecute criminal actions in the offline world may lead to online rules that will endanger our privacy. In the USA, the

American Civil Liberties Union has been in the forefront of this debate, which has become all the more urgent since the tragic events of 9/11.

In her extensive new introduction to the earlier paper, Professor Strossen reaffirms her earlier comments on the risks to liberty posed by overly aggressive, and too often ineffectual, attempts to regulate the Internet. Notwithstanding the rhetoric and presumed justification for stronger government power and regulation following in the wake of the terrorist attacks of 9/11, Professor Strossen argues that little has changed. Relying on claims of threats to national security to support extraordinary enforcement and surveillance powers that threaten freedom of speech and privacy are nothing new. She argues that safety and freedom are mutually reinforcing, and attacks on freedom in the name of safety have failed to promote safety. For example, policies targeted at limiting access to the Internet to protect children from sexually oriented content have failed to find support in the Courts which recognized such rules as injurious to free speech. Indeed, there exist much better alternatives for protecting children that are compatible with free speech on the Internet. Professor Strossen notes the heavy burden imposed on ISPs by the Patriot Act and the threat to personal privacy, as well as the Act's ineffectiveness in uncovering terrorist plots. Such policies are overly broad, allowing the government to collect too much information on too many innocent people while obscuring information that might be helpful for the few who may constitute a legitimate threat.

The Economic Challenge

In the first essay, the "Implications of Internet Commerce for Fiscal Policy," economics Professor Goolsbee focuses on the impact of E-commerce on tax policy. Traditional fiscal policy is based on geographically defined jurisdictional boundaries. For example, the collection of sales or value-added taxes is often more difficult in cyberspace. In the USA, this has caused a number of policymakers to fear that an important revenue source is being threatened by the emerging cybereconomy. A similar issue arises in Europe, where an even larger share of national tax receipts is derived from value-added taxation than in the USA. In response to this perceived danger, some policymakers have advocated in favor of adopting some form of Internet taxation. Professor Goolsbee recommends against such an approach, arguing that any losses in tax revenues through untaxed E-commerce is likely to be more than offset in the short term by the benefits from encouraging economic growth in the cybereconomy. In the longer term, what will be needed is a more coherent tax treatment for all types of transactions – whether they be online or in cyberspace. The current system of localized taxes is not efficient, and the Internet may provide the impetus for adopting a better and more rational system in the future.

In the second essay, "Spectrum Allocation and the Internet," economics professors Owen and Rosston turn to the important question of how we allocate wireless spectrum. The rise of the Internet was paralleled by the rise of wireless telephone services. Now, these two worlds are merging and the future of the Internet will incorporate the flexibility and mobility inherent in wireless access. Additionally, wireless technologies promise to play an important role in extending ubiquitous access coverage and enhancing competition in the last-mile access networks by which end-users connect to the Net. Additionally, the Internet and its complementary technologies offer myriad new technologies for utilizing spectrum more efficiently. To realize the potential for new wireless services and to take advantage of the emerging technologies, we need to liberalize traditional spectrum management policies. The old regulatory approach of allocating spectrum to specific uses, and then restricting the technologies used to support those uses, needs to be liberalized. The authors recommend adoption of a more flexible framework for allocating spectrum licenses that gives greater latitude to the action of market forces. Adopting such an approach will facilitate the continued growth of the Internet and will enhance economic efficiency and growth.

In the third essay, the "Role of Unlicensed in Spectrum Reform," Dr. Lehr reviews the current debate over the management of the radio frequency spectrum used by all wireless devices. In recent years, a growing number of policymakers have recognized the need to substantially reform the way spectrum is managed to make it more responsive to market forces and friendlier to the technical innovations that have occurred since the legacy framework was put in place almost a century ago. On the one hand, the explosive growth of wireless of all kinds has increased pressure for increased access to spectrum, increasing spectrum scarcity. On the other hand, modern radio system design makes it possible to share spectrum much more intensively, which holds the promise of helping to increase the supply of usable spectrum. Current regulatory frameworks, however, make it difficult to realize this potential by reducing opportunities and incentives to share spectrum more intensively. This is the regulatory "artificial scarcity" that spectrum management reform hopes to alleviate.

While many agree that market-based reform is needed, scholars differ how best to achieve that goal. One school argues that markets would be best realized by moving increasingly toward a private property-like regime in which spectrum licensees were given exclusive flexible usage rights to spectrum that could then be traded via spectrum markets. Another school has argued that spectrum is inherently a shared medium that should be managed more like a commons. One example of this approach is the designation of unlicensed spectrum bands, such as the 2.4 GHz spectrum used by WiFi devices.

Dr. Lehr explains why a mixed regime is valuable, and what the role for unlicensed spectrum is in such a mixed regime framework. Briefly, a mixed regime is needed to promote technical neutrality and a healthy wireless ecosystem. Each regulatory model offers distinct benefits and challenges that imply different industry economics. While practical considerations suggest that the dominant reform model is and should be flexible licensing of commercial spectrum, additional allocations of unlicensed spectrum are also needed to complement this. For example, unlicensed spectrum may serve as a petri dish for innovation in new services and business models, some of which may evolve into services that subsequently migrate to licensed spectrum. And, unlicensed spectrum will serve as a safety valve for users who may be foreclosed from licensed spectrum access, potentially because the promised secondary markets fail to evolve.

In the concluding essay, "P2P, Digital Commodities, and the Governance of Commerce," Dr. Alain Bourdeau de Fontenay and Eric Bourdeau de Fontenay, two economists, focus on the implications for the rise of peer-to-peer (P2P) networking in the Internet. While P2P came to public prominence as a consequence of Napster and the debate over the sharing of copyrighted MP3 music files, P2P has much more profound and deeper implications for the future of our communications infrastructure. The original architecture of the Internet was premised on the concept of an end-to-end network with the key attributes that define a service being located in the end-nodes. This is a distributed, user-centric as opposed to centralized, network-centric perspective on how communication networks ought to be organized and operated. P2P offers a fundamental challenge to how productive activity is organized within and between firms. It facilitates new ways for interacting and collaborating. P2P is reshaping the boundaries between commercial activities and those of informal, ad hoc communities.

In their paper, they focus on the music industry's misguided response to the emergence of P2P file sharing which has focused on the illegality of sharing copyrighted material based on the industry's presumption that P2P and free file sharing explain why CD sales fell. The Court, in siding with the RIAA, has chosen to support incumbent opposition to new technology. The authors point out a number of flaws in the empirical analysis that underlies this generally accepted truism, directing our attention to the deeper questions of how P2P and the other changes that both enabled it and which it enables have helped change music (i.e., more music in more places, more music to access/learn about, sampling). Indeed they argue that such fundamental changes in the character of the markets (wrought by technology, changing tastes, etc.) have changed the whole context and even changed the way the property rights associated with copyright ought to be interpreted. The emergence of new residual rights and stakeholders requires us to reexamine the nature of and the economic justification for copyright.

Conclusion

The essays included here discuss some of the newer policy issues (e.g., Jamison and Hauge's essay on net neutrality, Lehr's essay on unlicensed spectrum) as well as offering new perspectives on problems that have been around for a while (e.g., Pupillo's essay on intellectual property protection policies in the developing world, or Strossen's update to her earlier essay - also included - on the threat to personal privacy posed by government prosecution of cybercrimes). The essays that are reprinted highlight what continue to be major issues for Internet policy (e.g., Varian on the economics of privacy or Goolsbee on Internet taxation). Taken together, this collection of essays demonstrates the breadth of policy concerns raised by the Internet and the need for flexible policy approaches that can adapt as the Internet continues to grow and evolve. While the authors focus on different policy challenges, they agree on the need to clarify the policy environment to sustain a healthy Internet ecosystem into the future.

Notes

1. The chapters by Varian, Goolsbee, Strossen, and Owen and Rosston are reproduced from the earlier 2002 book.
2. The chapters by DeFontenay, Lehr, Noam, Pupillo, and Strossen are new contributions from authors involved in the earlier efforts.
3. The chapters by Cave, Frischmann, and Jamison and Hauge are new contributions from authors who are new to this project.

Part II
Policy Challenge

Chapter 2
Regulating Telecommunications in Europe: Present and Future

Martin Cave

Introduction

This chapter describes and assesses the new regime for regulating electronic communications services, which came into force in Europe in July 2003. The first two sections describe, respectively, the previous regime (the 1998 package) and the new regime. The third section discusses experience of the new system up to the end of 2007,[1] whereas the fourth evaluates its operation and the plans, already in place, to reform it.

Lessons of the 1998 Package

It is useful briefly to describe the 1998 legislative package which liberalized telecommunications markets throughout the European Union. For the 10 years or more before that, a series of green papers, directives, recommendations, and other interventions has imposed obligations on member states with respect to equipment markets, regulatory structures, value-added services, and regulation of infrastructure and service competition where it existed. But in 1998, the obligation was imposed on governments to liberalize entry into their telecommunications markets (except for those few countries for which extensions were granted).

The 1998 framework was inevitably fragmentary, as it developed over time. It also embodied rough-hewn remedies, designed to "take on" the incumbents. Overall it represented a crude but potentially effective toolkit. Liberalization and harmonization directives first had to be transposed into national legislation to take effect in the

M. Cave
Professor and Director of the Centre for Management under
Regulation, Warwick Business School, Coventry, England, UK
e-mail: Martin.Cave@wbs.ac.uk

W.H. Lehr and L.M. Pupillo (eds.), *Internet Policy and Economics*,
DOI 10.1007/978-1-4419-0038-8_2,

member states. The transposition process took nearly 2 years, but the Commission was able to report in October 1999 that it was largely complete. But the directives gave member states considerable latitude in implementation. For example, the Licensing Directive permitted ample variation in the requirements imposed on new entrants, and despite a requirement in the Interconnection Directive that interconnection charges be cost-based, interconnection charges within the EU varied significantly.

Achieving the goals of liberalizing the industry against the (initial) wishes of most incumbent operators and of many member states required substantial regulatory intervention from the Commission. Moreover, the regulatory framework had to be flexible enough to cover member states proceeding at quite different rates. In the early stages of liberalization – the transition to competition – it was necessary to constrain the former monopolists considerably.

For behavioral regulation, three instruments are required in the early stages of liberalization:

- *Control of retail prices*. This is necessary only when the historical operator exercises market power at the retail level and where in the absence of retail price controls, customers will be significantly disadvantaged.
- *Universal service obligation (USO)*. Governments have typically imposed a USO requiring the historical telecommunications monopolist to provide service to all parts of the country at a uniform price, despite the presence of significant cost differences. Firms entering the market without such an obligation have a strong incentive to focus on low-cost, "profitable" customers, putting the USO operator at a disadvantage, or the incumbent uses this as an argument against entry. There are, however, other ways to fulfill a USO, such as tendering for its provision.
- *Control of access prices*. In order to keep all subscribers connected with each other in the presence of competing network, operators require access to one another's networks to complete their customers' calls. This requires a system of interoperator wholesale or network access prices. Especially in the early stages of competition, entrants will require significant access to the dominant incumbent's network, and this relationship will almost inevitably necessitate regulatory intervention. As infrastructure is duplicated (at different rates in different parts of the network), the need for direct price regulation of certain network facilities diminishes. Interconnection was central to the development of competition within the EU, and the Commission has been heavily involved.

The 1997 Interconnection Directive required that charges for interconnection follow the principles of transparency and cost orientation. The first principle implied the publication of a reference interconnection offer. As a corollary, operators with significant market power (SMP) – defined as a 25% market share of a prespecified national market – were required to keep separate accounts for their wholesale or network activity and for other activities, including retailing. Cost orientation turned out to be an excessively vague phrase, permitting excessive interconnection charges. Until adequate cost data were available, the Commission published recommended "best current practice" interconnection charges, based on the average of the member states with the lowest charges. Charges dropped quickly in some countries, but not in all.

This falling trajectory, relative to cost, of access prices in Europe seems to have sustained a "service bias" in European telecommunications regulation. The regime sought to open up all avenues of competition but in practice was more preoccupied with opening existing infrastructures than with encouraging the construction of new ones. Entry of resellers has been vigorous and retail prices dropped fast. This does not seem to have provided medium-term incentives for an extensive deployment of alternative infrastructures. This situation was, of course, aggravated by the collapse in telecoms share prices after early 2001, which eliminated or weakened many alternative carriers. As a result, the new regime came into operation against the background of faltering competition in important parts of the fixed telecommunications market place. Nonetheless, the historic monopolists' market shares in fixed voice calls continued to decline, as shown in Table 2.1.

In relation to fixed broadband, penetration rates varied considerably, averaging 13.0 per 100 population for the EU15 in October 2005, and 11.5% for all 25 member states. Some member states were double that rate. In some countries, fixed broadband was available on both cable and telecommunications DSL infrastructures. On average, incumbent fixed telecommunications operators in 2005 controlled 50% of broadband lines. In Italy, it was 70%; in the UK, it was under 30%.

Competition in mobile markets was (and remains) more equal and more vibrant. As second and successive operators came into the market, prices fell and demand grew, assisted by innovative tariffs involving handset subsidies and prepay. The spread of mobile phones is shown in Table 2.2

Table 2.1 Incumbents' share (%) of fixed call markets in the European Union

	December 2003	December 2004	December 2005
Local calls	75.8	73.2	71.8
Long distance	70.6	69.2	67.0
International	62.9	58.7	56.7

Source: *European Electronic Communications Regulation and Markets 2006* (12th Implementation Report) Staff Working Document Vol 1 [SEC(2007) 403]

Table 2.2 Penetration rate (%) of mobile telephony in EU member states

2004	84.6
2005	95.0
2006	103.2

Source: *European Electronic Communications Regulation and Markets 2006* (12th Implementation Report) Staff Working Document Vol 1 [SEC(2007) 403]

The sector was lightly regulated. The absence of regulation, on balance, was highly beneficial, although the mobile industry's later development may have been affected by high licence fees paid by operators for 3G licences. The new regulatory regime thus came into effect against a background of significant successes in mobile but much more limited competition in fixed services.

The New Regime in Outline

After a tortuous and prolonged legislative process, the new European regulatory framework came into effect in July 2003. It is based on five Directives and on an array of other documentation. At one level, the new regime is a major step down the transition path between monopoly and normal competition, governed exclusively by generic competition law. Its provisions are applied across the range of "electronic communications services," ignoring preconvergence distinctions. It represents an ingenious attempt to corral the National Regulatory Agencies (NRAs) down the path of normalization – allowing them, however, to proceed at their own speed (but within the uniform framework necessary for the internal market). Since the end state is one governed by competition law, the regime moves away from the rather arbitrary and piecemeal approach of the current regulatory package toward something consistent with that law. However, competition law is to be applied (in certain markets) not in a responsive ex post fashion, but in a preemptive ex ante form. But ex ante regulation should only be applied when the so-called "three-criteria test" is fulfilled – the criteria being the presence of barriers to entry, the development of competition, and the absence of a tendency to effective competition.

The new regime therefore relies on a special implementation of the standard competition triple of: *market definition*, identifying *dominance*, and formulating *remedies*.[2] According to the underlying logic, a list of markets where ex ante regulation is permissible is first established, the markets being defined according to normal competition law principles. These markets are analyzed with the aim of identifying dominance (on a forward-looking basis). Where no dominance is found, no remedy can be applied. Where dominance is found, the choice of an appropriate remedy can be made from a specified list. The effect of this is to create a series of market by market "sunset clauses" as the scope of effective competition expands.

Market Definition

In 2003, the Commission issued a recommendation on relevant markets, defined broadly in the manner of competition policy. This identified 18 markets as candidates for ex ante regulation, by virtue of their satisfaction of three-criterion test. The 18 include 6 fixed retail markets, the main fixed voice wholesale markets, such as call origination and termination and interexchange transport, unbundled local loops, and wholesale broadband access (a product on the basis of which a competitor can combine some of its network assets with backhaul and local access provided by the incumbent to offer broadband service). The list also includes three mobile markets – call termination on individual networks, wholesale international roaming (a product which supports the use by mobile subscribers of their handsets when abroad), and the wholesaling of outgoing mobile services, called mobile access and call origination; this captures the product provided by a mobile operator to a mobile virtual network operator (MVNO) bases on its network. NRAs can also add or subtract markets, using specified (and quite complex) procedures.

NRAs, as well as the Commission and European Court of Justice, have undertaken many market definition exercises already, often using the now conventional competition policy approach. This often involves applying, at a conceptual level, the so-called hypothetical monopolist test, under which the analysts seek to identify the smallest set of goods or services with the characteristic that, if a monopolist gained control over them, it would be profitable to raise prices by 5–10% over a period, normally taken to be about a year. The monopolist's ability to force through a price increase obviously depends upon the extent to which consumers can switch away from the good or service in question (demand substitution) and the extent to which firms can quickly adapt their existing productive capacity to enhance supply (supply substitution). A consequence of the reliance of the proposed new regime on ex ante or preemptive regulation is that it is necessary to adopt a forward-looking perspective.

Dominance

The Commission proposed and the legislators accepted the classical "dominance", defined as the ability of a firm to behave to an appreciable effect independently of its customers and competitors, as a threshold for ex ante intervention, though dominance is known as SMP. The dominance can be exercised by a single firm, or collectively, or leveraged into a vertically related market.

Although single-firm dominance has come to be well understood, joint dominance (or tacit collusion) has been one of the more elusive concepts in European competition law. However, what is more noteworthy is the relative lack of candidates for joint dominance in fixed telecommunications markets. This arises because fixed market in Europe is typically effectively competitive or – more frequently – dominated (singly) by the historic monopolist. Joint dominance, however, has been attributed to mobile markets in some countries, where a small number of operators provide services behind effective barriers to entry created by spectrum assignment procedures.

The communications industry, like many industries, consists of a series of activities that can be performed either individually or by vertically integrated firms. There are well-established benign motives for firms to become vertically integrated. In particular, doing so may reduce costs, by eliminating the costs of transactions between two separate firms. It has also been argued that vertical integration by itself does not add additional market power. Thus, if a firm held a monopoly of an activity or process at any stage in an industry, it would be able to extract maximum profit from that monopoly, and would have no desire to engage in other activities, unless it was extremely efficient in performing them.

This simplified approach has now given way to more complex modeling of situations in which a vertically integrated firm may find it advantageous to distort competition downstream as a means of bolstering its upstream market power.[3] This is achieved by a variety of means involving the interaction of particular features of each market. For example, in one market (say, for delivery platforms), there may be consumer switching costs because consumers need to make significant investments in equipment. The second market may exhibit service differentiation. In such circumstances, making the service exclusive to the delivery platform may strengthen consumer lock-in and give the firm an ability to distort competition. To take another example, a dominant firm in the provision of network services for broadband may seek to use that market power to extend its dominance into the retail broadband market, for example, by obstructing competitor's in their efforts to use unbundled local loops rented from the incumbent to provide service to their own retail customers.

Remedies

Under the Directives, NRAs have the power to impose obligations on firms found to enjoy SMP in a relevant market. The NRAs act within a framework of duties set out in Article 8 of the Framework Directive. The measures they take shall be proportionate to the policy objectives identified. This can be construed as meaning that the intervention is appropriate, no more than is necessary, and, by implication, satisfies a cost-benefit test, in the sense that the expected benefits from the intervention exceed the expected costs. Article 8 additionally specifies policy objectives, which determine the weights appropriate for use in the cost-benefit analysis. For example, Article 8(2) requires NRAs to promote competition for electronic communications networks and services by maximizing users' choice and value for money, eliminating distortions or restrictions to competition and encouraging efficient investment and infrastructure. Article 7(4) requires NRAs to promote the interest of EU citizens by, inter alia, providing consumers with protection in their dealings with suppliers and requiring transparency of tariffs and conditions for use publicly available electronic communications services: NRAs must also contribute to the development of the internal market by avoiding different approaches to regulation within the EU. These provisions provide an important context in which NRAs must hone their interventions.

While the circumstances in which intervention is required are set out in the Framework Directive, discussion of the nature of the regulatory response is principally confined to the Access Directive.[4] Articles 8–13 outline the NRA's options. Thus, Article 8 (Imposition, Amendment, or Withdrawal of Obligations) reads as follows:

> 1: Where an operator is designated as having significant market power on a specific market ..., national regulatory authorities shall impose one or more of the obligations set out in Articles 9–13 of this Directive as appropriate....
>
> 4: Obligations imposed in accordance with this Article shall be based on the nature of the problem identified, and shall be proportionate and justified in the light of the objectives laid down in Article 8 of the [Framework Directive]....

The key remedies which then follow are now briefly described.[5]

Article 10 of the Access Directive

> *Obligation of non-discrimination. This requires the operator to provide equivalent conditions in equivalent circumstances to other undertakings providing similar services, and to provide services for its own services, or those of its subsidiaries or partners.*

This is primarily relevant to cases of an SMP operator which is vertically integrated into a competitive market, and the obligation is said to be needed to prevent exclusionary behavior by the firm with SMP, through the foreclosure of competition in the upstream and downstream market.

Article 11 of the Access Directive

> *Obligation of accounting separation. An NRA may require a vertically integrated company to make its wholesale prices and its internal transfer prices transparent, especially where the companies which it supplies and itself compete in the same downstream market.*

This represents a considerable ratcheting up of the regulatory burden on the firm with SMP. NRAs should ask themselves whether the additional burden is justified. The principal justification would be a situation in which a component of a vertically integrated incumbent was a persistent bottleneck (see Article 13 below).

Article 12 of the Access Directive

> *Obligation to meet reasonable requests for access to, and use of specific network facilities. An NRA may impose obligations on operators to grant access to specific facilities o r services, including in situations when the denial of access would hinder the emergence of a competitive retail market, or would not be in the end-user's interests.*

This represents an obligation to be implemented in circumstances similar to, but significantly broader than, those in which the essential facilities doctrine is applied under competition law. The extension to the test lies in the replacement of the precondition under competition law for mandatory access, that the asset is essential and cannot be replicated, by a much broader condition that NRAs can mandate access in circumstances where its denial "would hinder the emergence of a sustainable competitive market at the retail level, or would not be in the end-user's interest."

The obligation is silent about the pricing of such access, except to the extent that it prohibits "unreasonable terms and conditions" having a similar effect on denials of access. The range of pricing principles may therefore depart from simple cost-based prices to include other approaches such as retail minus pricing.[6]

Article 13 of the Access Directive

> *Price control and cost accounting obligations. This deals with situations where a potential lack of competition means that the operator concerned might be capable of sustaining prices*

at an excessive level, or applying a price squeeze, to the detriment of end users. National regulators should take into account the investment made by the operator and the risks involved.

It is generally accepted that the finding that a facility is essential implies the application of some appropriate pricing rule. The nature of that pricing rule is, however, by no means clear. In this context, Article 13 can be conceived as imposing the obligation of cost-oriented prices, the operator assuming the burden of proving that "the charges are derived from costs including a reasonable rate of return on investment…."

The circumstances identified as appropriate for the application of this rule are "situations where a market analysis indicates that a potential lack of effective competition means that the operator concerned might be capable of sustaining prices at an excessively high level, or applying a price squeeze to the detriment of end users."

Cost-oriented pricing for interconnection or access to customers should only be considered when dealing with an operator with SMP which is both persistent and incapable of being dealt with by other remedies, including particularly structural remedies. A classic case for its application might therefore be access to the local loop, either for call termination or for the purposes of leasing unbundled loops – provided that one operator enjoys monopoly or position of superdominance in the relevant geographical area. Even here the impact on incentives for infrastructure investment by competitors must be taken into account. Setting prices which are low in relation to forward-looking costs, or even creating an expectation that this will happen, can deal a fatal blow to infrastructure competition.

Article 17 of the Universal Service and Users' Rights Directive

Retail Price Regulation. Where on NRA determines that a retail markets is not effectively competitive and that carrier preselection will not suffice to solve the problem, it shall ensure that undertakings with significant market power in that market orient their tariffs towards costs, avoiding excessive pricing, predatory pricing, undue preference to specific users or unreasonable bundling of services. This may be done by appropriate retail price cap measures. Where there is retail tariff regulation, appropriate cost accounting systems must be implemented. Retail tariff control may not be applied in geographical or user markets where the NRA is satisfied that there is effective competition.

The implicit assumption of many regulators of and commentators on the communications industry is that if wholesale markets can be regulated to avoid the harmful effects of SMP, then regulation of retail markets can be confined to solving residual consumer protection problems, rather than problems relating to the abuse of market power. The underlying hypothesis is that entry into retailing activities will be sufficiently free from barriers to permit deregulation.

This proposition has not yet been properly tested, as many NRAs have been reluctant to accept the fundamental implication of the policy, which is that cost-based wholesale prices and competition in the retail market will bring retail prices into line with costs, thereby eliminating distributionally important pricing distortions associated with regulator-driven cross-subsidies (or departures from cost-orientation), involving different services or different customer groups. But the decision noted below to remove five of the six retail markets currently subject to ex ante regulation from the revised Recommendation issued in 2007 will make it much harder to impose retail price remedies.

Experience

As 25 member states have to notify 18 markets, a simple way of measuring success is to count the markets where the Commission has adjudicated on submissions by member states. On August 1, 2006, nearly 300 submissions had gone through that stage, and about 150 were still awaiting submission or approval. Of the latter group, the majority came from so-called accession states which only joined the EU in 2004. However, the numbers completed do allow a judgment of how the process is working. The assessment below is divided *process* and outcome components, the latter divided between *market analysis* and *remedies*.

Process

The first point to make is that the regime imposes very heavy burdens on NRAs. In the UK, which has virtually completed the process, an Ofcom official estimated that the reviews took about 60 person years of work. NRAs in smaller countries, which have the advantages of precedents, can reduce this considerably, but even in some of these, the volume of analysis undertaken and length of individual notifications have been enormous. It can be argued that some notifications have often contained unnecessarily exhaustive proofs of the obvious (e.g., that an incumbent supplying 95% of fixed lines is dominant in that market), but the existence of a national appeal mechanism, which has been widely used in several countries, encourages NRAs to undertake thorough analyses.

The European Commission's so-called Article 7 Task Force which receives the notifications (comprising officials from the Commission's Competition and Information Society Directorates) also has a heavy workload.[7] The Commission has one month to accept a notification, with comments, or retain it for a further two months' study internally and by other NRAs through the Communications Council. So far, only a handful of notifications have gone to the second stage, and the Commission has vetoed only a very few market analyses, where typically the NRA has departed from Commission-approved practice in some respect. A small number of notifications were withdrawn when rejection seemed imminent.

Many NRAs have prenotification meetings with the Commission at which work in progress is discussed. These are unquestionably helpful and (combined with previous Commission comment) have almost certainly reduced the number of notifications going to the second stage. NRAs reasonably infer that if an argument or piece of analysis submitted by another NRA has "got through," the same approach will work for it if the circumstances are sufficiently similar.

Although the Commission's legal basis for approving an NRA's choice of remedies is much weaker than its basis for approving market definitions and analyses, its responses to notifications have also included comments on proposed remedies.

Market Analysis

Despite the lengthy period taken over the analysis, the "surprise" value of many of the notifications is very low. Broadly, everyone knew that competition was slow to develop in fixed market, which tends to be dominated by the historic monopolist. This applies particularly to the smaller member states. The exceptions are international and, possibly, national retail calls (especially by business customers, where the data permit such a distinction) and wholesale transit or conveyance on "busy" routes. The high level of monopolization also applies to certain leased lines, the supply of which is tied to the generally monopolized public switched telephone network.

An area of emerging interest, especially in relation to fixed markets, is whether competitive conditions in a member state are sufficiently uniform to justify a geographic market definition which covers the whole country, or whether separate regions should be distinguished, served by differing numbers of operators. For example, transit might be competitive on thick (intercity) routes but not on other routes. Equally, in several member states, a cable network is in place in part of the territory, providing fixed voice and broadband services which compete with those of the historic telecommunications monopolist. NRAs have been reluctant to make such distinctions, but they may be necessary in the future if deregulation is to proceed.

Some comments on other markets are given below:

Fixed and mobile termination: in the Recommendation on relevant markets, these are defined as single-operator markets, carrying the implication that each operator is a 100% monopolist. This reflects the regime in Europe for both fixed and mobile calls, under which the calling partner pays the full cost of the call – the so-called calling party pays principle. This gives an operator the power to charge other operators, and, indirectly, their subscribers, a high price for the termination of calls on its network, as that is the only means by which a caller can contact the individuals they want to speak. NRAs have so far accepted this approach, and it has led to the extension of the cost-based regulation currently found on fixed networks to termination on mobile networks too. While cost models are being developed, several NRAs have proposed a "glide path" according to which termination charges gradually reduce over a few years to a cost-based level. There is some question as to whether mobile networks of different sizes should have the same termination changes. In some cases, smaller and more vulnerable networks are allowed in the interim to set higher charges. The Commission has been concerned about the wide spread of, especially, mobile termination rates, and seeks in 2008 to introduce greater standardization.

Mobile access and call origination: the Recommendation on relevant markets does not include retail markets for outgoing mobile services within the list of markets subject to ex ante regulation. However, it does include the underlying wholesale market, through which MVNOs or resellers of wholesale airtime sales would buy inputs from a mobile operator. Mobile operators do, however, supply themselves with such services, and this has formed a basis for discussion of whether there is single dominance on that market, as may apply if there is one mobile operator with a very high market share, or joint dominance exercised by two or more operators with similar market shares. Given the structure of mobile telephony in the EU, it is not wholly surprising that findings of joint dominance are made. This happened in Ireland, but the decision was later withdrawn for procedural reasons. It also happened in Spain, where it is subject to appeal.

Wholesale international roaming: these are national markets which permit a mobile subscriber to make calls in a visited country, but they have an international dimension: regulation in Greece will, by definition, benefit visitors from other countries, not Greeks. As a result, the European Regulators Group put measures in place encouraging NRAs to cooperate with one another or conducting their market analyses. But the continuing high level of international roaming charges, and the slow rate of progress in bringing them down, goaded the Commission to seek more direct means of price control by proposing a separate Regulation which came into effect in 2007, directly controlling the retail and wholesale prices of international roaming.

Wholesale broadband access ("bitstream") and unbundled loops: these two markets are central to the competitive supply of DSL-based broadband services. While markets for local loops are likely to exhibit dominance, there is room for more debate about whether single (or possibly joint) dominance can be found in the market for bitstream in member states where there are developed cable networks and more than one operator which has installed broadband equipment in local exchanges. Difficult problems of definition and analysis also arise where a dominant firm also installs a new fiber access network. Should this be included in the previously copper-based market, and should competitors have access to it?

Remedies

Here NRAs choose from, and in some cases add to, those listed above in the Access Directive, and in the case of retail markets, the price control regime specified in the Universal Service Directive. The European Regulators Group published an advisory paper on remedies in 2004 which is discussed below.

It is difficult to summarize what remedies have been imposed because each NRA tends to chose different variants. For example, under transparency, SMP operators may have to prenotify price changes, but the period of notice will vary. Equally, a retail price control might be designed, in a market from which competition is largely absent, to derive prices down to costs; but where competition is developing, it might simply act as a safety net, maintaining real or nominal prices at the current level, thereby preventing consumers from being seriously injured if competitors disappear.

It is apparent from a brief review of notified remedies, however, that NRAs almost invariably apply them in multiple combinations, and that in key wholesale markets, they often include the most draconian – cost-oriented pricings. This is often accompanied by the imposition of separate accounting, to facilitate cost allocation and deter discriminatory practices.

Evaluation and Proposed Reforms

The framework described here has many admirable qualities. It is founded in competition analysis and competition law. It takes account of the convergence of telecommunications, cable, and wireless platforms and requires regulation which is technologically neutral. It defaults to competition law, in the sense that a finding of SMP is necessary to trigger ex ante intervention. In both these respects, it is superior to the provisions of the US Telecommunications Act of 1996, which failed to adopt a consistent approach toward markets. But notwithstanding these advantages, the European regime has a number of flaws.

First, it imposes constant and costly analysis and reanalysis on regulators and firms. Market reviews and supposed to be undertaken 2–3 years, although the first review, which began in July 2003, is not yet compete. This constant repetition will impose direct costs on NRAs and firms, but it also introduces considerable uncertainty. For example, if a regulator finds, in the course of a market review, that an access provider no longer has SMP, it will no longer be able to mandate access; this possibility creates difficulties for an access-seeker trying to devise a long-term strategy.

Second, as noted above, there is the question of whether the hoped-for deregulation has materialized. As noted above, findings of the "no SMP" are very rare, perhaps reflecting regulators' excessive willingness to maintain their activity. As a result, remedies are required. But what should they be?

Ideally, remedies should promote a long-term deregulatory strategy. They should recognize that the relation between market power and regulation in a reciprocal one: while regulatory remedies are (and should be) tailored to the degree of power exhibited in any market over the relevant future period, so too the regulatory interventions chosen influence the development of the market. For example, a policy of mandating access to the incumbents' assets at low prices is bound to deter investment in competing infrastructure.

The challenge NRAs face in connection with choice of remedies is how best to use the flexibility available under the regime to design more focused remedies. In my view, this is best achieved by adopting a zero-based approach, that is, conjecturing how the market would operate without regulation. (This must in any case be done at the market analysis stage, where dominance is being tested for in a world without regulation.) Remedies to deal with problems can then be progressively added, and an estimate made of the incremental effect of each.

The alternative is to start not from zero regulation, but from the status quo, and evaluate the effect of perturbations from that point. The danger here is that this approach may be too conservative, in the sense that an NRA, not starting with a clean slate, might end up making no major change. An analysis of remedies adopted by NRAs to date suggests that this is occurring.

Thus, it would be preferable if NRAs adopted a more strategic approach to regulation, based upon incentives for new entrants progressively to make investments in infrastructure. This approach was set out by Mario Monti (then the European Commissioner responsible for competition) in a speech in December 2003.

> Competition would never be able to develop, in the short term, if entrants were not able to gain access to the incumbent operator's network to start offering services.
>
> In order to reconcile access-based and facilities-based competition it is necessary to take account of the time dimension. NRAs should provide incentives for competitors to seek access from the incumbent in the shorter term and to rely increasingly on building their own infrastructure in the longer term.

If this so-called "ladder of investment" approach were adopted, it would imply that NRAs would focus their wholesale regulation on a small number of access points, and then withdraw them as entrants progressively built infrastructure investment, either by withdrawing the access obligation or by raising the price of access to assets which competitors could realistically replicate themselves. This approach would allow NRAs to adopt a more strategic (and ultimately a more authentically deregulatory) approach to the choice of remedies.[8]

Despite its short existence, even now a consultation has begun on possible successors to the European Framework. The first element is the drafting of a revised Recommendation on relevant markets, came into effect in 2007. The second is a review of the regulatory framework as a whole; this will require legislation and is intended to take effect in 2010.

The revised Recommendation[9] reduced from 18 to 7, the number of markets automatically considered for ex ante regulation by national regulators. Five of the six retail markets were omitted, leaving only the fixed line rental. Transit, or interexchange conveyance, went, as did "mobile access and call origination," which was the basis for the regulatory remedy of mandating access to mobile operators' networks by MVNOs. This clearly represented a major step in the direction of deregulation.

In November 2007, the Commission published its own proposals to reform the regime as a whole.[10] In relation to the 2003 legislation, they embody modest changes and carryforward the underlying logic of the initial design. Many of the proposals are devoted to introducing more flexibility and the use of market methods in spectrum management – wireless technologies being seen as key to the future.

In other respects, there are two changes of interest:

- the Commission wants to assume more power over the selection of remedies; this will involve collaboration with the European Regulators' Group and the creation of a new European Telecom Market Authority with, initially at least, limited powers;
- the Commission proposes a new wholesale remedy under which a dominant firm might be required, in a limited set of circumstances, to reorganize its business processes in a way which more clearly separates its monopoly from its competitive

activities. This is known as functional or operational separation, and has been widely discussed in Europe and elsewhere since the UK incumbent, BT, separated its activities in this was in 2005.[11]

In summary, the European regulatory framework introduced in 2003 has passed its first tests, in the sense that its basic structure seems likely to go forward in the medium term, and it does appear to have delivered some a degree of enhanced competition and deregulation. It will face a series of challenges in the immediate future concerning the construction of next generation access networks, which are beginning to take root in Europe as elsewhere. The key question will be whether the access regime described above will deliver sufficient incentives for firms to make the very substantial investments in taking fiber either to the home or to the street cabinet – investments which are required to deliver genuinely high-speed broadband and to match developments in the USA, Japan, and other leading countries. This will require considerable skill on the part of the commission and national regulators in calibrating the interventions chosen. In other words, even though the framework is there, European regulators will have to show that they can operate it successfully.

Notes

1. For such analysis, see P. Buiges and P. Rey (eds) *The Economics of Antitrust and Regulation in Telecommunications: Perspective for the New European Regulatory Framework*, Edward Elgar (2003) and J. Scott Marcus. July 2002, *The potential relevance to the United States of the European Union's newly adopted regulatory framework for communications*, OPP Working Paper No. 36, FCC.
2. The first two of these processes are elaborated in, respectively, a Commission Recommendation (first edition 2003, second edition 2007) and Guidelines. A paper on remedies was published in 2004 (and revised in 2006) by the European Regulators Group, a grouping of NRAs, supported by the Commission.
3. For a review of these issues and some practical conclusions, see Ofcom's *Telecoms Strategy* Review. 2005 and M. Cave, P. Crocioni, and L. Correa. 2006. "Regulating non-price discrimination," *Competition and Regulation in Network Industries*, pp. 391–415.
4. Article 17 of the Universal Service Directive also considers retail price control – see below.
5. We omit Article 9 of the Access Directive, which mandates transparency or disclosure of information.
6. Under retail minus pricing, an access product is priced on the basis of subtracting from the retail price of the final service charged by the access provider the cost of the inputs now contributed by the access seeker.
7. Their very detailed account of the market reviews is given in *Communication on Market Reviews Under the EU Regulatory Framework, Staff Working Document* [COM (2007)401 final].
8. See also M. Cave. 2006. Encouraging infrastructure competition via the ladder of investment, *Telecommunications Policy* 223–232.
9. See European Commission, *Explanatory Note Accompanying Commission Recommendation on Relevant Product and Service Markets (Second edition)*, SEC(2007) 1483 final.
10. European Commission, *Proposal for a Directive*, COM(2007) 697 final.
11. See M. Cave. 2006. Six degrees of separation, Communications *and Strategies*, 64: 89–104.

Chapter 3
Infrastructure Commons in Economic Perspective

Brett M. Frischmann

Introduction

We live in an increasingly complex world with overlapping, interdependent resource systems that constitute our environment and affect our lives in significant, although sometimes in subtle and complex, ways. These overlapping systems include not only natural resource systems but also human-built and socially constructed resource systems that constitute the world we live in and experience. It is critical that we, as a society, continually strive to better understand our environment so that we can appreciate, construct, and manage it as best we can. Too often, we take for granted the fundamental infrastructure resources upon which these systems depend.

This chapter briefly summarizes a theory (developed in substantial detail elsewhere)[1] that explains why there are strong economic arguments for managing and sustaining infrastructure resources in an openly accessible manner. This theory facilitates a better understanding of two related issues: how society benefits from infrastructure resources and how decisions about how to manage or govern infrastructure resources affect a wide variety of public and private interests. The key insights from this analysis are that infrastructure resources generate value as inputs into a wide range of productive processes and that the outputs from these processes are often public goods and nonmarket goods that generate positive externalities that benefit society as a whole. Managing such resources in an openly accessible manner may be socially desirable from an economic perspective because doing so facilitates these downstream productive activities. For example, managing the Internet infrastructure in an openly accessible manner facilitates active citizen involvement in the

B.M. Frischmann
Associate Professor, Loyola University Chicago School of Law, Chicago, IL, USA
email: bfrischmann@gmail.com

W.H. Lehr and L.M. Pupillo (eds.), *Internet Policy and Economics*,
DOI 10.1007/978-1-4419-0038-8_3, © Springer Science+Business Media, LLC 2009

production and sharing of many different public and nonmarket goods. Over the last decade, this has led to increased opportunities for a wide range of citizens to engage in entrepreneurship, political discourse, social network formation, and community building, among many other activities. The chapter applies these insights to the network neutrality debate and suggests how the debate might be reframed to better account for the wide range of private and public interests at stake.

Infrastructure Resources and Commons Management

This section sets forth a general description of infrastructure resources and commons management. After providing a brief introduction to the modern conception of infrastructure and its traditional roots in large scale, human-made physical resource systems, the part discusses a few observations about traditional infrastructure resources, including the important observation that traditional infrastructures are generally managed as commons. This sets the stage for a more detailed discussion of commons management as a resource management strategy and lays the foundation for the theoretical discussion in the second section.

Defining Infrastructure

The term "infrastructure" generally conjures up the notion of a large-scale, physical resource facility made by humans for public consumption. Standard definitions of infrastructure refer to the "underlying framework of a system" or the "underlying foundation" of a "system."[2] In its report, Infrastructure for the 21st Century: Framework for a Research Agenda, the US National Research Council (NRC, 1987) identified a host of "public works infrastructure"[3] along with a more comprehensive notion of infrastructure that included "the operating procedures, management practices, and development policies that interact together with societal demand and the physical world to facilitate" the provision of a range of infrastructure-enabled services, including "the transport of people and goods, provision of water for drinking and a variety of other uses, safe disposal of society's waste products, provision of energy where it is needed, and transmission of information within and between communities" (NRC, 1987).

In recent years, infrastructure has been used even more widely to describe the underlying framework or foundation of many different types of systems, including information and social systems. What seems to be driving this expanding usage of the term is an emerging emphasis on the functional role of infrastructure in complex systems. Infrastructure resources are means to many ends in the sense that they enable, frame, and support a wide range of human activities. From a functional, systems-based perspective, infrastructure can best be understood as the foundational resources (or resource subsystems or platforms, depending on the field) that enable and/or structure more complex systems of human activity.

Traditional Infrastructure

A list of familiar examples of "traditional infrastructure" includes: (1) transportation systems, such as highway systems, railway systems, airline systems, and ports; (2) communication systems, such as telephone networks and postal services; (3) governance systems, such as court systems; and (4) basic public services and facilities, such as schools, sewers, and water systems. The list could be expanded considerably, but the point here is simply to bring to mind the range of traditional infrastructure resources that we rely on daily.

Three generalizations about traditional infrastructure are worth consideration.[4] First, the government has played and continues to play a significant and widely accepted role in ensuring the provision of many traditional infrastructures. The role of government varies, as it must, according to the context, community, and infrastructure resource in question. In many contexts, private parties and markets play an increasingly important role in providing many types of traditional infrastructure due to, among other things, a wave of privatization as well as cooperative ventures between industry and government (Levy, 1996: 16–17). Nonetheless, the key point (behind this generalization) is that the government's role as provider, subsidizer, coordinator, and/or regulator of traditional infrastructure provision remains intact in most communities in the USA and throughout the world.[5] The reason, which relates to the next two generalizations and to the analysis to come later, is that "free" markets often fail to meet society's demand for infrastructure.

Second, traditional infrastructures generally are managed in an openly accessible manner. They are managed in a manner whereby all members of a community who wish to use the resources may do so on nondiscriminatory terms (Lessig, 2001: 19–25; Rose, 1986: 752; Benkler, 2001a: 22–23, 47–48).[6] For many infrastructure resources, the relevant "community" is the public at large. As Cooper (2005: 14–15) has noted, "[r]oads and highways, canals, railroads, the mail, telegraph, and telephone, some owned by public entities, most owned by private corporations, have always been operated as common carriers that are required to interconnect and serve the public on a nondiscriminatory basis." This does not mean, however, that access is free. We pay tolls to access highways, we buy stamps to send letters, we pay telephone companies to route our calls across their lines, and so on.[7] Users must pay for access to some (though not all) of these resources. Nor does it mean that access to the resource is absolutely unregulated. Transportation of hazardous substances by highway or mail, for example, is heavily regulated. The key point (behind this generalization) is that the resource is accessible to all within a community regardless of the identity of the end-user or end-use.[8] With some exceptions (such as the narrowly defined priority given to a police officer driving with her siren and lights on), access to and use of most infrastructure resources are not prioritized based on such criteria. As discussed below, managing traditional infrastructure in this fashion often makes economic sense.

Third, traditional infrastructures generate significant spillovers (positive externalities)[9] that result in "large social gains" (Steinmueller, 1996: 117). As W. Edward Steinmueller observed:

> Both traditional and modern uses of the term infrastructure are related to "synergies," what economists call positive externalities, that are incompletely appropriated by the suppliers of goods and services within an economic system. The traditional idea of infrastructure was derived from the observation that the private gains from the construction and extension of transportation and communication networks, while very large, were also accompanied by additional large social gains.... Over the past century, publicly regulated and promoted investments in these types of infrastructure have been so large, and the resulting spread of competing transportation and communications modalities have become so pervasive, that they have come to be taken as a defining characteristic of industrialized nations.

The economics of traditional infrastructure are quite complex, as reflected perhaps in the fact that economists sometimes refer to infrastructure "opaquely" as "social overhead capital" (Button, 1986: 148). Not surprisingly, there are ongoing, hotly contested debates in economics about the costs and benefits of infrastructure – for example, about the degree to which particular infrastructure investments contribute (incrementally) to social welfare or economic growth, and about how to prioritize infrastructure investments in developing countries. Nonetheless, the key point (behind this generalization) is that most people, including economists, recognize that infrastructure resources are critically important to society precisely because infrastructure resources give rise to large social gains. As discussed in the second part, the nature of some of the gains – as spillovers – may explain why we take infrastructure for granted – the positive externalities are sufficiently difficult to observe or measure quantitatively, much less capture in economic transactions, and the benefits may be diffuse and sufficiently small in magnitude to escape the attention of individual beneficiaries.

Consider, for a moment, these three generalizations and how they might relate to each other. Might the accepted role for government associated with infrastructure market failure be related to society's need for nondiscriminatory community access or to the generation of substantial spillovers or to both? The societal need for nondiscriminatory community access to infrastructure and the generation of substantial spillovers each appear to independently constitute grounds for identifying a potential market failure and for supporting some role for government. But the confluence of both factors suggests that something more complex may be involved. Might society's need for nondiscriminatory community access to infrastructure be related to the generation of substantial spillovers?

Rose (1986: 723, 775–81), a prominent legal scholar, was the first to draw an explicit, causal connection between open access and these positive externalities.[10] In her path-breaking article, *The Comedy of the Commons: Custom, Commerce, and Inherently Public Property*, Rose (1986: 768–70) explained that a "comedy of the commons" arises where open access to a resource leads to scale returns – greater social value with greater use of the resource. With respect to road systems, for example, Rose considered commerce to be an interactive practice whose exponential returns to increasing participation run on without limit. Through ever-expanding commerce, the nation becomes ever-wealthier, and hence trade and commerce routes must be held open to the public, even if contrary to private interest. Instead of worrying that too many people will engage in commerce, we worry that too few will undertake the effort (Rose, 1986: 760–70).

Critically, as Rose (1986: 723, 774–818) recognized, (1) managing road systems in an openly accessible manner is the key to sustaining and increasing participation in commerce and (2) commerce is itself a productive activity that generates significant positive externalities. Commerce generates private value that is easily observed and captured by participants in economic transactions, as buyers and sellers exchange goods and services, but it also generates social value that is not easily observed and captured by participants, value associated with socialization and cultural exchange, among other things. Commerce is an excellent example of a productive use of roads that generates positive externalities and social surplus. There are many others such as visiting other communities to see friends, relatives, or recreate, or visiting state parks (Frischmann, 2008a; Branscomb and Keller, 1996: 1). These activities generate private value that is easily observed and captured by participants as well as social value that is not easily observed and captured by participants. Rose's critical insight is that certain resources ought to be managed in an openly accessible manner because doing so increases participation in socially valuable activities that yield scale returns. Building on Rose's important but since underdeveloped insight, the second section of this chapter further explores the relationship between open access to infrastructure and the generation of substantial spillovers. Before delving deeper into infrastructure theory, however, we need to explain "commons management."

Commons as Resource Management

The term "commons" generally conjures up the notion of a shared community resource, such as a public park or a common pasture. The term gained some notoriety with the publication of Garrett Hardin's essay, *The Tragedy of the Commons*, in *Science* (1968), and the term has more recently been used in a variety of different settings, ranging from various environmental resources to spectrum policy. Rather than take the reader on a detour to discuss various theories of the commons, this chapter adopts a functional approach to understanding commons. As with infrastructure, the idea is to identify and examine the functional role of commons in complex systems. From this perspective, commons can be understood as a strategy for managing certain resources in a nondiscriminatory manner.

We will use "open access" and "commons" interchangeably (and thus somewhat loosely) to refer to the situation in which a resource is accessible to all members of a community on nondiscriminatory terms, meaning specifically, that terms do not depend on the users' identity or intended use.[11] Conflating "open access" and "commons" may be troublesome to property scholars who are accustomed to maintaining an important distinction between open access and commons: open access typically implies absolutely no ownership rights or property rights. No entity possesses the right to exclude others from the resource; all who want access can get access (Hess and Ostrom, 2003: 121–22). Commons, on the other hand, typically involves some form of communal ownership (community property rights, public property rights, joint ownership rights, etc.), such that members of the relevant community obtain access "under rules that may range from 'anything goes' to quite crisply articulated formal rules that are effectively enforced" and nonmembers can be excluded.[12] There are at least three important distinctions: first, ownership (none vs communal); second, the definition of community (public at large vs a more narrowly defined and circumscribed group with some boundary between members and nonmembers); and third, the degree of exclusion (none vs exclusion of nonmembers). These distinctions become relevant to a more complex discussion of different institutional means for implementing a commons strategy, but we will not have that discussion here.

For now, we put aside these distinctions and simply focus on a common functional feature, nondiscrimination – the underlying resource is accessible to users within a community regardless of the user's identity or intended use. Thus, we intentionally abstract from the institutional form (property rights, regulations, norms, etc.) to focus on a particular institutional function (opening or restricting access to a resource). Tying form and function together obscures the fact that a commons management strategy can be implemented by a variety of institutional forms, which are often mixed (property and regulation, private and communal property, etc.), and not necessarily through one particular form of property rights. As I examine in other work, "infrastructure commons" – a shorthand for "infrastructure managed as commons" – of many different types are sustained through very different sets of institutional arrangements. Ultimately, the optimal degree of openness or restrictiveness depends upon a number of functional economic considerations related to the nature of the resource in question, the manner in which the resource is utilized to create value, institutional structures, and the community setting.

For our purposes, then, the term "commons" will refer to a de jure or de facto management decision "governing the use and disposition of" a resource (Benkler, 2003: 6). There are many ways in which a resource can come to be managed in an openly accessible manner. A resource may be open for common use naturally. The resource may be available to all naturally because its characteristics prevent it from being owned or controlled by anyone.[13] For example, for most of the earth's history, the oceans and the atmosphere were natural commons. Exercising dominion over such resources was beyond the ability of human beings or simply was unnecessary because there was no indication of scarcity (Rose, 2003: 93). A resource also may be open for common use as the result of social construction.[14] That is, laws or rules may prohibit ownership or ensure open access, or an open access regime may arise through norms and customs among owners and users. For example, the Internet infrastructure has been governed by norms creating an open access regime where end-users can access and use the infrastructure to route data packets without fear of discrimination or exclusion by infrastructure owners. Ultimately, "commons" is a form of resource management contingent upon human decision making. The decision about whether and how to manage a given resource as a commons might be made privately or publicly, politically or economically, through property rights, regulation, or some hybrid regime, depending on the context.

The general values of the commons management principle are that it maintains openness, does not discriminate among users or uses of the resource, and eliminates the need to obtain approval or a license to use the resource. Generally, managing infrastructure resources in an openly accessible manner eliminates the need to rely on either market or government actors to "pick winners" among users or uses of infrastructure. In theory, at least, this catalyzes innovation through the creation of and experimentation with new uses. More generally, it facilitates the generation of positive externalities by permitting downstream production of public goods and nonmarket goods that might be stifled under a more restrictive access regime.

Sustaining both natural commons and socially constructed commons poses numerous challenges, however. Environmental and information resources highlight the most well-known and studied dilemmas. Environmental resources suffer from the famous "tragedy of the commons" (Hardin, 1968), a consumption or capacity problem, which is familiar to many infrastructure resources. Information resources suffer from the famous "free-rider" dilemma, a production problem, which is also familiar to many infrastructure resources. The Internet suffers from both types of problems.

It is interesting how two frequently told stories of uncontrolled consumption – the tragedy of the commons and the free-rider story – came to dominate the policy discourse in the environmental and intellectual property areas and how both stories seem to lead to the conclusion that granting private property rights, typically with the power to grant access on discriminatory terms, is the best way to manage these resources (Ostrom, 1990: 3; Ghosh, 2004: 1332; Lemley, 2005). Both stories can be translated in game-theoretic terms into a prisoners' dilemma, another good story, although one that does not necessarily point to private property as a solution to the cooperation dilemma (Eastman, 1997: 749–51; Luban, 1995: 963; Crump, 2001: 375).

Whichever story one chooses to tell, the underlying economic problems are not insurmountable and should not stand in the way of managing infrastructure in an openly accessible manner. Social institutions reflect a strong commitment to sustaining common access to certain infrastructural resources. As theorized in the second part of this chapter and illustrated in the third, society values common access to infrastructure resources because these resources are fundamental inputs into many productive activities that generate benefits for society as a whole.

A Demand-Side Theory of Infrastructure

This section develops a demand-side model of infrastructure that provides a better means for understanding and analyzing societal demand for infrastructure resources. The goal is to better understand how value is realized and created by human beings that obtain access to infrastructure resources. I will take a functional perspective that is informed by welfare economics.

Defining Infrastructure from the Demand Side

Infrastructure resources are resources that satisfy the following demand-side criteria:

1. The resource is or may be consumed nonrivalrously;
2. Social demand for the resource is driven primarily by downstream productive activity that requires the resource as an input; and
3. The resource is used as an input into a wide range of goods and services, including private goods, public goods, and/or nonmarket goods.

Traditional infrastructure, such as roadways, telephone networks, and electricity grids, satisfy this definition, as do a wide range of resources not traditionally considered infrastructure resources, such as lakes, ideas, and the Internet.

The first criterion captures the consumption attribute of nonrival and partially (non) rival goods. In short, this characteristic describes the "sharable" nature of infrastructure resources. Infrastructure resources are sharable in the sense that the resources can be accessed and used concurrently by multiple users for multiple uses at the same time. Infrastructure resources vary in their capacity to accommodate multiple users, and this variance in capacity differentiates nonrival resources with infinite capacity from partially (non)rival resources with finite but renewable capacity. For nonrival resources of infinite capacity, the marginal costs of allowing an additional person to access the resource are zero.[15] For partially (non)rival resources of finite capacity, the degree and rate of rivalry may vary among users and uses, and consequently, the cost-benefit analysis is more complicated because of the possibility of congestion and, in some cases, depletion.[16] Nonrivalry opens the door to sharing, often, relatively cheap sharing, and potentially to widespread access and productive use of the resource.

The second and third criteria focus on the manner in which infrastructure resources create social value. The second criterion emphasizes that infrastructure resources are intermediate goods that create social value when utilized productively and that such use is the primary source of social benefits. In other words, while some infrastructure resources may be consumed directly to produce immediate benefits, most of the value derived from the resources results from productive use rather than passive consumption. A road system, for example, is not socially beneficial simply because we can drive on it. I may realize direct consumptive benefits when I go cruising with the windows down and my favorite music playing, but the bulk of social benefits attributable to a road system come from the activities it facilitates at the ends, including, for example, commerce, labor, communications, recreation, and civilization (Rose, 1986: 768–70).

The third criterion emphasizes both the *variance* of downstream outputs[17] and the *nature* of those outputs, particularly, public and nonmarket goods. The reason for emphasizing variance and the production of public and nonmarket goods downstream is that when these criteria are satisfied, the social value created by allowing additional users to access and use the resource may be substantial but extremely difficult to measure or capture in market transactions because of the prevalence of spillovers (positive externalities). The information problems associated with assessing demand for the resource and valuing its social benefits plague both infrastructure suppliers and users where users are producing many different public or nonmarket goods. This is an information problem that is pervasive and not easily solved.

Since introducing these criteria, I have found that people often focus on one or two and forget that all three work together to delineate a set of infrastructural resources. So let me briefly explain how they relate to each other. The first criterion isolates those resources that are potentially sharable at low (or at least manageable) marginal cost and the latter criteria further narrow the set to those resources that are more likely to give rise to an assortment of demand-side market failures associated with externalities, high transaction and information costs, and path dependency. I will discuss some of these failures below, but let me make clear that the demand-side focus is intended to draw attention to the functional means-ends relationship between infrastructure resources and society's capabilities to generate value in infrastructure-dependent systems.

Whether we are talking about transportation systems, the electricity grid, basic research (ideas), environmental ecosystems, or Internet infrastructure, the bulk of the social benefits generated by the resources derives from the downstream uses. Value is created downstream by a wide variety of users that rely on access to the infrastructure. Yet social demand for the infrastructure itself is extremely difficult to ascertain.

From an economic perspective, it makes sense to manage certain infrastructure resources in an openly accessible manner because doing so permits a wide range of downstream producers of private, public, and nonmarket goods to flourish. As Professor Yochai Benkler (2001: 47–48) has noted, "[t]he high variability in value of using both transportation and communications facilities from person to person and time to time have made a commons-based approach to providing the core facilities immensely valuable." The point is not that all infrastructure resources (traditional or nontraditional) should be managed in an openly accessible manner. Rather, for certain classes of resources, the economic arguments for managing the resources in an openly accessible manner vary in strength and substance.

Understanding the Outputs

When analyzing nonrival or partially (non)rival inputs, the outputs matter. The value of an infrastructure resource ultimately is realized by consumers of infrastructure-dependent outputs. It is thus the demand for these outputs that determines demand for the infrastructure. This section briefly distinguishes different types of outputs.

Private goods and public goods (both pure and impure) are supplied by the market mechanism with varying degrees of effectiveness. For private goods, the market mechanism generally works very well from both the supply and demand sides, assuming markets are competitive. Private goods are rivalrously consumed and generally do not give rise to externalities. For public goods, the market mechanism may work well in some cases, and in other cases, it may fail from both the supply and demand sides, even if markets are competitive. In some cases of potential market failure, the market may be "corrected" through institutional intervention. For example, if the costs of excluding nonpaying users are sufficiently high that undersupply is expected, legal fences may be employed to lessen the costs of exclusion and thereby improve incentives to invest in supplying the desired public good (Cornes and Sandler, 1996).

"Nonmarket goods" refer to those goods that are neither provided nor demanded well through the market mechanism; we do not "purchase" such goods (Flores, 2003: 27). We may recognize their value but we simply do not rely on the market as a provisional mechanism; institutional fixes do not work very well. Instead, we rely on other provisional mechanisms, including government, community, family, and individuals.

From the demand side, the important distinction between these outputs – in particular, what separates public goods from nonmarket goods – is the means by which they create value for society. The value of public goods is realized upon consumption. That is, upon obtaining access to a public good, a person "consumes" it and appreciates benefits (value or utility). The production of public goods has the potential to generate positive externalities. Whether the benefits are external to production depends upon the conditions of access and whether the producer internalizes the value realized by others upon consumption.[18]

For example, consider a flower garden.[19] A person who plants flowers in his front yard creates the potential for positive externalities that may be realized by those who walk by and appreciate their beauty. The view of the flowers is nonrival in the sense that consumption by one person does not deplete the view (or beauty) available for other to consume. Consumption depends upon access, however, and the realization of potential externalities depends upon whether the homeowner builds an effective fence (i.e., one that would obstruct the view from the sidewalk). If the homeowner builds an effective fence, then the door has been closed and the potential for externalities remains untapped potential. If, on the other hand, the homeowner does not build such a fence, then people who pass by obtain access to the view, consume it, and realize external benefits. I like to refer to such persons as incidental beneficiaries, although some would use loaded labels such as "free-riders" or even "pirates." At least in the context of an open view of a flower garden, however, we do not really expect people to stop and compensate the homeowner. The homeowner may anticipate and value the fact that persons passing by appreciate the visual beauty and wonderful smells of the garden, but generally the homeowner does not seek compensation or take into account fully the summed benefits for all.

By contrast, the value of nonmarket goods is realized in a more osmotic fashion and not through direct consumption. Nonmarket goods change environmental conditions and social interdependencies in ways that increase social welfare. Take, for example, active participation in democratic dialogue or education. While participants may realize direct benefits as a result of their activity, nonparticipants also benefit – not because they also may gain access to the good (dialogue or education), but instead because of the manner in which dialogue or education affect societal conditions (Frischmann, 2008b). As I discuss in the third section of the chapter, active participation in online discussions regarding political issues, such as the Iraq war and the 2008 election, benefit participants as well as those who never log onto the Internet.

An Infrastructure Typology

To better understand and evaluate the complex economic relationships, I define three general categories of infrastructure resources, illustrated in Table 3.1, based on the nature of the distribution of downstream activities: commercial, public, and social infrastructure. These categories are neither exhaustive nor mutually exclusive. Real-world infrastructure resources often fit within more than one of these categories at the same time. For example, the Internet is a combination of all three types of infrastructure, as explored in the third section, and is thus *mixed infrastructure*. The analytical advantage of this general categorization schema is that it provides a means for understanding the social value generated by these infrastructure resources, identifying different types of market failures, and formulating the appropriate rules to correct such failures.

Commercial Infrastructure

Commercial infrastructure resources are used to produce private goods. Consider the examples listed in Table 3.1. Basic manufacturing processes, such as die casting, milling, and the assembly line process, are nonrival inputs into the production of a wide variety of private manufactured goods. Basic agricultural processes and food processing techniques similarly are nonrival inputs into the production of a wide variety of private agricultural goods and foodstuffs. Many commercial infrastructure resources are used productively by suppliers purely as a delivery mechanism for manufactured goods, agricultural goods, foodstuffs, and many

Table 3.1 Typology of infrastructure resources

Type	Definition	Examples
Commercial infrastructure	Nonrival or partially (non)rival input into the production of a wide variance of private goods	1. Basic manufacturing processes 2. The Internet 3. Road systems
Public infrastructure	Nonrival or partially (non)rival input into the production of a wide variance of public goods	1. Basic research 2. Ideas 3. The Internet
Social infrastructure	Nonrival or partially (non)rival input into the production of a wide variance of nonmarket goods	1. Lakes 2. The Internet 3. Road systems

other commercial products. Ports, for example, act as an infrastructural input into the delivery of a wide range of private goods. Similarly, the Internet and highway systems are mixed infrastructures used by a wide range of suppliers to delivery private goods and services. The Internet and highway systems, in contrast with ports, also are used as inputs to support a wide range of other socially valuable activities.

For pure commercial infrastructure, basic economic theory predicts that competitive output markets should work well and effectively create demand information for the input; market actors (input suppliers) will process this information and satisfy the demand efficiently. Simply put, for commercial infrastructure, output producers should fully appropriate the benefits of the outputs (via sales to consumers) and thus should accurately manifest demand for the required inputs in upstream markets. Therefore, with respect to demand for commercial infrastructure, the key is maintaining competition in the output markets, where producers are competing to produce and supply private goods to consumers. Competition is the linchpin in this context because the consumptive demands of the public can best be assessed and satisfied by competitive markets.

Public and Social Infrastructure

Public and social infrastructure resources are used to produce public goods and nonmarket goods, respectively. For much of the analysis that follows, I have grouped public and social infrastructure together because the demand-side problems and arguments for commons management generally take the same form. For both public and social infrastructure, the ability of competitive output markets to effectively generate and process information regarding demand for the required input is less clear than in the case of commercial infrastructure.

Infrastructure users that produce public goods and nonmarket goods suffer valuation problems because they generally do not fully measure or appropriate the (potential) benefits of the outputs they produce and consequently do not accurately represent actual social demand for the infrastructure resource. Instead, for public and social infrastructure, "demand [generated by competitive output markets will] tend[] to reflect the individual benefits realized by a particular user and not take into account positive externalities" (Frischmann, 2001: 51). To the extent that individuals' willingness to pay for access to infrastructure reflects only the value that they will realize from an output, the market mechanism will not fully take into account (or provide the services for) the broader set of social benefits attributable to the public or nonmarket goods. Infrastructure consumers will pay for access to infrastructure only to the extent that they benefit (rather than to the extent that society benefits) from the outputs produced (Frischmann, 2001: 66). Difficulties in measuring and appropriating value generated in output markets translate into a valuation/measurement problem for infrastructure suppliers. Competitive output markets may fail to accurately manifest demand for public and social infrastructure because of the presence of demand-side externalities. To better understand this dynamic, the next section compares infrastructure and network effects, both of which involve demand-side externalities.

Network Effects

Most, if not all, traditional infrastructure resources are networks (Economides, 1996a: 673).[20] Economists have devoted substantial effort in recent years unraveling the peculiar economic features of networks, commonly referred to as "network effects." Nicholas Economides (2003), a pioneering network economist, provides the following simple explanation of networks:

> Networks are composed of complementary nodes and links. The crucial defining feature of networks is the complementarity between the various nodes and links. A service delivered over a network requires the use of two or more network components. Thus, the network components are complementary to each other.

Network effects are demand-side effects that often, although not always, result in positive externalities, which generally are referred to as network externalities (Katz and Shapiro, 1994: 93, 96–100; 1985: 436). Network effects exist when the utility to a user of a good or service increases with the number of other people using it, either for consumption or for production (specifically, to produce functionally compatible goods) (Lemley and McGowan, 1998: 488–94; Economides, 2003: 5). Standard examples of goods that exhibit direct network effects include telephones and fax machines.

Although network effects are prevalent for infrastructure resources and may generate significant positive externalities, network externalities are not the only type of demand-side externalities generated by infrastructure. The other positive externalities generated by infrastructure resources may be attributable to the production of public goods and nonmarket goods by users that obtain access to the infrastructure resource and use it as an input.

There is a critical difference between network effects and "infrastructure effects" and the resulting types of externalities. Network effects tend to increase consumers' willingness to pay for access to the resource (Economides, 1996a: 684; Economides, 2003: 6). By definition, network effects arise when users' utilities increase with the number of other users. Economists assume that consumers appreciate the value created by network effects and thus are willing to pay more for access to the larger network, which may lead to the internalization of some network externalities (Economides, 2003: 11). Thus, although the generally applicable law of demand holds that "the willingness to pay for the last unit of a good decreases with the number of units sold" (Economides, 1996b: 213; Economides, 2003: 6), the opposite may hold true for goods that exhibit network effects. The presence of network effects may cause the demand curve to shift upward as the quantity of units accessed (sold) increases, leading to an upward-sloping portion of the demand curve (Economides, 1996a: 682; Economides, 2003: 6).

Infrastructure effects do not necessarily increase users' willingness to pay for access to the infrastructure resource. As discussed above, a user's willingness to pay for access to the infrastructure resource is limited to the benefits that can be obtained by the user, which depends upon the nature of the outputs produced, the extent to which such outputs generate positive externalities, and the manner in which those externalities are distributed. Infrastructure effects resemble indirect network effects in the sense that a larger number (or a wider variance) of applications may lead to an increase in consumers' valuation of the infrastructure or network, but the externalities generated by public and social infrastructure are even more indirect in that they are diffuse, derived from public and nonmarket goods, and not simply a function of increased availability of desired end-users or end-uses. Further, the externalities generated by public and social infrastructure often positively affect the utility of nonusers, that is, members of society that are not using the infrastructure itself. In a sense, the positive externalities generated by the outputs are closely connected to the nature of the outputs and only loosely connected to the complementary relationship between the infrastructure and the output. This is important because the prospect of infrastructure suppliers internalizing complementary externalities is much less likely, making the possibility of a demand-side market failure much more likely.

The Case for Infrastructure Commons

To this point, we have developed a functional description of infrastructure that provides a better understanding of societal demand for infrastructure resources. The key insights from this analysis are that infrastructure resources generate value when used as inputs into a wide range of productive processes and that the outputs from these processes are often public goods and nonmarket goods that generate positive externalities benefiting society as a whole. Managing such resources in an openly accessible manner may be socially desirable when doing so takes advantage of nonrivalry and facilitates these types of downstream activities.

The case for commons management must be evaluated carefully and contextually. Broad prescriptions are not easily derived. To facilitate analysis, I developed an infrastructure typology to distinguish between commercial, public, and social infrastructure, based upon the nature of outputs and the potential for positive externalities. This section briefly sets forth the economic arguments for managing these different types of infrastructure in an openly accessible manner.

For commercial infrastructure, antitrust principles provide a sufficient basis for determining whether open access is desirable because competitive markets (for both inputs and outputs) should work well. Downstream producers of private goods can accurately manifest demand for infrastructure because consumers realize the full value of the goods (i.e., there are no externalities) and are willing to pay for such benefits. Accordingly, from the demand side, there is less reason to believe that government intervention into markets is necessary, absent anticompetitive behavior.

For public or social infrastructure, the case for commons management becomes stronger for a few reasons. First, output producers are less likely to accurately manifest demand due to information/appropriation problems. It is difficult for these producers to measure the value created by the public good or nonmarket good outputs; producers of such outputs are not able to appropriate the full value because consumers are not willing to pay for the full value (due to positive externalities), and such producers' willingness to pay for access to the input likely will be less than the amount that would maximize social welfare.

For purposes of illustration, let us engage in a brief thought experiment. For each infrastructure type, we will (1) imagine a ranking of uses based on consumers' willingness to pay and (2) imagine a similar ranking based instead on social value generated by the use. For commercial infrastructure, we should expect significant overlap if not identical ordering for the two rankings. For public and social infrastructure, the rankings likely are quite different because there may be many low willingness to pay users/uses that generate significant social value, much of which is externalized.

Social surplus (i.e., the amount by which the social value exceeds the private value) may result from a "killer app," such as e-mail or the World Wide Web, that generates significant positive externalities or from a large number of outputs that generate positive externalities on a smaller scale. That is, in some situations, there may be a particularly valuable public or nonmarket good output that generates a large social surplus, and in others, there may be a large number of such outputs that generate small social surpluses. Both types of situations are present in the Internet context. Although the "killer app" phenomenon appears to be well understood, the small-scale but widespread production of public and nonmarket goods by end-users that obtain access to the infrastructure appears to be underappreciated and undervalued by most analysts. Yet in both cases, there may be a strong argument for managing the infrastructure resource in an openly accessible manner to facilitate these productive activities.

The social costs of restricting access to public or social infrastructure can be significant and yet evade observation or consideration within conventional economic transactions. Initially, we may analyze the issue as one of high transaction costs and imperfect information. Yet, even with perfect information and low or no transaction costs with respect to input suppliers and input buyers, input buyers would still not accurately represent social demand because it is the benefits generated by the relevant outputs that escape observation and appropriation.

To the extent that infrastructure resources can be optimized for particular application – which is often the case, there is a risk that infrastructure suppliers will favor existing or expected applications. If we rely on the market as the provisional mechanism, there is a related risk that infrastructure suppliers will favor applications that generate appropriable benefits at the expense of applications that generate positive externalities. Even putting aside the generation and processing of demand signals, it remains unclear whether markets will operate efficiently with respect to the supply of public and social infrastructure. There may be significant transactions cost problems that may hamper markets. For example, transaction costs associated with price setting, licensing, and enforcement may increase as the variance of public good and nonmarket good outputs increases.

Of course, economists have long recognized that there is a case for subsidizing public and nonmarket goods producers directly because such goods are undersupplied by the market. The effectiveness of directly subsidizing such producers will vary, however, based on the capacity for subsidy mechanisms to identify and direct funds to worthy recipients. In some cases, open access to the infrastructure may be a more effective, albeit blunt, means for supporting such activities than targeted subsidies.

In a sense, managing infrastructure as a commons kills two birds with one stone: It eliminates the need to rely on either the market or the government to "pick winners" or uses worthy of access. On the one hand, the market picks winners according to the amount of appropriable value generated by outputs and consequently output producers' willingness to pay for access to the infrastructure. On the other hand, to subsidize production of public goods or nonmarket goods downstream, the government needs to pick winners by assessing social demand for such goods based on the social value they create. The inefficiencies, information problems, and transaction costs associated with picking winners under either system may justify managing public and social infrastructure resources in an openly accessible manner.

The Social Value of an Open Internet Infrastructure and Implications for the Network Neutrality Debate

This final section demonstrates how infrastructure theory applies to the Internet in the context of the particularly contentious "open access versus private control" debate. At the heart of this debate is whether the Internet will retain its end-to-end architecture and continue to be managed in an openly accessible manner. Ultimately, the outcome of this debate may determine whether the Internet continues to operate as a mixed infrastructure (commercial, public, and social), or whether it evolves into a commercial infrastructure optimized for the production and delivery of commercial outputs.

The Internet as Infrastructure

The Internet consists of many infrastructure resources. Scholars have delineated two macrolevel infrastructure resources. The physical infrastructure consists of a wide variety of physical networks interconnected with each other, whereas the logical infrastructure consists of the standards and protocols that facilitate seamless transmission of data across different types of physical networks (Benkler, 2000). The physical and logical infrastructure both act as essential inputs into downstream production of applications and content. In contrast with the upstream-downstream/

input-output model used in this chapter, Internet scholars tend to focus on layered models of the Internet that distinguish between complementary layers based on the functions each layer performs (Farrell and Weiser, 2004: 90–91; Werbach, 2002: 57–64; Benkler, 2000; Sicker and Mindel, 2002). The number of layers in particular models varies, but the following four-layered model in Table 3.2 is sufficient for our purposes. As the structure of this layered model implies, the physical and logical infrastructure are the foundational layers upon which the Internet environment we experience has been built. Thus, for purposes of this chapter (and ease of reference), I refer to the physical and logical infrastructure together as either the Internet or the Internet infrastructure and to the applications and content as downstream outputs.

The Internet meets all three demand-side criteria for infrastructure. The Internet infrastructure is a partially (non)rival good; it is consumed both nonrivalrously and rivalrously, depending upon available capacity.[21] The benefits of the Internet are realized at the ends. Like a road system and basic research, the Internet is socially valuable primarily because of the productive activity it facilitates downstream. That is, end-users hooked up to the Internet infrastructure realize benefits and generate value through the applications run on their computers and through the production and consumption of content delivered over the Internet. End-users thus create demand for Internet infrastructure through their demand for applications and content.

The Internet currently is a mixed commercial, public, and social infrastructure. As described below, the Internet is perhaps the clearest example of an infrastructure resource that enables the production of a wide variety of public, private, and nonmarket goods, many of which are network goods.

Like most traditional infrastructure, the Internet currently is managed in an openly accessible manner. The current Internet infrastructure evolved with the so-called "end-to-end" design principle as its central tenet.[22] As Barabara van Schewick and I recently explained: "To preserve the robustness and evolvability of the network and to allow applications to be easily layered on top of it, the broad version of this design principle recommends that the lower layers of the network be as general as possible, while all application-specific functionality should be concentrated at higher layers at end hosts" (Frischmann and van Schewick, 2007: 385–86).

Table 3.2 Four-layered model of the Internet

Layer	Description	Examples
Content	Information/data conveyed to end-users	E-mail communication, music, Web page
Applications	Programs and functions used by end-users	E-mail program, media player, Web browser
Logical infrastructure	Standards and protocols that facilitate transmission of data across physical networks	TCP/IP, domain name system
Physical infrastructure	Physical hardware that comprise interconnected networks	Telecommunications, cable and satellite networks, routers and servers, backbone networks

This design principle is implemented in the logical infrastructure of the Internet through the adoption of standardized communication protocols – the Internet Protocol suite – which "provides a general, technology– and application-independent interface to the lower layers of the network," that is, the physical infrastructure (Frischmann and van Schewick, 2007: 385–86; Farrell and Weiser, 2004: 91). End-to-end essentially means that infrastructure providers cannot differentiate or discriminate among data packets carried by their networks (Lemley and Lessig, 2001: 931). This design promotes the open interconnection of networks and focuses application development and innovation on the demands of end-users. For the most part, infrastructure providers are ignorant of the identity of the end-users and end-uses, and at the same time, end-users and end-uses are ignorant of the various networks that transport data packets. In a sense, shared ignorance is "built" into the infrastructure and precludes individualized exclusion or prioritization of end-users or end-uses. In essence, end-to-end design sustains an infrastructure commons.

There is considerable pressure for change, pressure to replace the existing "dumb," open architecture with an "intelligent," restrictive architecture capable of differentiating, and discriminating among end-uses and end-users. Pressure for change derives from many sources, including the Internet's evolution to broadband (infrastructure, applications, and content), the rapid increase in users, demand for latency-sensitive applications such as video-on-demand and IP telephony, demand for security measures and spam regulation measures implemented at the "core" of the Internet, and, more generally and importantly, demand for increased returns on infrastructure investments (Blumenthal and Clark, 2001: 71; Zittrain, 2008).

In response to these pressures, technologies have become available that enable network owners to monitor packets traveling across their networks to identify applications and end-users, and to manage, prioritize, and otherwise shape traffic based on identity of use or user (Cherry, 2005: 61; Cisco Systems, 2006). At the same time, the Federal Communications Commission (FCC) (2005) has removed most of the regulations that governed the behavior of providers of broadband networks in the past by classifying the provision of broadband Internet access services over cable or DSL as an "information service" that is regulated under Title I of the Communications Act.[23]

We should resist this pressure and think more carefully through the benefits of sustaining an Internet infrastructure commons.

Internet as Commercial, Public, and Social Infrastructure

Discussion of the costs and benefits of preserving the end-to-end design of the Internet focuses on issues relevant to commercial infrastructure, specifically, on competition in upstream and downstream markets (Farrell and Weiser, 2004; Yoo, 2004: 32–34) and in innovation markets (Wu, 2004: 75–79; Wu, 2003: 147–48; Wu and Lessig, 2003: 3–6). Framed in light of antitrust and regulatory economics, the current debate misses the forest for the trees.

The Internet is a mixed commercial, public, and social infrastructure. The public and social aspects of the Internet infrastructure are largely undervalued in the current debate. Bringing these aspects of the Internet into focus strengthens the case for preserving the end-to-end architecture of the Internet.

Consider what makes the Internet valuable to society. It is very difficult to estimate the full social value of the Internet, in large part because of the wide variety of downstream uses that generate public and nonmarket goods. Despite such difficulty, we know that the Internet is "transforming our society" (President's Info. Tech. Advisory Comm.,1999: 11–20). The transformation is similar to transformations experienced in the past with other infrastructure, yet things are changing in a more rapid, widespread, and dramatic fashion.

The Internet environment is quickly becoming integral to the lives, affairs and relationships of individuals, companies, universities, organizations, and governments worldwide. It is having significant effects on fundamental social processes and resource systems that generate value for society. Commerce, community, culture, education, government, health, politics, and science are all information- and communications-intensive systems that the Internet is transforming. The transformation is taking place at the ends, where people are empowered to participate and are engaged in socially valuable, productive activities. As Jack Balkin (2004: 2) has observed, the "digital revolution makes possible widespread cultural participation and interaction that previously could not have existed on the same scale."

The Internet opens the door widely for users, and, most important, it opens the door to many different activities that are productive. End-users actively engage in innovation and creation; speak about anything and everything; maintain family connections and friendships; debate, comment, and engage in political and nonpolitical discourse; meet new people; search, research, learn, and educate; and build and sustain communities.

These are the types of productive activities that generate substantial social value, value that evades observation or consideration within conventional economic transactions. When engaged in these activities, end-users are not passively consuming content delivered to them, nor are they producing content solely for controlled distribution on a pay-to-consume basis. Instead, end-users interact with each other to build, develop, produce, and distribute public and nonmarket goods. Public participation in such activities results in external benefits that accrue to society as a whole (online and offline) that are not captured or necessarily even appreciated by the participants.

Further, active participation in these activities by some portion of society benefits even those who do not participate. In other words, the social benefits of Internet-based innovation, creativity, cultural production, education, political discourse, and so on are not confined to the Internet; the social benefits spill over.

> Let me use a simple example. Consider the speech of a nonprofessional blogger pertaining to some political issue (for example, the Iraq war, civil rights, property tax reform). The speech may have external effects beyond those who write, read, or comment on the blog itself because the speech – the ideas and information communicated – may impact awareness and opinion within the community affected by the political issue being discussed, and perhaps

> ultimately, the speech may affect political processes. The likelihood that any particular speaker will have a noticeable impact may be small, but that is beside the point. Society benefits when its members participate because of the aggregate effects.... Speech affects community systems and community members, even community members who do not participate in the conversation (Frischmann, 2008b).

With respect to weblogs, in particular, political scientists, journalists, economists, and lawyers, among others, are beginning to appreciate and more carefully study the dynamic relationships between this new medium of communication and traditional, offline modes of communication and social interaction (whether economic, political, social, or otherwise).

Consider the fact that a significant portion of the content traveling on the Internet is noncommercial, speech-oriented information – whether personal e-mails and web pages, blog postings, instant messaging, or government documentation[24] – and the economic fact that such information is a pure public good generally available for both consumption and productive use by recipients. The productive use and reuse of such information creates benefits for the user, the downstream recipients, and even people that never consume or use the information. These benefits are positive externalities that are not fully appropriated or even appreciated by the initial output producer.

It is worth noting that welfare can be ratcheted up in incredibly small increments and still leads to significant social surplus. As participants educate themselves, interact, and socialize, for example, the magnitude of positive externalities may be quite small. Diffusion of small-scale positive externalities, however, can lead to a significant social surplus when the externality-producing activity is widespread, as it is on the Internet. This seems to reflect in economic terms the basic idea underlying Balkin's democratic culture theory (Balkin, 2004). This view also complements the arguments, persuasively made by Benkler (2001b), concerning the social value of diversity in both the types and sources of content.

Widespread, interactive participation in the creation, molding, distribution, and preservation of culture, in its many different forms and contexts, may be an ideal worth pursuing from an economic perspective because of the aggregate social welfare gains that accrue to society when its members are actively and productively engaged.

Reframing the Network Neutrality Debate

In 2003, Professor Tim Wu summarized the status of the ongoing "open access versus control" debate and couched it as one about "network neutrality," that is, whether, and if so how, the Internet should be made neutral. Together with Lawrence Lessig, Wu submitted an ex parte letter to the FCC explaining their view that network neutrality ought to be an "aspiration" for the FCC (Wu and Lessig, 2003). The debate has been ongoing and building upsteam ever since.

How does the end-to-end design principle discussed in the previous sections relate to network neutrality? Initially, implementing a commons via end-to-end network design might appear "neutral" to applications while shifting to an "intelligent" network design capable of allocating access to the infrastructure based on the identity of the uses (users) appears "nonneutral." Yet, as Wu, Lessig, and others have explained, end-to-end design precludes finely differentiated QoS[25] and thus disfavors latency-sensitive applications, such as IP telephony and video-on-demand. End-to-end thus involves bias and is not exactly neutral (Wu, 2003; Yoo, 2004: 32–34).

That end-to-end design entails some bias does not mean that shifting to finely differentiated QoS is unbiased. Quite to the contrary, bias may be inescapable. Just as the current end-to-end design favors data applications at the expense of time-sensitive applications, shifting to a fine-grained QoS regime also will exhibit a bias for particular applications, specifically for commercial applications that generate observable and appropriable returns. The bias would not be technologically determined (as in the case of end-to-end design), but rather would be determined by the predictable operation of the market mechanism. Given the ability to discriminate among end-users and end-uses on a packet-by-packet basis and the inability to perfectly price discriminate, infrastructure suppliers should be expected to act rationally and, to the extent feasible, bias access priority (via imperfect price discrimination) and/or optimize infrastructure design in favor of output markets that generate the highest levels of appropriable returns (producer surplus), at the expense of output markets that potentially generate a larger aggregate surplus (direct consumer surplus, producer surplus, and external surplus).

As Barabara van Schewick and I recently explained:

> Although often conflated, network neutrality is not equivalent to retaining the end-to-end architecture of the Internet. On one hand, the application-blindness of the network is only one consequence of applying the broad version of the end-to-end argument; thus, the broad version of the end-to-end arguments is much broader than network neutrality. On the other hand, network neutrality does not necessarily require end-to-end compatible protocols, such as the Internet Protocol.
>
> Still, the conflation of network neutrality with end-to-end is understandable because of the historical connection between the two principles. The blindness made possible by technology and end-to-end design disabled the ability of network providers to discriminate effectively among either uses or users. Technology has shifted so as to enable effective discrimination, and now the central issue to be resolved (through the political process) is whether to disable that ability through legal means (Frischmann and van Schewick, 2007: 385 n.7).

To properly address this difficult issue, the network neutrality debate must broaden its focus beyond the merits of sustaining a neutral network (framed almost exclusively in light of antitrust and regulatory economics) to the merits of sustaining the Internet as a mixed commercial, public, and social infrastructure. The debate ought to be about optimizing the Internet for society as a whole and it ought to take into account the full range of interests at stake, many of which are simply ignored by participants in the debate because they lie outside the purview of antitrust and regulatory economics. Again, as Barabara van Schewick and I recently explained: "There are many related normative commitments at stake in the network neutrality debate, including market values such as promoting allocative and productive efficiency, innovation, and economic growth but also various nonmarket values such as education and increased participation in cultural and political processes" (Frischmann and van Schewick, 2007: 426). Admittedly, this is a very difficult type of optimization problem, but it is one that arises frequently with infrastructure resources, and it is one that deserves a broader analytic frame than antitrust and regulatory economics alone provide.

Conclusion

Basic infrastructure is critical to the fabric of our society. That is, basic infrastructure contributes to more than just commercial goods which are often best provided by markets – basic infrastructure also contributes to social and public goods. This means there are significant "nonmarket" uses for the infrastructure that are not well reflected in demand for and willingness-to-pay for access to the infrastructure. Therefore, relying on market provisioning of these goods will result in underconsumption by public/nonmarket goods producers. Generally, attempts to directly subsidize these public/nonmarket goods producers are not appropriate because there are too many and the implications are too diverse. Open access is a (political) fix to ensure that willingness-to-pay is not used to allocate access to infrastructure. By disabling the capacity to exclude on the basis of market-value/willingness-to-pay, access to infrastructure is not biased against uses that produce public and social goods.

Notes

1. This chapter is an adaptation of a much longer and more detailed article, *An Economic Theory of Infrastructure and Commons Management* (Frischmann, 2005a). For my other work in this vein, see the series of articles listed as references.
2. See, for example, Black's Law Dictionary (7th ed. 1999: 784) (Infrastructure: "The underlying framework of a system, especially, public services and facilities (such as highways, schools, bridges, sewers, and water systems) needed to support commerce as well as economic and residential development."); Webster's Third New International Dictionary of the English Language Unabridged (1993: 1161) (Infrastructure: "[T]he underlying foundation or basic framework (as of an organization or a system): substructure; especially, the permanent installations required for military purposes."); Morris and Morris (1988: 309) (providing a historical account of how the term's meaning has evolved).
3. "'Public works infrastructure includes both specific functional modes – highways, streets, roads, and bridges; mass transit; airports and airways; water supply and water resources; wastewater management; solid-waste treatment and disposal; electric power generation and transmission; telecommunications; and hazardous waste management – and the combined system these modal elements comprise" (NRC 1987: 4 n.1).
4. Of course, there are exceptions to these generalizations.
5. The rebuilding of Iraq brings this point into stark relief. The task of reconstructing and rebuilding a country's traditional infrastructure – its transportation, communication, governance, and basic service systems – is a tremendous task requiring centralized coordination and substantial investment. Note that building these infrastructure systems is a necessary precursor to many other productive activities.
6. See, generally, Rose, 1986: 723–49 (discussing the history of public access rights to various infrastructure resources such as roadways and waterways).
7. As Lessig (2001: 244) notes: "The government has funded the construction of highways and local roads; these highways are then used either 'for free' or with the payment of a toll. In either case, the highway functions as a commons." Of course, as taxpayers, we ultimately foot

the bill for the provision of many infrastructure resources (Congressnal Budget Office 1998, 2003; Bassanini and Scarpetta, 2001: 9, 19).

8. In some industries, however, access to an infrastructure resource is priced at different rates for different classes of users. For example, telecommunications companies historically have treated businesses and individuals differently without much concern (Odlyzko, 2004: 336–37).
9. Basically, positive (negative) externalities are benefits (costs) realized by one person as a result of another person's activity without payment (compensation). Externalities generally are not fully factored into a person's decision to engage in the activity. According to Meade (1973: 15), "An external economy (diseconomy) is an event which confers an appreciable benefit (inflicts an appreciable damage) on some person or persons who were not fully consenting parties in reaching the decision or decisions which led directly or indirectly to the event in question." Arrow (1970: 67) defined externality as the absence of a functioning market. Cornes and Sandler (1996: 39, 40–43) discuss the views of both Meade and Arrow. Arrow, in particular, made clear the importance of understanding that the existence or nonexistence of externalities is a function of the relevant institutional setting, incentive structure, information, and other constraints on the decision-making and exchange possibilities of relevant actors. As Papandreou (1994: 13–68) explores in a detailed historical account of the term, "externality" means many things and has been a contested concept in economics for many years. It is, as Demsetz (1967: 348) described it, "an ambiguous concept." See also Frischmann (2007b) and Frischmann and Lemley (2007).
10. Harold Demsetz, however, came close. Demsetz suggested that "[c]ommunal property results in great externalities. The full costs of the activities of an owner of a communal property right are not borne directly by him, nor can they be called to his attention easily by the willingness of others to pay him an appropriate sum" (Demsetz 1968: 355). Demsetz focused on negative externalities (external costs) and failed to appreciate that communal property can result in great positive externalities (external benefits) and that such a result can be socially desirable.
11. Others have adopted similar definitions (Lessig, 2001: 19–20; Ostrom, 1990: 1–7; Burger et al., 2001: 1–6; Bollier, 2001: 2–3).
12. As Benkler (2003: 6) explains:
    Commons are a particular type of institutional arrangement for governing the use and disposition of resources. Their salient characteristic, which defines them in contradistinction to property, is that no single person has exclusive control over the use and disposition of any particular resource. Instead, resources governed by commons may be used or disposed of by anyone among some (more or less well defined) number of persons, under rules that may range from "anything goes" to quite crisply articulated formal rules that are effectively enforced.
13. Carol Rose (2003: 93) discusses the traditional Roman categories of nonexclusive property, one of which, *res communes*, was incapable of exclusive appropriation due to its inherent character.
14. David and Foray (1996: 91) note that the "activity of diffusing economically relevant knowledge is not itself a natural one." "Rather, it is socially constructed through the creation of appropriate institutions and conventions, such as open science and intellectual property…." *See also id.* at 93–99 (discussing the distribution of scientific and technological knowledge through institutions). The open source and creative commons movements are two prominent examples (Lessig, 2001: 164–65, 255–56; Reichman and Uhlir, 2003: 430–32).
15. The quintessential example of a nonrivalrous resource is an idea, which can be possessed, shared, and used widely. On the public good nature of ideas, see Frischmann and Lemley (2007) and the many sources cited therein.
16. It is worth emphasizing, however, that the possibility of congestion does not prelude managing such infrastructure as a commons. See, for example, Frischmann and van Schewick (2007) (exploring nondiscriminatory means for managing congestion on the Internet).
17. Another way to frame this would be to focus on the genericness of the input. Infrastructure are general purpose inputs that facilitate many different productive activities – as noted above, *means to many ends*.
18. Neither the law nor economic efficiency requires complete internalization (Frischmann, 2007b; Frischmann and Lemley, 2007).
19. The flowers themselves are private goods in the sense that they are rivalrously possessed and cannot be planted by multiple homeowners; each homeowner that wants to plant a tulip must

plant his own bulb. The example is intended to illustrate how the production of public goods – in this example, the beautiful view – has the potential to generate positive externalities and how realizing the potential is contingent. The example is *not* intended to suggest anything about whether or not flower gardens are efficiently supplied by markets.

20. Amitai Aviram (2003) observes that "Often (though not always) realization of network effects requires interconnection between the users. The institution that facilitates interconnection between users of a good or service exhibiting network effects, and thus enables the realization of the network effects, is called a *network*." Traditional infrastructure resources often act as such a network.
21. To be more precise, the physical infrastructure and certain components of the logical infrastructure such as domain name space are partially (non)rival in the sense that (1) the risk of congestion depends upon the amount of capacity, number of users, and other contextual factors, and (2) the risk can be managed in a fashion that sustains nonrivalry in consumption.
22. There are two versions of the end-to-end arguments: a narrow version, which was first identified, named and described in a seminal paper by Saltzer et al. (1981, 1984), and a broad version which was the focus of later papers by the authors (e.g., Reed et al., 1998: 69; Blumenthal and Clark, 2001: 71). While both versions have shaped the original architecture of the Internet, only the broad version is responsible for the application-blindness of the network and relevant to the network neutrality debate. van Schewick (forthcoming 2008) provides a detailed analysis of the two versions and their relationship to the architecture of the Internet. See also Lessig (2001: 34–35) and Lemley and Lessig (2001: 931).
23. See Appropriate Framework for Broadband Access to the Internet over Wireline Facilities, Report and Order and Notice of Proposed Rulemaking, 20 F.C.C.R. 14853 (2005). Before, the FCC's decision to classify the provision of broadband Internet access services over cable modems as an "information service" had been upheld by the Supreme Court, see Nat'l Cable & Telecomm. Ass'n v. Brand X Internet Servs., 125 S. Ct. 2688 (2005), aff'g Inquiry Concerning High-Speed Access to the Internet Over Cable and Other Facilities, Internet Over Cable Declaratory Ruling, Appropriate Regulatory Treatment for Broadband Access to the Internet Over Cable Facilities, Declaratory Ruling and Notice of Proposed Rulemaking, 17 F.C.C.R. 4798 (2002).
24. Consider, for example, the recent findings of the Pew Internet and American Life Project regarding content creation and distribution online. A significant percentage of Internet users produce and distribute content and interact online (44%). The types of productive activities range from posting content such as photographs to interactive products such as blogs (Lenhart et al., 2004).
25. The Internet currently provides best effort data delivery, which is a simple form of QoS. There are different types of QoS, some of which are "more consistent" with end-to-end than others (Lessig, 2001: 47).

References

Arrow, Kenneth J. (1970) The Organization of Economic Activity: Issues Pertinent to the Choice of Market Versus Nonmarket Allocation. In: Robert H.H. and Julius M. (eds.) Public Expenditure and Policy Analysis. Rand McNally & Co, USA.

Aviram, Amitai (2003) A Network Effects Analysis of Private Ordering. Berkeley Olin Program in Law & Economics, Working Paper Series 11079. Berkeley Olin Program in Law & Economics.

Balkin, Jack (2004) Digital Speech and Democratic Culture: A Theory of Freedom of Expression for the Information Society. New York University Law Review 79: 1–55.

Bassanini, Andrea and Stefano Scarpetta (2001) The Driving Forces of Economic Growth: Panel Data Evidence for the OECD Countries. OECD Economic Studies No. 33: 9–56.

Benkler, Yochai (2000) From Consumers to Users: Shifting the Deeper Structures of Regulation Towards Sustainable Commons and User Access. Federal Communications Law Journal 52: 561–579.

Benkler, Yochai (2001a) Property, Commons, and the First Amendment: Towards a Core Common Infrastructure. White Paper for the First Amendment Program, Brennan Center for Justice at NYU Law School. Available at http://www.benkler.org/WhitePaper.pdf

Benkler, Yochai (2001b) Siren Songs and Amish Children: Autonomy, Information, and Law. New York University Law Review 76: 23–113.

Benkler, Yochai (2003) The Political Economy of Commons. Upgrade IV: 6–9.

Black's Law Dictionary (7th ed. 1999). West Publishing.

Blumenthal, Marjory S. and David D. Clark (2001) Rethinking the Design of the Internet: The End-to-End Arguments vs. the Brave New World. ACM Transactions on Internet Tech. 1: 70–109.

Bollier, David (2001) Public Assets, Private Profits: Reclaiming the American Commons in an Age of Market Enclosure Available at http://www.bollier.org/pdf/PA_Report.pdf

Branscomb, Lewis M. and James H. Keller (1996) Introduction. In: Branscomb L.M. and Keller J.H. (eds.) Converging Infrastructures: Intelligent Transportation and the National Information Infrastructure. MIT Press Cambridge, MA.

Burger, Joannaet al. (2001) Introduction. In: Burger Joannaet al. (eds.) Protecting the Commons: A Framework for Resource Management in the Americas. Island Press.

Button, Kenneth (1986) Ownership, Investment and Pricing of Transport and Communications Infrastructure. In: Batten D.F. and Karlsson C. (eds.) Infrastructure and the Complexity of Economic Development. Springer-Verlag, Berlin.

Cherry, Steven (2005) The VoIP Backlash, IEEE Spectrum 42: 61–63.

Cisco Systems, Inc., Network-Based Application Recognition and Distributed Network-Based Application Recognition, Available at http://www.cisco.com/en/US/products/ps6350/products_configuration_guide_chapter09186a0080455985.html (last visited Sept. 30, 2006).

Congressional Budget Office (1998) The Economic Effects of Federal Spending on Infrastructure and Other Investments. Available at http://www.cbo.gov/ftpdocs/6xx/doc601/fedspend.pdf

Congressional Budget Office (2003) The Long-Term Budget Outlook. Available at http://www.cbo.gov/ftpdocs/49xx/doc4916/Report.pdf

Cooper, Mark (2005) Making the Network Connection: Using Network Theory to Explain the Link Between Open Digital Platforms and Innovation. Available at http://cyberlaw.stanford.edu/blogs/cooper/archives/network%20theory.pdf (last visited Jan. 20, 2005).

Cornes, Richard and Todd Sandler (1996) The Theory of Externalities, Public Goods, and Club Goods. 2 Cambridge University Press, Cambridge, UK.

Crump, David (2001) Game Theory, Legislation, and the Multiple Meanings of Equality. Harvard Journal on Legislation 38: 331–412.

David, Paul A. and Dominique Foray (1996) Information Distribution and the Growth of Economically Valuable Knowledge: A Rationale for Technological Infrastructure Policies. In: Teubal M., Foray D., Justman M., and Zuscovitch E. (eds.) Technological Infrastructure Policy: An International Perspective. Kluwer, Amsterdam.

Demsetz, Harold (1967) Toward a Theory of Property Rights. Am. Econ. Rev. Papers & Proc. 57: 347–359.

Eastman, Wayne (1997) Telling Alternative Stories: Heterodox Versions of the Prisoner's Dilemma, the Coase Theorem, and Supply-Demand Equilibrium. Connecticut Law Review 29: 727–825.

Economides, Nicholas (1996a) The Economics of Networks, International Journal of Industrial Organization 14: 673–699.

Economides, Nicholas (1996b) Network Externalities, Complementarities, and Invitations to Enter. European Journal of Political Economy 12: 211–233.

Economides, Nicholas (2003) Competition Policy in Network Industries: An Introduction. In: Dennis J. (ed.) The New Economy: Just How New Is It. University of Chicago Press.

Farrell, Joseph and Philip J. Weiser (2004) Modularity, Vertical Integration, and Open Access Policies: Towards a Convergence of Antitrust and Regulation in the Internet Age. Harvard Journal of Law & Technology 17: 85–134.

Federal Communications Commission (2005) Appropriate Framework for Broadband Access to the Internet over Wireline Facilities, Report and Order and Notice of Proposed Rulemaking. 20 F.C.C.R. 14853.

Flores, Nicholas E. (2003) Conceptual Framework for Nonmarket Valuation. In: Patricia A.C. et al. (eds.) A Primer on Nonmarket Valuation. Kluwer Academic Publishers, Boston, MA.

Frischmann, Brett M. and Barbara van Schewick (2007) Network Neutrality and The Economics of an Information Superhighway. Jurimetrics 47: 383–428.

Frischmann, Brett M. and Mark A. Lemley (2007) Spillovers. Columbia Law Review 107: 257–301.

Frischmann, Brett M. and Spencer Weber Waller (2008) Revitalizing Essential Facilities. 75 Antitrust Law Journal 1–65.

Frischmann, Brett M. (2000) Innovation and Institutions: Rethinking the Economics of U.S. Science and Technology Policy. Vermont Law Review 24: 347–416.

Frischmann, Brett M. (2001) Privatization and Commercialization of the Internet Infrastructure: Rethinking Market Intervention into Government and Government Intervention into the Market. 2 Columbia Science and Technology Law Review. Available at http://www.stlr.org/cite.cgi?volume=2&article=1

Frischmann, Brett M. (2005a) An Economic Theory of Infrastructure and Commons Management. Minnesota Law Review 89: 917–1030.

Frischmann, Brett M. (2007a) Cultural Environmentalism and The Wealth of Networks, University of Chicago Law Review 74: 1083–1143.

Frischmann, Brett M. (2007b) Evaluating the Demsetzian Trend in Copyright Law. Review of Law and Economics: 3(3). Available at http://www.bepress.com/rle/vol3/iss3/art2

Frischmann, Brett M. (2007c) Infrastructure Commons in Economic Perspective. First Monday: 12(6) (June 2007) Available at http://firstmonday.org/issues/issue12_6/frischmann/index.html

Frischmann, Brett M. (2008a) Environmental Infrastructure. Ecology Law Quarterly 35.

Frischmann, Brett M. (2008b) Spillovers, Speech, and the First Amendment. 2008 University of Chicago Legal Forum (forthcoming, Oct. 2008).

Ghosh, Shubha (2004) Patents and the Regulatory State: Rethinking the Patent Bargain Metaphor After Eldred. Berkeley Tech. L.J. 19: 1315–1388.

Hardin, Garrett (1968) The Tragedy of the Commons. Science 162: 1243–1248.

Hess, Charlotte and Elinor Ostrom (2003) Ideas, Artifacts, and Facilities: Information as a Common-Pool Resource. Law & Contemporary Problems: 66: 111–145.

Katz, Michael L. and Carl Shapiro (1985) Network Externalities, Competition, and Compatibility. Am. Econ. Rev. 75: 424–440.

Katz, Michael L. and Carl Shapiro (1994) Systems Competition and Network Effects. Journal of Economic Perspectives 93–115.

Lemley, Mark A. and David McGowan (1998) Legal Implications of Network Economic Effects. California Law Review 86: 479–611.

Lemley, Mark A. and Lawrence Lessig (2001) The End of End-to-End: Preserving the Architecture of the Internet in the Broadband Era. UCLA Law Review 48: 925–972.

Lemley, Mark A. (2005) Property, Intellectual Property, and Free Riding. Texas Law Review 83: 1031–1075.

Lenhart, Amanda, et al. (Feb. 29, 2004) Pew Internet & American Life Project, Content Creation Online.

Lessig, Lawrence (2001) The Future of Ideas: The Fate of the Commons in a Connected World. Random House, New York.

Levy, Sidney M. (1996) Build, Operate, Transfer: Paving the Way for Tomorrow's Infrastructure. John Wiley and Sons, NY.

Luban, David (1995) The Social Responsibilities of Lawyers: A Green Perspective. George Washington Law Review 63: 955–983.

Meade, James E. (1973) The Theory of Economic Externalities: The Control of Environmental Pollution and Similar Social Costs. Sijthoff-Leiden, Geneva.

Morris, William and Mary Morris (1988) Morris Dictionary of Word and Phrase Origins. 2 Harper Collins.
National Research Council (1987) Infrastructure for the 21st Century: Framework for a Research Agenda. National Academy Press, Washington, DC.
Nat'l Cable & Telecomm. Ass'n v. Brand X Internet Servs., 125 S. Ct. 2688 (2005), aff'g Inquiry Concerning High-Speed Access to the Internet Over Cable and Other Facilities, Internet Over Cable Declaratory Ruling, Appropriate Regulatory Treatment for Broadband Access to the Internet Over Cable Facilities, Declaratory Ruling and Notice of Proposed Rulemaking, 17 F.C.C.R. 4798 (2002).
Odlyzko, Andrew (2004) The Evolution of Price Discrimination in Transportation and Its Implications for the Internet. Review of Network Economics 3: 323–346.
Ostrom, Elinor (1990) Governing the Commons: The Evolution of Institutions for Collective Action. Cambridge, UK.
Papandreou, Andreas A. (1994) Externality and Institutions. Clarendon Press, Oxford.
President's Info. Tech. Advisory Comm. (1999), Information Technology Research: Investing in Our Future. Available at http://www.ccic.gov/ac/report/pitac_report.pdf
Reed, David P. et al. (1998) Commentaries on "Active Networking and End-to-End Arguments." IEEE Network 12(3): 66–71.
Reichman, J.H. and Paul F. Uhlir (2003) A Contractually Reconstructed Research Commons for Scientific Data in a Highly Protectionist Intellectual Property Environment. Law & Contemporary Problems 66: 315–462.
Rose, Carol (1986) The Comedy of the Commons: Custom, Commerce, and Inherently Public Property. University of Chicago Law Review 53: 711–781.
Rose, Carol (2003) Romans, Roads, and Romantic Creators: Traditions of Public Property in the Information Age. Law & Contemp. Probs. 66: 89–110.
Saltzer, Jerome H. et al. (1981) End-to-End Arguments in System Design. 1981 Second International Conference on Distributed Computing Systems 509–512.
Saltzer, Jerome H. et al. (1984) End-to-End Arguments in System Design. ACM Transactions on Computer Sys: 2: 277–288.
Sicker, Douglas C. and Joshua L. Mindel (2002) Refinements of a Layered Model for Telecom munications Policy. Journal on Telecommunications & High Technology Law 1: 69–94.
Steinmueller, W. Edward (1996) Technological Infrastructure in Information Technology Industries. In: Teubal M., Foray D., Justman M., and Zuscovitch E. (eds.) Technological Infrastructure Policy: An International Perspective. Kluwer, Amsterdam.
van Schewick, Barbara (forthcoming 2008) Architecture and Innovation: The Role of the End-to-End Arguments in the Original Internet. PhD Dissertation, Technical University Berlin 2005, MIT Press, Boston.
Webster's Third New International Dictionary of the English Language Unabridged (1993).
Werbach, Kevin (2002) A Layered Model for Internet Privacy. Journal on Telecommunications & High Technology Law 1: 37–68.
Wu, Tim (2003) Network Neutrality, Broadband Discrimination. Journal on Telecommunications & High Technology Law2 141–175.
Wu, Tim (2004) The Broadband Debate: A User's Guide. Journal on Telecommunications & High Technology Law3: 69–95.
Wu, Timothy and Lawrence Lessig (2003) Letter from Timothy Wu, Associate Professor, University of Virginia School of Law, & Lawrence Lessig, Professor of Law, Stanford Law School, to Marlene H. Dortch, Secretary, FCC 3 n.3 (Aug. 22, 2003). Available at http://faculty.virginia.edu/timwu/wu_lessig_fcc.pdf
Yoo, Christopher S. (2004) Would Mandating Broadband Network Neutrality Help or Hurt Competition? A Comment on the End-to-End Debate. Journal on Telecommunications & High Technology Law 3: 32–34.
Zittrain, Jonathan (2008) The Future of the Internet and How to Stop It. Yale University Press, New Haven.

Chapter 4
Dumbing Down the Net: A Further Look at the Net Neutrality Debate

Mark A. Jamison and Janice A. Hauge

Introduction

It is commonplace for sellers of goods and services to enhance the value of their products by paying extra for premium delivery service. For example, package delivery services such as Federal Express and the US Postal Service offer shippers a variety of delivery speeds and insurance programs. Web content providers such as Yahoo! and MSN Live Earth can purchase web-enhancing services from companies such as Akamai to speed the delivery of their web content to customers.[1]

Recently, there has been concern over the desires of some Internet Service Providers (ISPs) such as AT&T and Verizon to offer Internet content providers faster, premium delivery of content and services to end user customers and to charge the content providers for the superior transmission. This is the part of what has been termed the net neutrality issue, which is actually a loose collection of issues that vary in their mixture and meaning over time.[2] However, the provision of and charging for premium transmission speed of Internet packets consistently appear in the public debate.[3] Proponents of net neutrality argue that the network itself is simply infrastructure that should not add value to the service, and thus innovation should occur only at the edges of the network.[4] Net neutrality advocates also hold that the network should be a commons that broadband users are allowed to use in ways that are not illegal and that do not harm the network, and that networks should not discriminate between uses, users, and content. In contrast, network providers such as AT&T argue that offering premium transmission services will improve customer choice and that ISPs would not degrade service to content providers not purchasing the premium transmission speed.[5]

In order to analyze the potential effects of policy proposals to ensure net neutrality, it is important to consider positively (rather than normatively) conditions under which the various hypothesized outcomes might occur. In this chapter, we focus on

M.A. Jamison (✉)
Director of the Public Utility Research Center (PURC) and Director of Telecommunications Studies, University of Florida, Gainesville, FL, USA
email: mark.jamison@cba.ulf.edu

W.H. Lehr and L.M. Pupillo (eds.), *Internet Policy and Economics*,
DOI 10.1007/978-1-4419-0038-8_4, © Springer Science+Business Media, LLC 2009

the findings of analytical research on the effects of networks offering and charging for premium transmission service, and on the effect of regulation on network providers' offerings. In the second section, we provide background on the Internet and on the net neutrality debate. The third section considers how premium transmission is provided and priced, and how content providers provide their services. The fourth section addresses how the offering and provision of premium transmission affects network innovation, network subscription, and incentives for the network provider to hinder rivals. The final section is the conclusion.

Background

Net neutrality became part of the public debate over the roles of networks in 2003 with the Supreme Court reversal of the Ninth Circuit court ruling in *Brand X Internet Services v. FCC*.[6] The decision upheld the Federal Communications Commission's (FCC's) conclusion that cable modems, as an information service, are not subject to regulation as telecommunications carriers.[7] This decision resulted in asymmetric regulatory treatment of two substitutable services: Internet access via cable modem and Internet access via DSL (digital subscriber line), which is offered by telephone companies. This led to intense lobbying on the part of telephone companies to have DSL treated in a manner similar to cable access. The FCC issued a ruling in 2005[8] that exempted DSL from the "statutory access requirements applied to traditional telephone [service]."[9] The ruling effectively deregulated methods of Internet access in the USA, at least with respect to traditional telecommunications regulation.

Currently, ISPs and Internet backbone providers carry traffic on a best effort basis, which in general means that the first packets into a switching point are the first packets out. Net neutrality proponents see this best-effort approach as a central principle for an application-blind Internet, which they apparently believe is important for content development and innovation. They fear that network providers might exercise market power to "pick and choose" what Internet users would "be able to see and do on the Internet."[10] Recent quotes by telephone company executives have provided fuel for this fear: Verizon CEO Ivan Seidenberg stated, "We have to make sure that they [application providers] don't sit on our network and chew up bandwidth… We need to pay for the pipe."[11] The FCC under Chairman Powell and Chairman Martin has believed that it is doing an adequate job of overseeing and promoting competition among ISPs,[12] but net neutrality proponents believe that the FCC and the federal courts will not exercise rigorous oversight of ISPs absent legislation.[13] Proponents believe that the FCC's actions to date are inadequate, and Proponents fear that without legislative or regulatory safeguards, the phone companies will determine which content providers are to be successful and which are not.

The broader debate is over what regulations, if any, are to be imposed on the Internet industry. Content providers (such as Google and Microsoft) are concerned about ISPs offering preferred delivery of data. Such offerings would be designed so that for a fee, the ISPs would guarantee "head of the line" privileges for a customer's data,[14] even though there is some doubt as to the technical feasibility of such a plan if it were implemented.[15] From these content providers' perspectives, there are two basic implications: (1) Any content provider that did not pay the extra fee might have the quality of service for its data degraded,[16] and (2) ISPs that are vertically integrated into the content business might give their own packets priority service or otherwise deliberately disadvantage their content rivals. Said another way, priority delivery of content could be a means by which ISPs could use price discrimination to earn higher profits while compelling content providers to pay the additional fee or risk degradation of service. Furthermore, network neutrality proponents believe that such an exercise of market power in infrastructure would stifle application-level innovation and harm consumers. Proponents of net neutrality use the case of Madison River Communications to illustrate their point. Madison River Communications is a rural telecommunications company that blocked its DSL customers from accessing VoIP[17] service. After these actions were brought to regulators' attention, the FCC issued an order directing Madison River to allow its DSL customers to access VoIP service.[18]

The FCC also responded more broadly to concerns about net neutrality in other proceedings. Even though the FCC does not apply traditional telephone-like regulation to Internet access providers, it does retain some ancillary authority over Internet providers under its current statutes. Using that authority, the FCC recently adopted a set of policy principles applicable to Internet providers, namely:

- "To encourage broadband deployment and preserve and promote the open and interconnected nature of the public Internet, consumers are entitled to access the lawful Internet content of their choice.
- To encourage broadband deployment and preserve and promote the open and interconnected nature of the public Internet, consumers are entitled to run applications and use services of their choice, subject to the needs of law enforcement.
- To encourage broadband deployment and preserve and promote the open and interconnected nature of the public Internet, consumers are entitled to connect their choice of legal devices that do not harm the network.
- To encourage broadband deployment and preserve and promote the open and interconnected nature of the public Internet, consumers are entitled to competition among network providers, application and service providers, and content providers."[19]

The FCC did note that these principles are "...subject to reasonable network management,"[20] which means that the principles did not necessarily bind the FCC to agree with net neutrality proponents. However, the FCC's policy statement may produce more questions than clarity.[21]

Consider the controversy over Comcast's management of peer-to-peer (P2P) traffic. Vuze, a company providing a platform for the downloading of high quality video (e.g., from National Geographic and PBS), has filed a petition for rulemaking requesting the FCC to prevent broadband network operators from degrading or blocking Internet content, a practice Vuze calls "throttling."[22] Specifically, Vuze alleges that Comcast, a large cable operator, was throttling bandwidth-intensive traffic such as video distribution. Comcast used deep packet analysis to identify bandwidth-intensive applications, and then used that information to "shape" or manage network traffic by delaying or disrupting those applications.[23] Comcast defended the practice, stating that it only delayed P2P traffic where the end user's computer was being used only for uploads even when the user was not present, and that this was done only when the network traffic reached specified levels of congestion.[24] Comcast also pointed out that its actions protected the quality of other consumer applications, such as VoIP and Internet gaming.

In support of their position, the ISPs also argue that under the status quo they have no incentive to upgrade their networks, and limited ability to recoup costs of initial investments in the Internet. Conversely, if ISPs are able to offer (and charge for) premium transmission, the incentive and ability to invest in the network would be greater. Although these arguments may be overstated, we explain below that offering premium transmission should improve overall network performance.

Thus far, much of the net neutrality debate has been more rhetorical than rigorous. Relying upon the analytical research that does exist, we consider the implications of net neutrality policies on network capacity, innovation, network subscription, and incentives for the network provider to hinder rivals.

Provision of Transmission and Content

Transmission Speed

In this section, we describe how network providers can provide premium transmission services alongside standard transmission services. Consider what happens when consumers visit web sites. Each visit or hit triggers the delivery of the site's content to the consumer. The speed with which the content's packets transverse the network is determined by the physical speeds of the transmission and switching facilities of the network and by the amount of congestion that the packets encounter. Congestion occurs when more packets enter a point in the network during a given period of time than the point can process. With current technologies, the physical speeds are barely consequential; however, packets do encounter congestion in the network.

The amount of time that a packet takes to clear a point of congestion, called the wait time, is determined by the capacity of the network at that point, the number of packets that are trying to pass through that point, and the priorities given to the packets that are in the queue waiting to be processed. The capacity of the network at a particular point is defined as the number of packets the point can process during a unit of time. In some sense, the net neutrality debate is about what happens at these congestion points or in their associated queues.

To understand this aspect of the debate, consider the situation where all packets are treated the same.[25] In this situation, every packet entering a queue during a given time experiences the same expected wait time: the packets simply line up in the queue as they arrive and wait to be processed. Mathematically, the expected or average wait time is represented as the number one divided by the difference between the network capacity and the arrival rate of packets during the time period, where the arrival rate is defined as the number of packets to arrive during the time period divided by the number of units of time during the period. As this formula illustrates, average wait time decreases (conversely, increases) if the difference between network capacity and arrival rate increases (conversely, decreases).[26]

Now consider what happens if some packets are given preferential treatment, that is, some packets receive the standard transmission service and others receive a premium service. There are various methods by which this could be done.[27] One method is called the one-processing rate system with priority. In this system, the premium group's content moves ahead of the standard group's content in the queue, but does not stop the standard group's content from being delivered once the standard group's content is in the service process. Another method is a two-processing rate situation. In this method, each group is given its own processing rate and these rates are chosen such that the average wait time for the premium service is less than the average wait time for the standard service. In either the one-rate system or the two-rate system, or indeed in any system, the packets with premium transmission experience less wait time than the packets receiving standard transmission. Providing premium transmission for some content may affect the average wait time in a network and the average wait time for content not receiving premium service, depending on how the premium service is provided.[28] Some network providers have committed to not degrading service for any content provider if premium service is offered. We call this the nondegradation condition.

Nondegradation Condition. Under this condition, the network operator keeps its commitment that standard transmission service will be the same regardless of whether premium service is offered.

When the nondegradation condition holds, a network provider will increase network capacity when providing premium transmission service.[29] This result follows directly from queuing theory.[30] In the one-rate system, the premium group always gets ahead in line and the second group experiences a decrease in its service speed, because it loses its place in line, unless the total system speeds up. Thus network capacity has to be increased if the first group experiences an improvement in service whereas the second group experiences no degradation in its service. With the two-rate system, the standard group would experience an increase in wait time unless total network capacity was increased so that the second group's access to delivery capacity was not diminished. Thus, when the nondegradation condition holds, the network's provision of premium transmission results in an increase in network capacity, all other things remaining equal.

Content Provision

There are many ways of categorizing the content on the Internet, but there are basically two ways that have been shown to be relevant for analyzing the net neutrality issue.

One type of content is that whose value decays as it passes through the network because the value of the content is time sensitive. We call this d-content, for decaying-content. Examples of d-content include auction sites such as e-Bay and sites for trading financial securities. For auction sites, some bidders wait until near the close of the auction before entering their final bids. Timely information on other bids is valuable because it decreases uncertainty about what others are willing to pay for the item that is offered for auction. This value provides an incentive for a bidder to purchase broadband Internet access so that information is not delayed by the connection to the network, and it provides an incentive for an auction site to seek ways to speed its delivery of bid data so as to attract bidders. Similarly, securities traders such as day traders depend on timely price information as they attempt to profit from small changes in securities prices. A site that offers timelier price information and faster trades would be more valuable to traders than a site that provided slower service, all other things being equal.

The second type of content is that which does not decay with the time it takes to transit the network. We call this n-content, for nondecaying content. Examples include the Social Science Research Network (SSRN) and news sites. For these types of sites, visitors value their time and so prefer faster delivery to slower delivery, but the value of the substance of a research paper downloaded from SSRN and the value of the substance of a news article on a recent court decision are unaffected whether it takes 3 or 10 seconds to download the information.

The type of content affects how consumers receive value from the content site. In the case of n-content, the value is simply the difference between the positive value of the content and the value of the time consumed to obtain the information. This is the consumer utility function developed by Mendelson (1985) to represent the value consumers receive from computing services. It has been further applied to analyzing broadband pricing and net neutrality issues.[31] In the case of d-content, wait time affects consumer utility in two ways. First, wait time decreases consumer utility directly by the time consumed to obtain the information, just as with n-content. Second, wait time decreases consumer utility indirectly by causing decay in the value of the content.

Why does it matter whether content is d-content or n-content? The content type affects which sites have greater preferences for premium transmission. Consider the situation for providers of d-content. When a d-content provider considers whether to purchase premium transmission, she compares the impact of her choice on her revenue to the impact of her choice on her costs. She chooses to purchase the premium transmission if she believes the revenue impact is greater than the cost impact because this improves her overall profit. But d-content providers vary in their abilities to provide useful d-content. For example one auction site might have proprietary algorithms that make it easier to use than rival sites. This raises the question of whether all d-content sites experience the same marginal impacts on revenue and cost. They do not. In situations where the marginal effect of wait time on the value of d-content is positively correlated with the content provider's innate ability to provide content and its investment in content, then lower value sites have a higher preference for premium service than do higher value sites. If instead the marginal effect of wait time on d-content value is negatively correlated with innate ability and content investment, then preferences for premium service depend on the relationship between these marginal effects and how the amount paid for premium service varies with wait time and the number of visits to the site.[32]

Now consider how n-content sites would view the choice between premium and standard transmission. An n-content provider would perform the same marginal analysis as a d-content provider: the n-content provider chooses to purchase the premium transmission if he believes the revenue impact is greater than the cost impact because this improves his overall profit. But innate abilities of n-content providers do not affect transmission preferences in the same way that they affect d-content providers.[33] The n-content providers with lower innate abilities consistently value premium transmission more than do n-content providers with greater innate abilities. The reason is that the extra cost of premium transmission to the high-ability n-content provider is greater relative to the extra revenue than for the low-ability n-content provider.

Transmission Tariff

There are two issues with the transmission tariff that affect analyses of net neutrality. One issue is whether content providers are able to extract what is called an information rent. The other issue is the design of the tariff. We discuss these issues in this section.

An information rent is a net benefit that a seller (conversely, buyer) can obtain because she has information about either her ability or her effort that the buyer (conversely, seller) does not have, or if he does have the information he cannot use it. To illustrate this situation, consider how a network provider might design a tariff for premium transmission. If the network provider gives each content provider a choice between standard transmission and premium transmission, and if the tariff is generally available to all content providers, then in order to induce a particular content provider to purchase premium transmission, the tariff prices for premium transmission must allow the content provider to receive just as much profit when she uses premium transmission as when she uses standard transmission. This profit is called the information rent.

Why would a network provider design its tariffs this way? Why not simply force each content provider to use the type of transmission that maximizes profit for the network provider? There are two reasons. First, recall that content providers vary in their innate abilities and that these abilities affect the value of premium transmission. The network provider might not know enough about each content provider's innate ability to know which type of transmission service would be preferred from the network provider's perspective. Second, the network provider might be regulated in the sense that either a sector or competition regulator requires the network provider to offer the same tariff to all content providers. In either case, the network provider's tariff must induce content providers to self-select the appropriate service.

Studies differ in whether it is reasonable to assume that content providers will receive an information rent. We assert that it is unreasonable to assume an information rent for two reasons. First, economic models of network content assume that customers are able to assess content value, which reveals each content site's innate ability. It seems reasonable to conclude that managers of the network operator also are able to observe content value given that they, too, are consumers. Furthermore, there are no regulations that require network operators to offer generally available tariffs to content providers; network providers and content providers negotiate individual contracts.[34]

The issue of tariff design is also important because the conclusions about how content providers' abilities affect their preferences for premium transmission depend upon tariff design. The profit-maximizing tariff design, given the assumption that there are no information rents, charges for premium delivery of packets based on the advertising revenue that the packets generate for content providers. This tariff structure is profit maximizing for the network provider because it exacts all of the content providers' profits.[35]

Effects of Premium Transmission on Innovation, Subscription, and Incentives to Harm Rivals

Innovation at the Edges

Net neutrality advocates hold that allowing network providers to supply and charge for premium transmission would hinder innovation at the edges of the network, including content sites. Interpreting innovation to mean an increase in the value and diversity of content available at the edges of the network, we assert the opposite is true for n-content. More specifically, the variety of n-content at the edges of the network increases when the network provider provides premium transmission services, and the value that consumers receive from the sites that purchase the premium transmission service is greater than it would be otherwise.[36]

To understand why this holds, recall that premium transmission improves the profitability of n-content providers with innately lower value content. This means that there are potential n-content providers who have such low innate abilities that they are unprofitable unless premium transmission is available. So, one result of premium transmission is an increase in the variety of content made available on the network. Furthermore, consumers receive greater utility from content sites that purchase the premium speed than they would receive if the premium service were not available. This happens because content providers will purchase the premium speed only if it increases revenues, which happens only if the premium speed increases consumer visits on these sites by increasing the utility that consumers receive from the sites that purchase the premium service.

A corollary from the finding that premium transmission stimulates innovation at the edges is that when lower value n-content sites purchase the premium speed, profits decrease for the sites that do not purchase it. This occurs because advertising prices decline with a downward sloping demand curve for advertising on content sites. This price decrease lowers revenue, and thus profits, for every content site that does not increase its hits by purchasing the premium transmission service. The declining price of advertising and subsequent reduction in content provider profits helps us understand why content providers with very large web presence are some of the strongest proponents of net neutrality. Although they may have numerous reasons for advocating net neutrality, at least one effect of premium transmission is that high-ability incumbent providers of n-content stand to lose market share and advertising revenue to smaller web sites that are the more likely purchasers of premium services.

Network Subscription

We now turn our attention to the effects of premium transmission service on demand for network subscription. Research indicates that more consumers subscribe to the network service when premium transmission service is offered and at least one content site purchases the service than if the network provider did not offer the premium service.[37] We assert that this is simply a consequence of network effects. More consumers subscribe to the network service because the value of the network is greater when premium service is provided than when it is not. The network provider benefits in two ways from the premium transmission service. First, it receives greater profit by being able to charge premium prices for something that at least some content providers value, whereas without the premium prices there would be no direct benefit to offering a higher speed service. Second, the number of consumers subscribing to network access is greater, which in turn leads to more hits on the content sites, which stimulates the demand for premium transmission. The greater diversity of content sites also stimulates demand by consumers for network access and increases the number of content sites interested in purchasing the premium transmission service.[38]

Incentives to Harm Rivals

Finally, a common concern of net neutrality proponents is that a vertically integrated network provider, that is, one that provides both content and network services, would discriminate against its content rivals. We argue that this would not be the case at least for n-content. The network provider's profit from being the content provider is no greater than its profit from selling premium transmission to a nonaffiliated entity providing that same content.[39] Indeed, this may be a situation in which regulation would lead to incentives to discriminate: if regulation were to impose a nondiscriminatory tariff requirement on the network and such a tariff requirement resulted in an information rent for content providers, then the network provider might be able to decrease the information rent and improve its profit by vertically integrating and discriminating against its content rivals.

Conclusion

In this chapter, we have analyzed the effects of a network provider offering premium transmission speeds for content providers. We have found that at least some of the claims of the net neutrality advocates do not hold. Specifically, we find that offering premium service stimulates innovation on the edges of the network because lower-value content sites are better able to compete with higher-value sites with the availability of the premium service. The greater diversity of content and the greater value created by sites that purchase the premium service benefit advertisers because consumers visit content sites more frequently. Consumers also benefit from lower network access prices. We also explain that a vertically integrated network provider does not have an incentive to discriminate against its n-content rivals.

Notes

1. http://www.akamai.com/html/customers/customer_list.html, downloaded July 1, 2008.
2. See Wu (2004) for an explanation of the various issues included under the general name of net neutrality.
3. See Hahn and Wallsten (2006).
4. Net neutrality proponents have pressed their case at the FCC and, as of the time of this writing, are seeking federal legislation to impose mandatory net neutrality. See http://www.google.com/help/netneutrality.html, downloaded July 5, 2008.
5. See Whitacre (2006).
6. Case filed October 6, 2003.
7. National Cable & Telecommunications Assn. V. Brand X Internet Services (04-277) 345 F.3d 1120. The Supreme Court stated that the FCC had the authority, under its Title I jurisdiction, to impose regulation on the Internet industry in the future, if necessary.
8. See *Appropriate Framework for Broadband Access to the Internet over Wireline Facilities, Report and Order and Notice of Proposed Rulemaking*, 20 FCCR 14853.
9. Yoo (2006: 1858).
10. See statement of Google CEO Eric Schmidt, http://www.google.com/help/netneutrality_letter.html, downloaded July 5, 2008.
11. Quoted on arstechnica.com website, January 6, 2006.
12. *See High-Speed Services for Internet Access: Status as of June 30, 2006* available at www.fcc.gov/wcb/stats for data supporting the FCC assertion that the broadband market is competitive.

13. For a more detailed discussion of the lack of oversight from the federal courts and FCC, see Prepared Statement of Earl W. Comstock for US House of Representatives Committee on the Judiciary Telecommunications and Antitrust Task Force, submitted April 25, 2006. See also the testimony of Paul Misener, Earl W. Comstock, and Timothy Wu before US House of Representatives Committee on the Judiciary Telecommunications and Antitrust Task Force, April 26, 2006.
14. "Head of the line" is reference to one approach to providing some packets with premium transmission. There are other approaches as well.
15. See testimony of Gary R. Bachula, Vice President, Internet2 before the US Senate Committee on Commerce, Science, and Transportation. Testimony given February 7, 2006.
16. See Paul Misener's testimony before the US House of Representatives Committee on the Judiciary Telecommunications and Antitrust Task Force, April 26, 2006.
17. VoIP is the acronym for Voice over Internet Protocol. VoIP allows people to use the Internet for telephone calls by sending voice data using IP (Internet Protocol) technology rather than via the traditional (copper wire) method of telecommunications.
18. See Madison River Communications Order FCC 4295 (2005).
19. Policy Statement, FCC 05-151, released September 23, 2005.
20. Policy Statement, p. 3, footnote 15.
21. Jamison and Sichter (2008).
22. Vuze Petition for Rulemaking, November 14, 2007.
23. A coalition of parties, including Free Press and the Consumer Federation of America filed a Petition for Declaratory Ruling on November 1, 2007, requesting the FCC to rule that Comcast's practices violated the Commission's Policy Principles.
24. Comments of Comcast, FCC WC Docket 07-52, February 12, 2008.
25. To simplify discussion, we consider an *M/M/1* queuing system, which is a queuing system where interval and distribution times are exponentially distributed and there is one server. The first *M* represents that the arrival process for packets is random, the second *M* represents that the processing service time is exponential, and the *1* represents that there is one server. For more detailed explanations, see Gross and Harris (1998).
26. Other implications of this formula for wait time are: (1) Average wait time approaches infinity as the arrival rate of the packets approaches the network capacity; and (2) At least some congestion is expected unless the network capacity is such that the network can simultaneously process the maximum number of packets that content providers and consumers can send at one time. When average wait time is infinity, the average packet does not expect to make it through this network point during the time period. This does not mean that no packets make it through – clearly some do make it through because the network processes information – but the queue continues to grow in length throughout the time period.
27. For more detailed explanations, see Chapter 3 in Gross and Harris (1998).
28. See Gross and Harris (1998: 150).
29. See Jamison and Hauge (2008a).
30. See Gross and Harris (1998: 141–151).
31. See Bandyopadhyay and Cheng (2006) for applications in analyzing broadband pricing, and Jamison and Hauge (2008a, 2008b) for applications in analyzing net neutrality issues.
32. These relationships have not been worked out in the literature, so we provide an analytical proof in the Appendix.
33. Jamison and Hauge (2008a, 2008b) formally illustrate this result.
34. Neither Hermalin and Katz (2007) nor Jamison and Hauge (2008a, 2008b) investigate how their information rent assumptions affects their analyses.
35. See Jamison and Hauge (2008b) for formal presentation of this result.
36. See Jamison and Hauge (2008a, 2008b) for formal presentation of this result.
37. Both Hermalin and Katz (2007) and Jamison and Hauge (2008a) find this result.
38. Jamison and Hauge (2008b).
39. See Jamison and Hauge (2008b) for formal derivation of this result.

Appendix

Following the model we develop in Jamison and Hauge (2008a), content provider ι's profit function is

$$\max_{I,S} \pi_{\iota} \equiv v(\iota) \bullet n(a \bullet - r(S)) - w \bullet I \tag{1}$$

where $v(\iota)$ is the value a consumer experiences when she visits ι's site, n is the number of consumers with access to the network, a is the revenue per hit that ι receives from advertisers, $r(S)$ is the price per hit charged by the network operator for providing speed S for ι's packets, I is the amount of information that ι places on its site, and w is ι's cost per unit of information. Normalizing the number of hits per consumer to the value each consumer receives from the site, $v(\iota)\cdot n$ represents the number of hits that ι receives from all consumers. For ease of exposition in this proof, we treat S as a continuous variable. We deviate from our earlier model by assuming that information value decays with delay.

Assuming that content providers are price takers, first-order conditions from (1) for an internal solution include

$$v_I \bullet n(a-r) - w = 0 \tag{2}$$

and

$$v_S \bullet n(a-r) - r_S v \bullet n = 0 \tag{3}$$

Taking the total derivates of (2) and (3) with respect to I, S, and ι and applying Cramer's rule gives us

$$\begin{bmatrix} v_{I,I} n \cdot (a-r) & n[v_{I,S}(a-r) - r_S v_I] \\ n[v_{S,I}(a-r) - r_S v_I] & n(v_{S,S}(a-r) - 2r_S v_S - r_{S,S} v) \end{bmatrix} \begin{bmatrix} \mathrm{d}I \\ \mathrm{d}S \end{bmatrix} = \begin{bmatrix} -v_{I,\iota} \cdot n(a-r) \\ n[v_{S,\iota}(a-r) - r_S v_{\iota}] \end{bmatrix} \mathrm{d}\iota$$

and

$$\frac{\mathrm{d}S}{\mathrm{d}\iota} = \frac{v_{I,I}(a-r)[v_{S,\iota}(a-r) - r_S v_{\iota}] + v_{I,\iota}(a-r)[v_{S,I}(a-r) - r_S v_I]}{v_{I,I}(a-r)(v_{S,S}(a-r) - 2r_S v_S - r_{S,S} v) - (v_{I,S}(a-r) - r_S v_I)^2} \tag{4}$$

The denominator in (4) is positive because of the assumption that second-order conditions are met. But, the sign of the numerator is ambiguous. Note that $v_{I.I}(a-r) < 0$ because $v_{I.I} < 0$ by assumption and $a-r > 0$ from (2), making $v_{I.I}(a-r) > 0$. Furthermore $v_{I.\iota}(a-r) > 0$ because $v_{I.\iota} > 0$ by assumption and $a-r > 0$. If $v_{S.\iota}(a-r)-r_S v_{\iota} > 0$ and $v_{S,I}(a-r)-r_S v_I > 0$, then the numerator is positive and higher ability content providers have a greater preference for premium service than do lower types, i.e., $(\mathrm{d}S/\mathrm{d}\iota) > 0$. More generally, $(\mathrm{d}S/\mathrm{d}\iota) > 0$ if

$$v_{I,I}[v_{S,\iota}(a-r)-r_S v_\iota] > -v_{I,\iota}[v_{S,I}(a-r)-r_S v_I] \qquad (5)$$

References

Bandyopadhyay, S. and H. K. Cheng 2006. "Liquid Pricing For Digital Infrastructure Services." *International Journal of Electronic Commerce* 10(4), 47–72.

Federal Communications Commission 2007. "High Speed Services for Internet Access: Status as of June 2006."

Gross, Donald and Carl M. Harris. 1998. *Fundamentals of Queueing Theory*. 3rd Edition. New York, NY: John Wiley & Sons.

Hahn, Robert and Scott Wallsten. 2006. "The Economics of Net Neutrality." *The Economists' Voice* 3(6), 1–7.

Hermalin, Benjamin, E. and Michael L. Katz. 2007. "The Economics of Product-Line Restrictions with an Application to the Network Neutrality Debate." *Information Economics and Policy* 19, 215–248.

Jamison, Mark A. and Janice Hauge. 2008a. "Getting What You Pay For: Analyzing the Net Neutrality Debate." University of Florida, Department of Economics, PURC Working Paper.

Jamison, Mark A. and Janice Hauge. 2008b. "Will Packets Wait? The Effects of Net Neutrality on Network Performance and Consumers." University of Florida, Department of Economics, PURC Working Paper.

Jamison, Mark A. and James Sichter. 2008. "US Experiences with Business Separation in Telecommunications." University of Florida, Department of Economics, PURC Working Paper.

Mendelson, Haim. 1985. "Pricing Computer Services: Queueing Effects." *Communications of the ACM* 28(3), 312–321.

Whitacre, Ed. 2006. Keynote Session at TelecomNEXT, Mandalay Bay and Convention Center Las Vegas, NV.

Wu, Tim. 2004. "The Broadband Debate, a User's Guide," *Journal on Telecommunications and High Technology Law*, 3(1), 69–96.

Yoo, Christopher S. 2006. "Network Neutrality and the Economics of Congestion," The Georgetown Law Journal, 94, 1847–1858.

Part III
Development Challenge

Chapter 5
Why Broadband Internet Should Not Be the Priority for Developing Countries

Eli Noam

With broadband Internet connectivity progressing and rapidly moving to a fiber access platform, the focus of attention has shifted to those left behind. The shorthand word for this concern is the classic "digital divide." Underlying virtually every discussion about a gap in broadband penetrations is the implicit assumption that overcoming such a divide is a priority (Meschi et al., 2004; Crandall et al., 2007). But maybe we first should pause for a moment and understand the implications of ending this divide. If we do that, we might end up changing our perspective on Internet policy in an important way: away from a focus on high-speed *broadband Internet connectivity*, and towards universal connectivity and the creation of *E-transactions*, *E-commerce*, and *E-content*.

With present trends continuing, Internet connectivity will soon be near universal in rich countries, like electricity or television. For the affluent world, therefore, the universality of Internet connectivity will not be an issue. It is more likely that an Internet differentiation will emerge for high-speed broadband. Next-generation high-speed broadband Internet access that is powerful enough for quality video entertainment requires an upgrade of the infrastructure – whether telecom, cable, or wireless. Income, location, and demand factors will be factors for bandwidth consumption. High-speed broadband quality will therefore be the digital-divide issue for wealthy countries.

But the transformation of the divide into a gentle slope in rich countries does not mean that the issue will not persist for the poor countries of the developing world (International Telecommunication Union, 2007). In an interdependent world, this is problematic not just for the South but also for the North because such a gap will inevitably lead to international friction.

In talking about high-speed broadband for poor countries, it is easy to feel like a modern day Marie Antoinette. *Let them eat megabytes*. Of course, high-speed Internet is important. Who outside of North Korea would deny that? But is it a priority? It is important to distinguish between three kinds of gaps. The first gap is

E. Noam
Professor of Finance and Economics, Columbia University Graduate School of Business, and Director of the Columbia Institute for Tele-information, New York, NY, USA
email: noam@columbia.edu

W.H. Lehr and L.M. Pupillo (eds.), *Internet Policy and Economics*,
DOI 10.1007/978-1-4419-0038-8_5,

that of *telecommunications connectivity*. This gap is being closed by investment in infrastructure and by policy reform. In consequence, the telephone penetration of the developing countries has been improving, especially through wireless networks (International Telecommunication Union, 2008). Governments have been making telecom connectivity a priority.

The second type of gap is for *basic Internet access*. The vast majority of Internet hosts are domiciled in OECD countries. Telecom and Internet are related, of course. Internet usage is more expensive in most developing countries, both relative to income and in absolute terms. Progress is being made in basic Internet connectivity in LDCs (Meschi et al., 2004). But closing this gap also will prove to be, relatively speaking, an easy task. In fact, it is an easier gap to overcome than the gap in telecom infrastructure. Once telephone lines exist, it is not very difficult to connect a computer or a simple Internet device to them. Some specific policies to encourage basic Internet usage are (1) establish flat rate telecom pricing on local calls and data plans for wireline and wireless, (2) accept widespread use of IP telephony, (3) create public Internet access points such as kiosks at public places, government departments, or post offices, and (4) use e-mail for some government businesses with citizens.

But what about broadband connectivity (Badran et al., 2007)? There is a real difference here to basic narrowband connectivity insofar as major network upgrades are needed. Of course, it is preferable to have an Internet connection that runs at 10 Mb/s rather than a slow dial-up service which might be almost 1,000 times slower. But such an upgradation is not cost free. It costs about $250 of new investment and labor per DSL Internet subscribed and over $1,000 for a still more powerful fiber-based Internet connection. For poor countries, is this money well spent at a time when few people in poor countries have phone connectivity of any kind? The money for broadband upgrade could instead support basic connection of new users to a network.

Should broadband upgrade, or should basic connectivity receive priority? Broadband benefits the urban professional classes; universal service benefits the rural areas and the poor. Faced with the unpalatable choice, and with the high-tech siren songs of equipment vendors and network companies, most policymakers will simply deny the existence of this choice.

Even in rich countries, the migration to broadband has taken a definite historic path. First, basic telecom connectivity for everyone was achieved, a process that took a century, until the 1970s (Noam, 1992). Wireless mobile communications followed. Narrowband Internet started in earnest with the Web in the early 1990s, and has now reached near saturation for those likely to use it. Broadband Internet has now reached a majority of households. Fiber upgrades are being initiated today. In other words, rich countries at first expanded their basic services across society and only then embarked on bursts of upgrades.

If high-speed broadband were a second telecom priority for poor countries, second to basic connectivity, will they suffer for it? Not really. First, the expanding base of basic phone and wireless users would also raise the number of narrowband or intermediate speed Internet users. The extra speed of broadband is convenient but not essential. There are few things one could not do on narrowband outside its use for music and video. Yes, there are important applications, such as telemedicine and distance education that require great speed and upgraded infrastructure. For those, broadband may be justified in institutional settings, and they could grow into shared community high-speed access points. But that does not mean that high-speed broadband is essential as a residential and consumer service.

The second prong of an Internet strategy for developing countries should be to focus on applications, in particular on E-commerce (Lefebvre and Lefebvre, 2002). Progress in overcoming the first and second gaps described above may exacerbate the third gap, that of E-applications and E-transactions. To understand why this is so, let us make three observations about the global dynamics of E-transactions and E-content:

(1) The price of international transmission is dropping rapidly.
(2) Domestic Internet penetrations are increasing rapidly.
(3) Most E-commerce applications have strong economies of scale.

Low-cost global transmission leads to a great rise in electronic transactions with consequences for business. Traditional ways of doing business will not disappear, just as the mom-and-pop store did not vanish when supermarkets emerged; but the energy and dynamism will be in electronic modes of commerce. And here, firms from rich countries will be most successful. They will be technologically at the leading edge, with risk capital at their disposal. They also will enjoy the advantages of being an early entrant and having a large home market. Once a firm establishes a successful model for the domestic market, invests the fixed costs, and brings transmission prices to near zero, there is no reason to stop at the border.

The implications are that E-commerce will be dominated by firms from electronically advanced countries. Closing the first two gaps exacerbates the third gap by creating the highways and instrumentalities for rich countries to sell in poor countries. Of course, it is not purely a one-way street. The Internet also provides poor countries with opportunities to participate and share information. We all have heard stories about how a local craftsman in a remote village can now access the world market for his wood carvings. And it is true that for certain types of products, marketing becomes easier. But for most mass products, the complexities of sophisticated E-commerce sites are great. They are greater still for information products and services, and will be even greater in a broadband Internet environment where the production costs of attractive E-sites are high.

What counts is not absolute but relative cost reductions, and the relative advantage of E-commerce goes to advanced countries. One lesson we have learned the hard way is that it is expensive to do E-commerce well. E-commerce operations are difficult. They are vastly more involved than simply running a Web site and a shopping cart. Multiple systems need to be in place and integrated. Some of the elements needed include supply chain EDI, payment systems, integration with financial institutions, fulfillment systems, customer data mining, production, customization, community creation, and the creation of consumer lock-in by additional features. Intermediaries need to be reshaped. Processes are accelerated domestically and internationally at lightning speed, with great reliability, easy scalability, and flexibility of configuration.

All this is truer still for the emerging high-speed broadband Internet. The costs for consumer E-commerce sites will rise considerably. Text and stills will not be good enough in a competitive environment, and expensive video and multimedia will be required.

What are some of the implications? Instead of being the frictionless competitive capitalism that people have rhapsodized about, many parts of the new economy will actually be fortresses of market power. Economies of scale are returning. On the supply side, the fixed costs of E-commerce operations tend to be high, but the variable cost of spreading the service to the entire world is relatively low – the classic attributes of "natural" monopoly. On the demand side, there are "positive network externalities" of having large user communities. Put these three things together – high fixed costs, low marginal costs, and network effects – and there are real advantages to being large.

The Internet is a revolution, and it is characteristic of revolutions to create many losers. Banks will be threatened by electronic global financial institutions. Universities will find students migrating to online education. TV broadcasters will be bypassed by global video servers, etc. Most institutions will lose the protection of distance and will be exposed to world markets.

It is characteristic of losers, especially if they are domestically still large and powerful, to seek protection through the political sphere. There will be, therefore, an inevitable global political backlash against E-commerce. This backlash is likely to take the form of restrictions by countries on the wrong side of the gap for E-commerce, and there will be a strong likelihood for new-style international trade wars.

The main alternative to future conflicts over trade is for developing countries to create progress in E-commerce that makes the electronic highways into two-way routes. But what can a developing country do, concretely? This is much more difficult than catching up with telecom and Internet densities because it is a question of general societal modernization, not just of an infrastructure construction program.

There is no single strategy, no silver bullet. But here are several suggested elements.

(1) *Telecom policy of entry and investment* based on market forces. Use government as a lead user, to help create domestic critical mass and experts. There is a history here: The US military was successful in getting the Internet started in the first place. Government operations such as procurement should move to the Web. This would create transparency, reduce procurement cost, and force domestic suppliers to move to electronic marketing. Governments could also provide some services electronically, such as the filing of forms and applications or posting information on subjects such as health, education, taxes, and agriculture.
(2) *Focus on export.* It takes much time to develop new domestic consumer markets. The focus should instead be on the global market, mostly business-to-business. In most developing countries, the domestic consumer market is relatively small, but the global Internet market is huge and open. The creation of national free trade zones for E-commerce is one concrete step in that direction.

(3) *Develop niche markets*. Leverage cultural proximity. Examples could be:

- *Regional hub*: Tunisia for North Africa
- *Language*: Brazil for Portuguese speakers
- *Economics*: Dubai for the oil industry

(4) *Reform the legal system* to make E-transactions possible. Commercial codes need to be adapted to the online environment. Rules applying to liability, contract, privacy, and security issues ought to be updated.
(5) *Strengthen the physical delivery infrastructure and investments in it.* One cannot sell abroad if one cannot ship it quickly. This is one of the secrets of Singapore's success. This includes the physical delivery infrastructure of harbors, airports, and export facilities.
(6) *Strengthen the investment climate.* Provide tax incentives for E-commerce and E-exports, offer low international telecom rates, support microcredit institutions, encourage local entrepreneurship and co-ops, and support the venture capital industry and incubators.
(7) *Support technological education.* Investments are important, but not as important as IT skills and a new economy mindset. There are 3.8 R&D scientists and technicians per thousand people in developed countries and only 0.4 percent per thousand in developing countries.
(8) *Create wealth incentives.* Permit E-commerce entrepreneurs to become rich through the Internet, thereby fueling the emergence of local start-ups.
(9) *Encourage foreign investment.* Scarcity of capital is a common problem for developing countries, especially in a global recession such as now. Do not erect barriers to foreign investment that can help fund the development of domestic E-commerce capabilities.
(10) *Provide back-office functions* to major E-commerce sites as a way to establish experience. India and Jamaica are examples.

The challenge to developing countries is *to get moving*, but in the right direction. To deal with the first gap, that of telecommunications connectivity, by investment and policy. This will also close the second gap, that of narrowband Internet access. And to deal aggressively with closing the third, the E-commerce gap, because it is the real, critical, and fundamental threat – as well as major opportunity – to poor countries, and to economic relations around the world.

The conclusion is therefore that the IT priorities of poor countries should be to expand basic network connectivity both through wireline and wireless, by public investments and by market structures that encourage private investment in self-sustaining network growth. It should also be to develop a base of relatively narrowband applications and content providers. High-speed broadband platforms such as residential fiber, however, make sense only selectively. Their society-wide spread should not be the priority. Indeed, absent the development of domestic providers of transactions, it might actually backfire in terms of national economic development. It is more glamorous for advanced and articulate users, providers, and international funders to focus on leading edge networks. But sometimes it makes more sense to build back roads and auto repair shops than superhighways.

References

Badran MF, Sherbini AE, and Ragab A (2007) What determines broadband uptake in emerging countries? An empircal study. International Telecommunication Union. http://www.itu.int/md/D06-DAP2B.1.3-INF-0001/en Accessed 19 May 2008.

Crandall R, Lehr W, and Litan R (2007) The effects of broadband deployment on output and employment: A cross-sectional analysis of US data. Issues in Economic Policy. http://www.brookings.edu/~/media/Files/rc/reports/2007/06labor_crandall/200706litan.pdf Accessed 19 May 2008.

International Telecommunication Union (2008) Mobile cellular subscribers. http://www.itu.int/ITU-D/icteye/Reporting/ShowReportFrame.aspx?ReportName=/WTI/CellularSubscribersPublic&RP_intYear=2007&RP_intLanguageID=1 Accessed 19 May 2008.

International Telecommunication Union (2007) Top 30 economies in terms of broadband subscribers per 100 population. http://www.itu.int/ITU-D/ict/statistics/at_glance/top20_broad_2007.html Access 19 May 2008.

Lefebvre L and Lefebvre E (2002) E-commerce and virtual enterprises: issues and challenges for transition economies. Technovation 22: 313–323.

Meschi M, Waverman L, and Fuss M (2004) The Impact of Telecoms on Economic Growth in Developing Countries. http://www.london.edu/assets/documents/PDF/L_Waverman_Telecoms_Growth_in_Dev_Countries.pdf Accessed 19 May 2008.

Noam E (1992) Telecommunications in Europe. Oxford University Press, New York.

Chapter 6
Intellectual Property, Digital Technology and the Developing World

Lorenzo Maria Pupillo[1]

Introduction

Information and Communication Technologies (ICTs) is a field in which tremendous advances have been made in a very short time. Software, hardware, semiconductor, and telecommunications industries have been at the forefront of innovation in recent years. The emergence of these new technologies has produced a continuous adaptation of Intellectual Property Right (IPR) instruments over the last decade. Although these new trends originate almost exclusively in the developed world, it is important for developing countries to participate in the ongoing international debate on IPRs and ICTs and to take into account new technologies when reforming their IPR systems.

For the majority of developing countries, industries such as software, publishing, and entertainment contribute in a limited way to national output. There are, however, large developing countries such as India, China, and Brazil that have created important motion picture and television industries. Furthermore, developing countries such as India have been able to develop a successful software industry and others such as China, Egypt, Indonesia, and Lebanon are following a similar pattern. Other developing countries would definitely benefit from stronger IPR protection.[2]

In today's information economy, copyright law plays a key role in governing information and media flows. It covers a wide array of human creativity that fosters the development of industries such as publishing, film, television, radio, music, and software. Copyright law protects certain works and rewards their creators by granting exclusive control over specific uses of the work through a government-granted monopoly that lasts for the life of the author plus 50–100 years. However, copyright law creates exceptions to and limitations upon its exclusive rights in order to guarantee socially desirable uses of protected works. Usually, these exceptions include the "first sale doctrine,"[3] the "idea/expression" distinction (copyright protects only

L.M. Pupillo
Executive Director, Public Affairs Telecom Italia and Affiliated Researcher with
Columbia Institute for Tele-information, Columbia University, New York, NY, USA
email: lorenzo.pupillo@telecomitalia.it

W.H. Lehr and L.M. Pupillo (eds.), *Internet Policy and Economics*,
DOI 10.1007/978-1-4419-0038-8_6, © Springer Science+Business Media, LLC 2009

the expression on an intellectual creation, whereas the idea of the work can be freely copied), and "fair use" (exceptions for copying for personal use, research, criticism, education, archival copying, library use, and news reporting).

What is the major impact that the shift from analog and physical media (books, CDs, video) to digital and online media has on copyright law? How are the off-line copyright exceptions and limitations going to be managed? Also, as ICTs have changed not only the methods by which copyrighted material is distributed but also the form of appearance of the work as well as the way the work is used, is it time to introduce a digital first sale doctrine?

Research on these matters originating from the Apple *iTune* case seems to suggest that under current US, International, and European Law, the first sale doctrine is unlikely to apply to digital works distributed over the Internet.[4] Therefore, what are the implications for developing countries? And how is the fair use doctrine going to change in the digital world?

To tackle these issues, it can be very helpful to look at one of the copyright markets most exposed to the digital revolution, the entertainment industry, in order to understand the structural changes going on in this industry and the legal and technical solutions that the copyright industries are suggesting to respond to the Internet challenges. Furthermore, the entertainment industry, especially the music industry, seems to play an increasingly important role in the economic development and in shaping national identities of many countries in the African continent or in Latin America and the Caribbean.[5]

This chapter provides an overview of how the converging ICTs are challenging the traditional off-line copyright doctrine and suggests how developing countries should approach issues such as copyright in the digital world, software (Protection, Open Source, Reverse Engineering), and data base protection.

The balance of the chapter is organized into three sections. After the introduction, the second section explains how digital technology is dramatically changing the entertainment industry, what are the major challenges to the industry, and what are the approaches that the economic literature suggest to face the structural changes that the digital revolution is bringing forward. Starting from the assumption that IPRs frameworks need to be customized to the countries' development needs, the third section makes recommendations on how developing countries should use copyright to support access to information and to creative industries.

Entertainment Industry, Digital Technology, and Economics

Copyright and Entertainment Industry[6]

Today, especially for teenagers and young adults, entertainment is an experience characterized as being inexpensive, plentiful, strongly open to the culture of sharing, and available anywhere and anytime. Music, for instance, is quite inexpensive because it is obtained for free, illegally downloaded, from many Web sites and peer-to-peer (P2P) copying services.

More precisely, downloading music requires the users to have a computer and pay for an Internet connection. Thus, the *average cost* of each sound recording is positive but the *marginal cost* – the cost of obtaining each additional recording – is almost zero. For this reason, it is possible to have access to an extremely broad collection of music and movies that make plentiful the entertainment experience. The abundance of material available fosters the culture of sharing. Consumers have been mixing and making copies of music through analog cassettes and CDs for years. But today, the huge availability of content and the digital technology available off-line and online makes the scale of this phenomenon completely different.

Furthermore, the expectation is for entertainment available anywhere, anytime. Portable Radio and TV, portable cassette, and CD players have been around for quite some time. However, the dominant behavior has always been to see movies in theaters with large screen, watch TV at home, listening to music through a stereo system. Now, new technologies are challenging these established habits giving the users the possibility to control their "media environments," that is, the times and places in which they experience media.[7]

This overall improvement in the way in which people enjoy entertainment has been made possible by the widespread use of digital technology. Beside the increased quality of music and video recording, the digital technology brought out two basic differences compared with the analog systems:

1. digital copies are identical to the originals, whereas the analog ones were of lower quality;
2. digital recordings can be stored and manipulated by general-purpose computers.

The effects of these characteristics of the digital technology have been amplified in scope and magnitude by the massive diffusion of the Internet, opening up possibilities still yet to be fully exploited.

First, it would be possible to deliver entertainment far more efficiently then today. At present, of $18, the undiscounted retail price in the USA of a CD with permanent music recordings, only about 12% goes to the artist whereas 39% goes to the retail store that sells the disk to the customer and about 49% goes to the record company.

Digital technology enables reduction of production and distribution costs for music, diminishing the musician's dependence upon record companies and enabling them to distribute the music themselves. Although it is difficult to quantify in detail those savings, it is clear that "*those potential savings would then allow us either to increase the amount of money allocated to the composers and performers who create the music or to reduce substantially the prices paid by consumers for access to the music, or both.*"[8]

Second, there would be additional benefits that these technologies can bring. Consumers through the Internet can have immediate access to the music they like by choosing an individual song instead of the entire collection of an album. Overall their ability to "sample" the music and decide what to buy is greatly enhanced. Furthermore, there is an increase in cultural diversity coming from a greater variety of songs and movies available through the Internet and the possibility of choosing instead of accepting what the "blockbuster market" offers. Artists will benefit too from the new technological environment. The decline in the cost of high-quality recording equipment and the reduced dependency on the record companies will open to them new possibilities and business opportunities.

But these technologies could also completely undermine the current flow of revenues to the entertainment industry. So far, a combination of legal rules and impediments because of the analog technology has avoided the access to audio and video recordings for free. Indeed, consumers had to pay a fee such as the price of CDs, the rental of VHS cassette or the price to buy a video recording, and the cost of tickets for the movies. But if it becomes possible to get for free this content from the web, the consumers' willingness to pay for these product will drop, reducing dramatically the revenues for the industry. Is this a threat or an opportunity? As we mentioned before, the new technologies potentially expand the revenues earned by artists and reduce the prices paid by consumers. And what about the recording companies?

The industry has envisaged so far legal and technical solutions to manage this situation. However, every time in the last years that the technology has offered consumers an innovative and more convenient access to recorded entertainment, the companies loosing from the rapid diffusion of these technologies resisted the changes through law reform, and technological countermeasures.

Enforcing the existing rules more aggressively or even strengthening exclusive rights had only limited effects, and instead, it has generated enormous transaction costs. On the technical side, the diffusion of technical protection measures such as Digital Rights Managements (DRM), although attractive in theory, seem to have two important flaws: (1) discouraging innovation and flexibility in designing electronic equipment and (2) low level of acceptance by consumers unwilling to give up the flexibility they are currently enjoying.

Is there a way out to this deadlock and is it possible to envisage alternative routes extending beyond the legal-technical tandem approach that appears to be quite defensive and ineffective in dealing with these issues? The economic literature seems to suggest more forward-looking approaches that appear to deal better with the structural changes that the digital revolution is bringing forward. These models may also offer new avenues to be followed by developing countries. As suggested in Farchy (2004),[9] we can distinguish market, public, and cooperation economies approaches.

Market Economies Approaches

The structural changes that the new digital world is putting forward, call for embracing the new technologies as a medium to create new markets and open up new services that use the delivery potential of the Internet. Many majors have been quite slow in reacting to the free downloading of music or video with a service offering, but now they are starting to realize the possibilities of differentiating their offer on the *web developing fee-paying services.*[10] Indeed, P2P noncommercial services, although free, are characterized by many inconveniences: excessive spam, risk of viruses, fakes, spyware, uncertain quality of files, and high transaction costs. The right mix of pricing and product differentiation can make a service successful. In the last few years, there have been a numbers of legal online music sites but the most successful has been the iTune Music Store (iTMS) from Apple.

Price discrimination has always been suggested by economists as a way to better capture the consumers' willingness to pay for services. Using price discrimination, publishers, for instance, indirectly earn appropriate revenues by selling copyrighted works – books and journals – to libraries at higher prices than to individual consumers, in order to offset future losses due to photocopying.[11] Today, the developments of DRM technologies suggest that price discrimination can become available for copyrighted work in digital format. DRM systems could make possible for copyrights owners to charge consumers accordingly to the specific use of copyrighted work they are willing to pay for.

Many industry and government people strongly believe in the potentiality of these new pricing possibilities and increasingly support DRM solutions. However, some qualifications to this approach should be noted.[12] Although in theory perfect, price discrimination can be efficient in the static sense, that is, distributing each creative work among consumers in the best way, the dynamic effects on the production of creative works are still unknown.

The increased amount of resources that DRM will make available does not guarantee a better supply of creative works. Some copyrighted works are still too new to be commercially viable and still need support from public funding or private endowments. Furthermore, "*relatively little is known about what motivate people to engage in creative activity and how those influences differ from the perhaps more pecuniary motivations of those who acquire the copyright to creative works for purpose of reproduction and distribution.*"[13]

For instance, Nadel (2004) claims that because the creators may be more likely motivated by nonpecuniary factors, such as creative drive, desire for attribution and recognition, while distributors may be more inclined to follow monetary incentives, the existence of copyright exclusive rights may motivate distributors of copyrighted works to engage in marketing activities that promote only existing works without having significant effects in ensuring the supply of new creative works.[14]

Therefore, Nadel (2004) suggests that there are many relevant business models for financing the creation of content that can be seen as alternatives to §106's prohibition against unauthorized copying.[15] These business models are based on a combination of new and existing technologies, social norms, and copyright laws less restrictive than §106. The basic idea is to use the new technologies that the Internet and the digital technology are making available to reduce publisher costs and to provide buyers with limited access to the content. The most relevant models are *Pre-sales to Consumers* and *Versioning and Offering Services in Place of Products.*

Social norms can also provide a funding alternative to the current "socially harmful broad legal protection of §106." A social norm is "a rule governing an individual's behavior that third parties other than state agents diffusely enforce by means of social sanctions."[16] Instead of scaring customers into avoiding the use of new technologies by threatening lawsuits, publishers should use their expertise to teach consumers to consider reasonable payments to creative artists as fair and the right thing to do. They should even encourage a stronger social customs of donations to creative artists. Indeed, consumers are already used to do some of it: they donate money to street musicians, pay "what they can" for live performances and museums, and more generally, they are willing to pay more to support special goals such as buy merchandise from their own country, or buy "green" (environmental friendly products).

Of course, right now, due to the current widespread perception that the actual pricing structure of digital music is unfair, the alternative of voluntary contribution is not credible. However, the success of the Apple's iTunes suggests that consumers are willing to pay reasonable prices if given the chance.

A combination of voluntary payments, reduction of distribution and production costs by using digital technologies and de-escalation of today's marketing practices could allow many new artists to finance new creative works.

Public Economies Approaches

Governments have always provided funding for the provision of culturally and scientifically valuable content, when the market is unable to provide it in an optimal way (funding of merit goods). In particular, David (1993)[17] suggests three ways in which the government can handle the underproduction problems related to the special nature of creative works: IPR allocation but also direct state production and subsidies.

According to Farchy (2004), while perfectly acceptable in many countries for scientific research, direct state production in the cultural sector is not well received. Subsidies, instead, while not applicable to all content, can be an effective way of offsetting the losses of more vulnerable copyrights holders. Furthermore, Eckersley (2003) shows that using subsidies can lead to better results in terms of social welfare than a DRM-backed system of exclusive rights, especially because the cost of DRM technologies is infinitely higher in terms of implementation and ensuring security against infringement.[18]

Another approach that the government can take is to set both the price of creative content and the terms on which that content must be made available. This is called "*Compulsory Licensing*." It implies for the owners to drop their rights in exchange of a lump-sum payment set by law or by negotiated contract. The compensation is not proportional to revenues anymore. Compulsory licensing makes easier access for users by eliminating the need to seek authorial consent.

The rationale for compulsory licensing is that it represents a way to allow copyright owners to exercise meaningful control over their works due to the fact that the high transaction costs of this process makes it almost impossible to use private management or voluntary collective administration. For instance, P2P advocates have suggested using compulsory licensing to compensate recording artists for file sharing and therefore make legal the use of copyrighted material on P2P networks.

Compulsory licensing has many drawbacks. Setting a fixed price for some types of copyrighted works is, from an economic standpoint, less efficient than using differential pricing. Indeed, the price for copyrighted work to be used under compulsory licensing is the same not only for all consumers but also for all works covered. Furthermore, once compensation has been collected, the collecting societies have to share it among the authors, the performing artists, and producers with all the difficulties that this process implies.[19]

Another way of compensating copyrights owner is to create an administrative compensation system (levies) that would provide an alternative to the copyright regime. In Europe, right now, there is already a legislation,[20] started with the written work and then extended to music and audiovisual, that authorizes private copying in return for a sum paid to the rights owner to compensate for the loss of revenues from conventional sources.[21]

Introducing new taxes also has its shortcomings. It leads to market distortions: blank media manufactures will be penalized because not all their production is used for copying protected content and so should not be taxed. Furthermore, which ancillary products markets should be taxed? Recording devices, blank media, Internet subscriptions? And at what rate over time?

Cooperation Economies Approach

Instead of claiming their exclusive rights and being compensated accordingly, authors can freely decide to drop these rights. The idea of "free" movement started in the field of software and gained momentum during the 1990s, contributing to significative commercial success of products such as Linux. Farchy (2004) claimed, "the voluntary 'loss' of exclusive rights is only ever temporary, but it allows a set of creators to produce 'common' works without each of them having to bear the financial burden of paying for protected elements. With less restrictive terms and conditions, the emphasis is on the right to authorize not the right to prohibit." These ideas, call for a creation of a community of user–creators able to take a work and modify, enrich, and redistribute it.

Farchy (2004) suggested that a clear distinction exists between the sharing of works with an author's consent, where the roles of users and creators are largely one and the same, from the sharing of end products by mere users such as the P2P networks ones. In the former case, the free sharing is made with the author's agreement, whereas in the latter, without it. Furthermore, it is necessary to emphasize that it is fruitful to apply the philosophy of free software to cultural productions as long as it implies a voluntary approach and there is a cooperation-based collective creations. The free software philosophy can never under any circumstances be extended to productions requiring extremely large fixed costs, such as movies production.

IPRs Policies and Digital Technology in the Developing World

So far, we have focused our attention to the entertainment industry and to the USA, but these processes to different extent are affecting many countries worldwide and are not limited to music recording and movies production but are or will soon transform other sectors such as television, publishing, games. From the issues already discussed and the findings presented, it is clear that there are no magic solutions. As Farchy (2004) claimed:

> It is not a matter of two conflicting models (free P2P versus DRM) but a production-remuneration continuum extending from the absolutely free through public forms of redistribution to direct payment by the user. Different ways of exploiting works will probably need to be identified, exclusive copyright being just one possible form of remuneration that is well-suited to some periods and types of content yet less so to others. DRM-protected exclusive rights are fine for a few market niches: premium content with fixed costs and audience that is more than ready to pay.[22]

If this more flexible approach to copyright is suggested for developed countries, it should be strongly recommended for developing countries where markets and products development are still at an early stage, and scarcity of resources will make difficult to have access to information at affordable costs.

As far as copyright law is concerned, many developing countries tend to adopt the copyright law of the country that affected their language or culture under colonial influences. They adopt the law but quite often they do not enforce it. Furthermore, they adopt copyright law without exceptions to and limitations upon exclusive rights. This approach, in the digital world, is very counterproductive because the technical protection measures, such as DRM, tend to eliminate the flexibility that the analog world was offering in implementing copyright laws.

Therefore, developing countries should consider to adopt in their own copyrights laws the following safeguards:

1. Create preambles to the copyrights law that link this law to the constitution of each country.
2. Adopt exceptions and limitations to the copyrights in order to guarantee socially desirable uses of protected works and guarantee access to knowledge and technology.[23]
3. Verify the effects of rulemaking: find out periodically, for instance, every 3 years, the effects of copyright law on consumers, industry, and creators

Contract–Copyright Interplay

To promote a socially beneficial use of creative works, the copyright law creates an initial balance between the rights afforded to creators to reward them for their efforts and the consumers of these works. Contract law, on the contrary, enforces private agreements between parties who agree to perform certain actions. For instance, computer software and Internet-based commerce recently introduced a new form of contract known as "Clickwrap."[24] In the online world, commercial ventures such as Apple *iTunes* benefit when they can use contractual agreements to rearrange this balance. The success of this online music distribution model depends on the interplay between contract and copyright law. If contract law can override copyright, and governments do not impose mandatory contract terms, license agreements can plug the holes created by copyright. The contract-copyright interplay can specify, for example, in the *iTunes* case, what actions are permitted and prohibited with the downloaded songs.

Laws governing the interplay between contract and copyright in the world vary geographically according to the different copyright regimes and commercial laws. In the USA, although the Constitution gives Congress the power to reward authors with exclusive rights, the courts increasingly agree that copyright law does not override contract law and permit contracts to assign or waive copyright protections and defense.[25] It means that ventures such as iTunes can quite effectively use contractual agreements with consumers to alter the balance of rights and defenses available under contract.

In Europe, the situation is more complex due to the differences in copyright and commercial law among the countries. To harmonize the regimes, the European Parliament has approved the EU Copyright Directive (Directive 2001/29/EC) that still leaves a great deal of flexibility for national implementations. To standardize the laws for online contracts, the EU has approved two directives: The Distance Contract Directive (Directive 97/7/EC) and the Electronic Commerce Directive (Directive 2000/31/EC). The Distance Contract Directive grants consumers a right of withdrawal from any distance contract and this right cannot be waived by contract.

Overall, in Europe, a venture such as *iTunes* must consider the implications of limited harmonization of copyright and contract law that might imply high cost for complying with particularized state laws.[26]

This brief discussion on the copyright–contract interplay in the USA and Europe has interesting implications for copyright regimes in the developing countries.

First, it states once again that the existence of differences in copyright regimes in the developed countries strengthens the case for tailoring the national implementation of international copyright treaties to each individual country's development stage.

Second, the awareness of the importance of the *copyright–contract interplay* in the online world could suggest more balanced solutions in the IP policy reform in developing countries for promoting wider access to information and the dissemination of knowledge and knowledge-based products.

Copyright and Creative Industries in Developing Countries

Many development agencies have emphasized that it is important for developing countries to protect and benefit from the exploitation of their own past and current creative work.[27] This is true in many countries with a wealth of musical and artistic tradition as long as there is a local infrastructure for cultural industries.[28] Therefore, copyright protection may be a necessary but not a sufficient condition for the development of growing domestic industries in publishing, entertainment, and software sectors. Instead, in larger developing countries such as India, China, Brazil, or Egypt, copyright protection is more important for the development of national industries in the creative sectors.

To implement these policies, some developing countries have established collective management societies, which represent the rights of artists, writers, and performers and collect royalties from licensing their copyrighted works.[29]

The DIFID report (2002) claims that only a minority of developing countries have established these collective societies and that there are quite different views about their role. Some industry groups, for instance, argue that the establishment of Reprographic Rights Organizations in developing countries could facilitate the access to copyrighted material through photocopying at rates compatible with the local economy.

Some other commentators argue that, in practice, these organizations would collect far more royalties for foreign rights holder from developed countries than for local artists and authors. Furthermore, these collective management organizations quite often wield significant market power, promote anticompetitive practices, and increase corruption.

Therefore, developing countries should decide on the creation of these societies, based on the costs and benefits of implementing them, taking also into account the current debate on the reforms of these institutions.

Copyright and Access to Information and Knowledge Dissemination

One of the most critical issues on the agenda of developing countries remains how to balance the copyright protection of creative work, especially knowledge and knowledge-based products, with the need to close the knowledge divide between rich and poor countries.

We are facing a striking situation in the governance of knowledge, technology, and culture. From one side, the Internet and the new digital technologies are allowing an unprecedented way of accessing and distributing information. Technologies such as Google, for instance, provides millions of people with powerful tool to find copyrighted and not information for free. From the other side, technological protection measures designed to enforce IPRs in digital environments threaten fundamental exceptions in copyrighted laws for disabled people, libraries, educators, authors, and consumers, and undermine privacy and freedom.[30] Furthermore, because the majority of countries that have ratified the WIPO Internet treaties are developing countries that already have low internet use and penetration, it is highly prejudicial for them to adopt copyright laws that make access to digital content more difficult or costly. Additionally, because many developing countries have identified education as priority to mainstream ICTs in the development agenda, their copyrights legislation may need to be modified to allow the implementation of policies that use Internet to access educational materials available in digital format.[31] A case in point is the adoption of ad hoc legislation for Distance Education.[32]

To guarantee access to online publications and to copyrighted material representative from the copyrighted-based industries are suggesting special initiatives such as donation schemes and low price "budget" editions of books or computer software, as the way to go instead of weakening of international copyright rules or national IPR enforcement rules in developing countries.[33]

However, this issue of differential pricing or subsidized access to copyrighted work for institutions (libraries, schools) in developing countries needs some qualifications. These initiatives come from the following backdrop. Facing the situation that IPRs tend to increase the income of knowledge producers such as Bill Gates, would not it be fair to put limitations on IPRs, which would reduce the income of very rich people while allowing poorer people to consume knowledge-intensive goods at a cheaper price?

Economists say that, in such cases, there is a dichotomy between distributive concerns and efficiency, and economic theory[34] suggests that redistribution always dominates restrictions to IPRs. Therefore, let us not touch IPRs, but instead redistribute money to the poor. While for medicines or books this idea can make sense, using a similar idea for proprietary software, however, is quite controversial. Indeed, given the characteristics of the software market (economies of scale, network externalities, customer lock-in, and path dependence), the greatest worry is that a "further spread of proprietary software even if initially at lower prices or 'free', will create further technological lock-in for such countries."[35]

Copyright and Online Service Providers Liability

The transmission of data from one point of the network to another involves several parties. An issue of concern is the question of who should be liable for copyright infringements online. Indeed, the convergence of Information and Communications Technologies has blurred the traditional boundary between content carriers and content providers.

The liability could arise in one of two ways: the service provider itself may have engaged in unauthorized acts of reproduction or communication to the public or it may have contributed to make possible the act of infringement by another. The transnational dimension of the Internet makes this process even more complex. Indeed, it requires compatible approaches to the way in which this issue is treated internationally. Furthermore, by prosecuting the infringing carriers of digital information, the expansion of the value-added services that make the Internet valuable may be inhibited.

During the Conference on the WIPO Internet Treaties in 1996, the issue was extensively debated but the treaties are essentially neutral on this matter, with the issue of liability left to the national legislation to determine.[36]

Two basic approaches are used worldwide: addressing the copyright issue only or taking a more "horizontal approach," that is, covering not only copyright infringement but also other laws such as libel or obscenity.

The European Community has adopted a horizontal approach with the Directive on Electronic Commerce legally binding since January 2002.[37] In articles 12–14, three kinds of providers are described with their respective liabilities. In case of mere conduit (access provisioning) and caching, providers are exempted from any liability. In the case of hosting, providers are only exempted if they have no actual knowledge of "apparent" illegal content and, if so, act expeditiously to remove the content. The European liability rule is quite vague.[38]

The alternative approach of implementing copyright-specific laws to determine online service provider liability has been adopted by countries such as the USA. As part of the 1998 Digital Millennium Copyright Act (DMCA), the "Online Copyright Infringement Liability Limitation Act" establishes "safe harbors" to shelter providers from liability for copyright infringement if five conditions occur:

- a complaint must identify himself and the infringements exactly
- plaintiff and the customer must act "in good faith," on penalty for perjury
- the provider must block the material upon receipt of the complaint and inform the customer
- materials must be put back in 10, maximum 14 business days after a counter notice
- identification data can only be obtained with a subpoena

According to Sjoera Nas (2004), the comparisons with the Safe Harbor provisions shows that the "European legislation leaves plenty of room for doubt and misguided judgment by providers. There are no criteria to validate complaints and counter notices and there are no arrangements for the hand-over of customer data, besides general privacy principles that do allow voluntary hand-over. Moreover, there is no obligation in Europe to inform the customer and there are no legal guarantees to protect the freedom of speech."

The implications of these different approaches between Europe and the USA have also been tested through experiments with *notice and take down* to see if the different legal regimes made any difference in practice. The Liberty experiment in 2003[39] comparing the reaction of UK and US providers showed that it is a lot harder to take down a Web site in the USA. In the Multatuli Project (2004),[40] seven of ten Dutch providers took down the contested material almost immediately without further investigations.

What type of solutions can be suggested to developing countries? This issue should be investigated in more details, using the experiences from other countries, considering national legislations and cultural specificities and keeping in mind the following recommendations:

- An excessive burden on the providers can have negative effects on the development of the Internet value-added services market.
- The unbalanced situation among developing countries as far as civil rights are concerned suggests to avoid giving to providers the power to easily remove material and content from the web.
- The idea of involving a third party as guarantor (such as an agency) in this process could be considered, at least for the largest developing countries.

Database Protection

The creation of digital databases and technologically enabled tools for the aggregation and classification of data are, today, one of the fastest growing activities not only for E-commerce but also for research, education, and knowledge dissemination. The diffusion of Internet facilitates their distribution and easy use.

Under the TRIPS agreement (Art.10), databases as compilations of data "... whether in machine readable or other form [.] constitute intellectual creations,. shall be protected as such. Such protection, [.] shall not extend to the data or material itself...." Since copyright does not protect the facts contained in a particular work but only the selection and the arrangement of those facts as long as they are original, some legislators decided to protect databases under sui generis regimes. The EU followed this approach in 1996 (Directive 96/9/EC).

This model was contested by many research organizations, educational institutions, and internet companies as going too far in providing protection for assemblages of data.[41] Therefore, developing countries should avoid adopting this type of sui generis protection of databases as it unduly restricts access to knowledge and information.

Furthermore, as far as data protection is concerned, alternative solutions that developing countries can follow needed to be envisaged. The area that can be worthwhile to consider is the *compensatory liability approach*. Because there is a difference between protecting an innovation and protecting an investment (such as the creation of a data base, indeed considered factual data), under a compensatory liability approach, everyone would be allowed to use a database (i.e., there is no need for an authorization) but would need to share the cost of developing it (i.e., there is a compensation).

This approach is suggested by Reichman (2000)[42] and applied to the case of sharing database for scientific data.[43] Furthermore, the WIPO's Intergovernmental Committee on Intellectual Property and Genetic Resources, Traditional Knowledge and Folklore, mentions this approach as one of the options followed by member States for the protection of Traditional Knowledge.[44]

Computer Software

In the early days of computer technology, computer software was not protected by copyright law. Firms relied on trade secret law[45] to protect the code written by programmers (source code) and on contract law for selling the code readable by the machine (object code) to users. Although in the USA, the debate on a different protection regime for software started in the mid-1950s, only in 1980 did the USA – and later a number of governments in the developed countries – decided to classify computer software as analogous to the traditional copyright category of "literary works" and subject to protection as a literary copyright.[46]

Both the 1995 TRIPS Agreement (Art.10) and the 1996 WIPO Copyright Treaty (Art.5) state that computer programs (both source and objects codes) should be protected by copyright. Although the TRIPS allows developing countries to delay the application of this part of the agreement until 2006, it is very likely that the final outcome will be that all countries will adopt copyright protection for computer software.

In this context, developing countries should draft appropriate national copyrights laws making full use of the flexibility allowed in the TRIPS. This implies the necessity to consider the following issues.

Patentability of Software and Business Methods

During the infancy of the computer era, characterized by many important software innovations, software was not protected by patent law in the USA or elsewhere.[47] Indeed, in the USA, both legal and policy reasons against patenting software were brought forward. Courts had long held that neither mathematical algorithms nor methods of doing business were patentable subject matter. A program is, of course, a type of mathematical algorithm, and many programs implemented methods of doing business.

From a policy standpoint, many commentators including CONTU (Commission on New Technological Uses of Copyrighted Works) posed the question of whether patent protection for software might unduly restrict competition and reduce dissemination of information.[48] In 1981, however, in the *Diamond v. Diehr* case (450 US 175), the US Supreme Court paved the way for the recognition of the patentability of computer software.

Interestingly, today the only country that allows software patentability, besides Japan, is the USA. In Europe, article 52C of the European Patent Convention bans such patents. However, there is growing debate on this issue between large multinational software companies and small- and medium-size software developers, in particular, about the effects of software patenting on innovation. The pressure to require the patenting of software is not diminishing.

The USA, after signing the TRIPS, started promoting bilateral agreements with many countries under the flag of "free trade," that, among other matters, warrant a stronger than TRIPS required IPRs protection, such as software patents. A case in point is the US-Jordan Free Trade Agreement (2000).[49]

Therefore, developing countries should not include software patents in their IPRs national regimes. Indeed, if there are concerns on the negative effect of software patenting on innovation in the USA,[50] it is reasonable to worry about these effects on innovation in the countries of the South and, in particular, for the small and medium enterprises run by national entrepreneurs.

Similar caution is recommended for approaching the subject of business methods patents.[51] These patents fall into three categories. First, the computer business method category, which includes patent claims required to perform traditional business functions via computers which were previously carried out without computers. Second, the E-commerce category, related to internet applications and E-commerce, such as Amazon's *one-click* order patent. And third, other new business methods not included in the previous two categories.

The extension of patents to business methods has been very controversial in the USA. In particular, there are strong concerns on the stifling effect that such patents may have on the development of E-commerce and innovation in cyberspace. But there are also very practical drawbacks for using such patents. First, the number of applications for this type of patents has added a huge burden to the administration of the patent system in the USA.[52] Second, these patents are also much more likely to be litigated than any other category of patents.

Therefore, developing countries should not enforce the patenting of business methods for two main reasons: first, there is not enough evidence of a positive effect on innovation; second, the administrative cost for managing these patents is too high for countries that already have very limited resources to devote to IPR protection and enforcement. For instance, such countries could adopt, as India has done, a per se rule against the patentability of business methods.

Reverse Engineering of Software Beyond Interoperability

In trade secrecy law, the balance between initial and follow-on innovation is guaranteed through the legitimacy of reverse engineering. "Reverse engineering is the scientific method of taking something apart in order to figure out how it works. Reverse engineering has been used by innovators to determine a product's structure in order to develop competing or interoperable products. Reverse engineering is also an invaluable teaching tool used by researchers, academics, and students in many disciplines, who reverse engineer technology to discover, and learn from, its structure and design."[53] For this reason, reverse engineering on products which are purchased legally is not only allowed but considered a way of encouraging innovation. Under the TRIPS, developing countries have the flexibility to allow reverse engineering of software. Therefore, they should consider whether their national copyright laws should permit the reverse engineering of computer software beyond the requirements for interoperability.[54]

Indeed, reverse engineering has been the traditional method of technology transfer and, in the past, has enabled local innovators to develop off-the-shelf technologies to reflect local conditions.[55]

Open Source Software

With regards to software, developing countries should explore alternatives to proprietary solutions, the most relevant being the Open Source Software, as a complement to the dominant offering of proprietary software.[56] Although in the last few years, there has been a growing global discussion on this topic among proprietary software companies, NGOs, International Organizations, industry analyst, and regulatory bodies, much of this discussion has generated creation of myths, misperceptions, and concerns.[57]

Economists have only recently begun to analyze formally the competition between open source and proprietary software. The research available to date reaches conclusions that are consistent with the view that banning the use of proprietary software (for all consumers or even for government consumers) would, in general, make consumers worse off.[58] In this discussion, it is important drawing a distinction between "use" of *Open Source Software* and "promotion" of it by developing countries' governments.

Decisions about use of software should normally be based on standard commercial considerations such as prices, features, flexibility, ease of use, and other characteristics. From this standpoint, *Open Source Software* seems particularly suitable for the needs of developing countries.[59] However, policies toward specific government promotion of *Open Source Software* need very careful screening.[60]

Each government must find the best mix between proprietary and Open Source software. In order to achieve this goal, decision makers need to understand the consequences of their choices and must also recognize that true government neutrality is impossible. The software industry cannot exist without government regulation of intellectual property, contracts, and licenses. The government is also an important consumer of the industry's products.[61] Therefore, support to software research and training, standard setting and compatibility as an overall public policy, is strongly recommended.[62]

Notes

1. This chapter is a revision and an adaptation of a broader work done for the Infodev Program in the Global ICTs Department at the World Bank, where the author was Adviser, in secondment from Telecom Italia. The views expressed in this chapter reflect the author's view and do not necessarily reflect the views of the organizations which the author belongs to. I thank Infodev for the support and Carsten Fink, Kerry McNamara, and Sanford Malman for helpful comments.
2. *See* UCTAD – ICTSD Policy Paper (2003), pages 69–70; Maskus K.E. (2000), "Strengthening Intellectual Property Rights in Lebanon" in B. Hoekman and J.E. Zarrouk, editors, *Catching Up with the Competition*. University of Michigan Press; Harabi N. (2004), "Copyright Industries in Arab Countries," University of Northwestern Switzerland, mimeo.
3. "Certain copyright's holder's rights end after the first sale of a particular copy of the copyrighted work i.e., an owner of books or records is permitted to resell, rent, or lend these works, donate them to libraries without the need to obtain the permission of copyright holders or the need to make royalty payments.[.] the first sale doctrine[…]does not allow a purchaser of copyright material to copy it." The Berkman Center Green Paper (2004) V.1.2, page 48.
4. *See* The Berkman Center Green Paper (2004) V.1.2, page 62.
5. *See* Penna F.J. et al. (2004), The Africa Music Project, *Poor People's Knowledge*, Finger and Schuler, editors, World Bank. ICTSD and UNCTAD Policy Discussion Paper, pages 70–71.
6. *Copyright and entertainment industry* draws from Fisher W. (2004), *Promises to Keep-Technology, Law and the Future of Entertainment*, Stanford University Press, Chapters 1–3.
7. *See* Steinmueller W.E. (2008), "Peer to Peer Media File Sharing: From Copyright Crisis to Market?" in E. Noam and L.M. Pupillo, editors, "Peer to Peer Video: The Economics, Policy and Culture of Today's New Mass Medium," Springer.

8. *See* Fisher W. (2004), page 24.
9. *See* Farchy J. (2004), "Seeking alternative economics solutions for combating piracy," mimeo.
10. A totally different approach from the music industry has been followed by the games industry. Games publishers are actually working with peer-to peer networks to sell legal copies of their product alongside the illicit copies. Trymedia, an antipiracy software firm, offers about 300 legitimate games on P2P networks and has experienced 20 millions downloads in 18 months. The global market for legally downloaded games is estimated now worth $150 million annually and that it will double every year. P2P is seen as a sales channel for games. Companies such as Trymedia, Softwrap, and Macromedia are also offering software to games publishers that stops games from being copied or limits the access to them only on a trial mode. Therefore, they can play a demo version before buying. P2P networks allow to enhance the "viral sharing of content between friends" that has always been the biggest promoter for software content. Trymedia's Zicherman says: "If you can convert 5% of users into legitimate buyers, then you'll be ahead." Converting pirates to sales is their goal!
11. The basic idea of indirect appropriability is that "originals from which copies are made might undergo an increase in demand as those making copies of originals capture some of the value from those receiving the copies and transfer this value into their demand for the originals that they purchase. [.] Such price discrimination was practically unheard of prior to the advent of photocopier, and the most heavily copies journal were also those with the greatest price differential," *see* Liebowitz (2004), page 14 and on "sharing arrangements" Shapiro and Varian (1999), page 47. However, Liebowitz (2004) claims that in the case of file sharing systems, the mechanism that allows indirect appropriability to function will not work.
12. *See* "Copyright Issues in Digital Media," CBO paper, August 2004, page 23.
13. *See* note 12.
14. *See* Nadel M.S. (2004), "How Current Copyright Law Discourages Creative Output: The Overlooked Impact of Marketing," *Berkeley Technology Law Journal*, Vol. 19, Spring. In particular, he contends that in the current lottery-like environment of many media markets, copyright law disproportionately inflates the revenues of the most popular creations, which leads publishers to spend increasing amounts on promotional campaigns, which, intentionally or not, drowns out economically marginal creations. This discourages, rather than encourages, investment in many new creations.
15. US Code: Title 17 § 106. Exclusive rights in copyrighted works. See<http://assembler.law.cornell.edu/uscode/html/uscode17/usc_sec_17_00000106-000-.html>. This section draws from Nadel (2004), pages 822–845.
16. *See* Ellickson R.C. (2001), The Market for Social Norms, 3 AM.L. & Econ. Rev. 1.3.
17. David P.A. (1993), "Intellectual property institutions and the panda's thumb: Patent copyrights, and trade secrets in Economic Theory and History," M.B. Wallerstein, M.E. Mogee, and R.A. Scone, editors, *Global Dimensions of Intellectual Property Rights in Science and Technology*, National Academy Press, Washington DC.
18. Eckerseley P. (2003), The Economic Evaluation of Alternatives to Digital Copyright - Serciac. www.serciac.org
19. Michael Botein and Edward Samuels remain skeptical about the feasibility of implementing compulsory licensing, for instance, to authorize and regulate peer-to-peer distribution of copyrighted works, because considering the history of copyright licenses in a number of different contexts, they conclude that compulsory licensing has not been successful in implementing policy goals. Instead they suggest that privately negotiated contracts may be more efficient than governmental intervention. *See* Botein M. and Samuels E. (2008), "Compulsory licensing v. private negotiations in Peer to Peer file sharing," in Noam E. and Pupillo L., editors, "Peer to Peer Video: The Economics, Policy and Culture of Today's New Mass Medium," Springer 2008.
20. *See* EU Directive 2001/29/EC. Member States may allow for a limitation to the exclusive reproduction right "*in respect of reproductions on any medium made by a natural person for private use and for ends that are neither directly nor indirectly commercial, on condition that the right holders receive fair compensation which takes account of the application or non application of technological measures*" (article 5.2 (b)), http://europa.eu.int/information_society/eeurope/2005/all_about/digital_rights_man/doc/directive_copyright_en.pdf

21. As mentioned previously, a similar system was used under the Audio Home recording Act of 1992 in the USA. Indeed, it imposed a levy on the sale of the digital audio recording devices with receipts going to copyrights owners.
22. Farchy (2004), page 6.
23. *See* Okedij R.L. (2006), "The International Copyright System: Limitations, Exceptions and Public Interest Considerations for Developing Countries," ICTSD, Issue Paper n. 15.
24. "In a clickwrap contract, the software or Internet site presents the user or potential purchaser with contractual terms governing the use of the software or site. The user must agree to those terms and click a button or link demonstrating her assent to use the software or site," The Berkman Center Green Paper (2004) V. 1.2, page 13.
25. See The Berkman Center Green Paper (2004) V.1.2, pages 15–17.
26. See The Berkman Center Green Paper (2004) V.1.2, pages 18–23.
27. See, for instance, "Creative Economy - Report 2008," United Nations.
28. In many developing countries in Africa, but also in Latin America, many writers and artists have to rely on foreign publishers or record companies. *See* ICTSD & UNCTAD Report (2004), page 70.
29. The creation of collective administration is quite common in developed countries, and is not limited to performing rights but it is often advocated as a solution to many copyrights and enforcement problems. The idea behind collective administration is that some aspects of copyright administrations are natural monopolies, that is, that individual administration is impracticable or not economical. It follows that the collective administration is considered the most efficient way for licensing, monitoring, and enforcing those rights. This view is challenged by Katz (2004). Furthermore, he argues that Internet and the DRM technologies, facilitating the online licensing of music, undermine the natural monopoly characteristics of this market, facilitating the formation of a competitive market place for performing rights. Katz A. (2004), "The Potential Demise of another Natural Monopoly: New Technologies and the Future of Collective Administration of Copyrights," University of Toronto, Faculty of Law, Research Papers.
30. *See* Geneva Declaration on the Future of the World Intellectual Property Organization, http://www.cptech.org/ip/wipo/genevadeclaration.html
31. *See* Okediji R.L. (2003) "Development in the Information Age: The Importance of Copyright," Comment-Bridges – www.ictsd.org
32. For instance, On October 4, 2002, the US Congress enacted the "Technology, Education and Copyright Harmonization Act" commonly known as the "Teach Act." It protects copyrighted works, while permitting educators to use those materials in distance education. *See* Crews K.D. (2003), "New Copyright Law for Distance Education: The Meaning and Importance of the TEACH Act," www.copyright.iupui.edu/teach_summary.htm
33. *See* DFID report (2002), pages 101–102.
34. *See* Gilles Saint-Paul (2002), page 2.
35. "Microsoft, as part of its proposed settlement with a number of US states following its recent US anti-trust prosecution, suggested that it donates tens of thousand of free software licenses to school and low-income communities located in those states. Yet, some states rejected this offer and the donations after calculating that, over the long-term, the licensing costs would be substantial." See Story A. (2004), pages 20 and 34. For a discussion on "Lock in and Information Technology," see Shapiro C. and Varian H.R. (1999), chapter. 5.
36. *See* WIPO (2002), "Intellectual Property on the Internet: A Survey of Issues," page 44.
37. This section draws from Sjoera Nas (2004), "The Multatuli Project-ISP Notice and Take Down," http://www.bof.nl/docs/researchpaperSANE.pdf
38. This rule was inspired by a 1999 decision of the court of the Hague on the case of the religious sect Scientology against the Dutch author Karin Spaink and 20 providers. This decision included a statement that providers could be held liable if three conditions are met: (1) the provider is notified; (2) the notification leaves no reasonable doubt about the infringement of copyrights; and (3) the provider does not take down the material. Furthermore, beside the E-commerce directive and national jurisprudence, provider liability is also determined in

some countries by the penal code, according to the horizontal approach (not only copyright but also obscenity and so on).

39. *See* http://pcmlp.socleg.ox.ac.uk/archive/index.html
40. *See* Sjoera Nas (2004).
41. *See* Anne Linn (2000) "History of Database Protection: Legal Issues of Concern to the Scientific Community," *National Research Council* at http://www.codata.org/codata/data_access/linn.html
42. Reichman J.H. (2000), "Of Green Tulips and Legal Kudzu: Repackaging Rights in Sub patentable Innovation," Vanderbilt Law Review, Vol. 53(6), 1743.
43. Reichman J.H. and Uhlirf P.F. (2003), "A contractually Reconstructed Research Commons for Scientific Data in Highly Protectionist Intellectual Property Environment," Law& Contemp. Probs.
44. WIPO (2004), "Traditional Knowledge Policy and Legal Options," page 18.
45. Trade secrets consist of commercially valuable information about production methods, companies' financial data, etc. The law protects these information against acquisition by commercially unfair means and unauthorized disclosure. Reverse engineering, for instance, is considered a fair method to acquire these information.
46. In the USA The CONTU's (Commission on New Technological Uses of Copyrighted Works) recommendation of using copyright protection for software was not without criticism. In particular, Commissioner John Hersey wrote a strong dissent. He feared that big companies "lock their software into their hardware," adversely affecting independent software vendors who would like to sell programs to run on all hardware. See Cohen J.E. et al. (2002), *Copyright in a Global Information Economy*, Aspen Law and Business, page 242.
47. This section draws from Cohen J.E. et al. (2002), page 269.
48. Even before the CONTU report (1980), in 1960s, US President Lyndon Johnson established the President's Commission on the Patent System to examine, among other issues, whether computer software should be protected by patent. In 1966, its final report strongly rejected this proposal. See Story A. (2004), Intellectual Property and Computer Software, *ICTSD-UNCTAD Issue Paper n.10*, page 10.
49. *See* Story (2004), page. 25.
50. *See* Bessen J. and Hunt R.M. (2004), "An Empirical Look at Software Patents," *Working Paper N. 03-17R*. They find evidence that software patents substitute for R&D at the firm level.
51. This section draws from Okediji R.L. (2004), Development in the Information Age, *ICTSD-UNCTAD Issue Paper n.9*, pages 20–21.
52. It is interesting to notice that in the recent report from the US National Research Council of the National Academies on patents, among the reasons to believe that patent quality has suffered, it is mentioned "…some dilution of the application of the non-obviousness standard in biotechnology and some limitations on its proper application to business methods patent applications." *A Patent System for the 21st Century* (2004), page 3.
53. *See* Reverse Engineering, Chilling Effects, at http://www.chillingeffects.org/reverse
54. "Under certain circumstances, the EU Software directive permits a person in rightful possession of the program to reverse engineer the program by decompiling it (go from object code to source code) to obtain information necessary to ensure interoperability between the decompiled program and another independently created one. The right to engage in such conduct is limited to cases in which the necessary information is not available elsewhere." See Cohen J.E. et al. (2002), page 271.
55. *See* May (2004b), page 17.
56. "Open Source Software (OSS) is software for which the source code is available to the public, enabling anyone to copy, modify, and redistribute the source code. Access to the source code allows users or programmers to inspect and understand the underlying program; they can even extend or modify the source code, subject to certain licensing restrictions. Commercial Software, by contrast, is software distributed under commercial license agreements, usually for a fee. While there are many different approaches to commercial software licensing, it is

frequently the case that the user of commercial software does not receive the copyrighted software source code and typically cannot redistribute the software itself or extensions to that software. Companies that develop commercial software typically employ intellectual property protection to maintain control over the source code they develop." See Varian H.R. and Shapiro C. (2003), "Linux Adoption in the Public Sector: An Economic Analysis," page 3, http://www.sims.berkeley.edu/~hal/Papers/2004/linux-adoption-in-the-public-sector.pdf

57. *See* Dravis P. (2003), "Open Source Software: Prospective for Development," *infoDev*, page 7.
58. See Evans D.S. and Reddy B.J. (2003), "Government Preferences for Promoting Open-Source Software: A Solution in Search of a Problem," *9 Mich. Telecomm. Tech. L. Review* 313, page 371.
59. *See* Sida (2004), Open Source in Developing Countries; Story A. (2004a); Story A. (2004b); Varian and Shapiro (2003), page 13; Dravis (2003); Okediji (2004).
60. *See* Schmidt K.M. and Schnitzer M. (2002), "Public Subsidies for Open Source? Some Economic Policy Issues of the Software Market," http://opensource.mit.edu/papers/schmidt-schnitzer.pdf
61. *See* Varian H.R. et al. (2003), "Public Sectors Software Adoption: What Policymakers Need to Know About Open Source Software," *mimeo*, IDEI Conference on Internet and Software Industries.
62. It is interesting to notice that recently, the open-source model has been applied to goods other than software. *See* "Beyond Capitalism," *The Economist*, June 12th–8th, 2004.

Part IV
Privacy Challenge

Chapter 7
Economic Aspects of Personal Privacy

Hal R. Varian

Introduction

The advent of low-cost technology for manipulating and communicating information has raised significant concerns about personal privacy. Privacy is a complex issue that can be treated from many perspectives; this chapter provides an overview of some of the *economic* issues surrounding it.[1]

I first describe the role of privacy in economic transactions, in which consumers will rationally *want* certain kinds of information about themselves to be available to producers and will want other kinds of information to be secret. Then, I go on to consider how one might define property rights with respect to private information in ways that allow consumers to retain control over how information about them is used.

A Simple Example

The most fundamental economic transaction is that of *exchange*: Two individuals engage in a trade. For example, one person, "the seller," gives another person, "the buyer," an apple; in exchange, the buyer gives the seller some money.

Let us think about how privacy concerns enter this very basic transaction. Suppose that the seller has many different kinds of apples (Jonathan, Macintosh, Red Delicious, etc.). The buyer is willing to pay at most r to purchase a Jonathan, and 0 to purchase any other kind of apple.

In this transaction, the buyer would want the seller to know certain things, but not others, about him. In particular, the buyer would like the seller to know *what it is that he wants* – namely a Jonathan apple. This helps the buyer reduce his search costs, as the seller can immediately offer him the appropriate product.

H.R. Varian
School of information,
University of California at Berkeley, Berkeley, CA
hai@sims.berkeley.edu

W.H. Lehr and L.M. Pupillo (eds.), *Internet Policy and Economics*,
DOI 10.1007/978-1-4419-0038-8_7, © Springer Science+Business Media, LLC 2009

The transaction is made more efficient if detailed information about the consumer's tastes is available to the seller.

On the contrary, the buyer in general will *not* want the seller to know r, the maximum price that he is willing to pay for the item being sold. If this information were available to the seller, the seller would price the product at the buyer's maximum willingness to pay, and the buyer would receive no surplus from the transaction.

Roughly speaking, the buyer wants the seller to know his tastes about which products he may be interested in buying, but he doesn't want the seller to know how much he is willing to pay for them. Armed with this simple insight, let us investigate some more realistic examples.

Search Costs

When many people talk about "privacy rights," they really are talking about the "right not to be annoyed." I don't really care if someone has my telephone number as long as they don't call me during dinner and try to sell me insurance. Similarly, I don't care if someone has my address, as long as they don't send me lots of official-looking letters offering to refinance my house or sell me mortgage insurance. In this case, the annoyance is in the form of a distraction – the seller uses more of my "attention" than I would like.

In the "information age," attention is becoming a more and more valuable commodity, and ways to economize on attention may be quite valuable. Junk mail, junk phone calls, and junk e-mail are annoying and costly to consumers.

In the context of the apple example described above, it is as though the seller of apples has to tell me about each of the different kinds of apples that he has to sell before I am able to purchase.

It is important to recognize that this form of annoyance – essentially excess search costs – arises because the seller has *too little* information about the buyer. If the seller knows precisely whether or not I am interested in buying insurance or refinancing my mortgage, he can make a much better decision about whether or not to provide me with information about his product.

In the context of the apple example, it is in the interest of *both* parties to know that the buyer will purchase only a certain kind of apple. The seller has every incentive to present this information to the seller, and the buyer has every incentive to solicit this information from the seller.

This is, in fact, how the direct mail market works. If I subscribe to a computer magazine, I will end up on a mailing list that is sold to companies that want to sell me computer hardware and software. If I refinance my house, I am deluged with letters offering me mortgage insurance. In these cases, the seller is using information about me that is correlated with my likelihood of purchasing certain products. [See Blattberg and Deighton (1991) for discussion of some current trends in direct marketing.]

In this context, the more the seller knows about my preferences, the better it is. If, for example, I am interested in buying a computer printer, it may well be in my interest and in the seller's interest for this fact to be known. If I am only interested in a laser printer, this is even more valuable information, as it further reduces search costs for both buyer and seller. If I already have a laser printer that I am happy with, the seller may find that valuable to know as he will not have to incur costs trying in vain to sell me a new printer.

Secondary Users of Information

When a mailing list is sold to a third party, the relationship between the buyer's original interests and the seller's interest may become more tenuous. For example, suppose that the list of computer magazine subscribers is sold to an office-furniture supplier. Some of the people on this mailing list may or may not have an interest in office furniture.

Even though the first two parties in the transaction – the individual who may want to buy something and the seller who may want to sell him something – have incentives that are more or less aligned, the transaction between the original owner of the mailing list and those to whom it is sold do not have such well-aligned incentives.

Economists would say that an *externality* is present. The actions of the party who buys the mailing list will potentially impose costs on the individuals on that list, but the seller of the mailing list ignores those costs when selling it.

These costs could be mitigated, to some degree, if the individual who is on the mailing list has a voice in the transaction. For example, the individual could forbid all secondary transactions in his personal information. Or, more generally, the individual could allow his information to be distributed to companies who would send him information about laser printers, but not about office furniture.

These considerations suggest that the difficulty in the "annoyance" component of privacy concerns could be significantly improved if the communications channels between the buyers and the sellers were clearer, the information conveyed were more accurate, and third-party transactions were restricted to only those transactions that the original consumers authorize.

Incentives Involving Payment

Let us now consider a more difficult case, the case where the buyer's revealing information about himself is detrimental. Suppose that the buyer wishes to purchase life insurance but knows information about his health that would adversely influence the terms under which the seller would offer insurance. In this case, the buyer does not want information released that would influence the price at which the insurance would be offered.

Suppose, for example, that the potential buyer of insurance is a smoker, and the seller's knowledge of this information would result in a higher life insurance premium. Should the buyer be required to truthfully release the information? Since the information here concerns the price at which the service (insurance) is offered, the incentives are perfectly opposed: The buyer would not want to reveal that he is a smoker, while the seller would want to know this information.

Note, however, that a nonsmoker *would* want this particular information about himself revealed. Hence, the insurance company has an easy solution to this problem: They offer insurance at a rate appropriate for smokers, and then offer a discount for nonsmokers. This would succeed in aligning information incentives for the buyer and seller.

More generally, suppose that the price that the seller would like to charge is higher for people with some characteristic C. Then people who have that characteristic have bad incentives to reveal it, but people who do not have that characteristic have good incentives to reveal it. It is in the interest of the seller to construct the transaction in a way that the information is revealed.

Contracts and Markets for Information

We have seen that several of the problems with personal privacy arise because of the *lack* of information available between concerned parties. Perhaps some of these problems could be mitigated by allowing for more explicit ways to convey information between buyers and sellers.

For example, it is common to see boxes on subscription cards that say, "Check here if you do not want your name and address redistributed to other parties." This is a very primitive form of contract. A more interesting contract might be something like, "Check here if you would like your name distributed to other parties who will provide you with information about computer peripherals until December 31, 1998. After that, name and address will be destroyed. In exchange, you will be paid $5 for each list to which your name and address is distributed."

Although it might be hard to fit this sort of contract on a subscription response card, it would easily fit on a Web page. The contract being offered implicitly assigns property rights in an individual's name and address to him or herself, unless the individual chooses to sell or, more properly, rent that information.

This particular legal policy seems quite attractive: Assign a property rights in information about an individual to that individual, but then allow contracts to be written that would allow that information to be used for limited times and specified purposes. In particular, information about an individual could not be resold, or provided to third parties, without that individual's explicit agreement.

This idea appears to have been most thoroughly explored by Laudon (1996). He goes further than simple contracting and suggests that one might sell property rights in personal information on markets. As Laudon points out, there is already a large market in personal information. But the property rights are held by those who collect and compile information about individuals – not by the individuals themselves. These third parties buy and sell information that can impose costs on those individuals, without the individuals being directly involved in the transactions. In economic terminology, there is, again, an *externality*.

The personal information industry in the USA is primarily self-regulated, based on so-called Fair Information Practices.[2]

- There shall be no personal-record systems whose existence is secret.
- Individuals have rights of access, inspection, review, and amendment to systems containing information about them.
- There must be a way for individuals to prevent information about themselves gathered for one purpose from being used for another purpose without their consent.
- Organizations and managers of systems are responsible for the reliability and security of their systems and for the damage done by them.
- Governments have the right to intervene in the information relationships among private parties.

The European Community has more explicit privacy regulation. For more on international regulations, see the Electronic Privacy Information Center's page on International Privacy Standards.[3]

It is worth observing that the Fair Information Practices principles would be implemented automatically if the property rights in individual information resided solely with those individuals. Secret information archives would be illegal; individuals could demand the right of review before allowing information about themselves to be used, and those who want to utilize individual information would have to request that right explicitly from the individual in question, or from an agent acting on his or her behalf.

Laudon goes on to propose that pieces of individual information could be aggregated into bundles that would be leased on a public market that he refers to as the "National Information Market." For example, an individual might provide information about himself to a company that aggregates it with 999 other individuals with similar demographic and marketing characteristics. Such groups could be described by titles such as "20- to 30-year-old males in California who are interested in computers," or "20- to 30-year-old married couples who are interested in home purchase."

Those who want to sell to such groups could purchase rights to use these mailing lists for limited periods. The payments they made would flow back to the individual users as "dividends." Individuals who find the annoyance cost of being on such lists greater than the financial compensation could remove their names. Individuals who feel appropriately compensated could remain on the lists.

Although they are many practical details of implementation that would need to be solved to implement Laudon's market, it is important to recognize that information about individuals is commonly bought and sold today by third parties in market-like environments. The National Information Market simply gives individuals an economic stake in those transactions that they currently do not have.

Personal Information

There may be information about me that I don't want revealed just because I don't want people to know it. For example, many people are very touchy about personal financial information. They don't want other people to know how much income they make, or how much they paid for their house or car.

In some cases, there is a social interest to making such information public. Consider the following two examples.

A computer consultant in Oregon paid the state $222 for its complete motor vehicles database, which he then posted to a Web site, prompting charges of privacy violations from people who complained that he had invaded their privacy. The database allows anyone with an Oregon license plate number to look up the vehicle owner's name, address, birth date, driver's license number, and title information. The consultant's motive in posting the information, which anyone can obtain for a fee by going to a state office, was to improve public safety by allowing identification of reckless drivers. Oregon Governor John Kitzhaver says that instant access to motor vehicle records over the Internet is different from information access obtained by physically going to state offices and making a formal request for information: "I am concerned that this ease of access to people's addresses could be abused and present a threat to an individual's safety."[4]

Victoria, the first city in Canada to put its tax-assessment rolls on the Internet, has pulled the plug after British Columbia's Information Commissioner announced an investigation into the practice, believing it violates privacy laws.[5]

In each of these cases, there is a public interest in having the information publicly available. Making information available about owners of motor vehicles may help ensure safer operation. Making the selling prices of houses available may help ensure the accuracy of tax assessments. My neighbors may care about the assessment of my house, not because they particularly care about *my* tax assessment, but because they care about *their* tax assessment.

Whether such information should be publicly available would depend ideally on an individual cost–benefit analysis. If I am willing to pay more to keep my assessment private than my neighbors are willing to pay to see it, we have a potential way to make everyone better off: I pay my neighbors for the right to keep my assessment private. If they value seeing my information more than I value keeping it private, then they pay me for the right to see it.

This sort of transaction is not really practical for a variety of reasons, but the same principle should apply in aggregate. One has to compare the "average" potential benefits from making this sort of information public to the potential costs of keeping it private. The presence of a market where individuals can sell information about themselves helps to provide a benchmark for such cost-benefit calculations.

Certain kinds of information can be collected and distributed without revealing the identity of individuals. Froomkin and Michael (1996) explores some of the legal issues involving anonymity and pseudonymity [see Camp et al. (1996) for a computer science view]. Karnow (1994) proposes the interesting idea of "e-persons," or "epers," which provide privacy while conveying a relevant description of the individual.

Costs of Acquiring Public Information

Many sorts of public information have been available at some transactions cost. In order to find housing assessments, for example, it typically has been necessary to travel to a city or county office and look up the information. Now that increasing numbers of consumers are computerized, it is possible to acquire this information much more inexpensively. Information that was previously deemed useful to have publicly available under the old transactions technology may now be deemed to be *too* available.

This situation, it seems to me, has a reasonably simple solution. The information could be made available in digital form, but at a price that reflects the transactions costs implicit in acquiring the information by means of the old technology. The price paid for the information could then be used to defray the cost of making it publicly available.

For example, suppose that, on average, it takes a citizen one hour to go to the county records department, look up a tax assessment, and photocopy the relevant material. Then a reasonable charge for accessing this information online might be on the order of $25.20 or so per assessment requested.

This sort of charging schedule essentially restores the status quo, provides some funds for local government, and offers an additional choice to individuals. People who don't want to pay $25 can make the trip to the county records office and access the same information there "for free" (i.e., paying no monetary cost).

Assignment of Rights

I have argued that an appropriate way to deal with privacy issues is to determine a baseline assignment of rights, but allow individuals to trade those rights if they desire to do so. If there are no transactions costs in trading or negotiation, the initial assignment of privacy rights is arbitrary from the viewpoint of economic efficiency.[6]

To see this, suppose that it is worth 50 cents a week to me to have my name omitted from a junk e-mail list, and that it is worth 20 cents a week to the owner of the junk e-mail list to have my name on it. If the owner of the e-mail list has the right to put my name on it without consulting me, then I would have to pay him some amount between 20 and 50 cents to have him remove it. On the contrary, if he has to seek my permission to use my name, it would not be forthcoming, since the value to him of having my name on the list is less than the value to me of having it off. Either way the property rights are assigned, my name would end up off the list.

If there *are* significant transactions costs to making contracts such as these, the standard Coasian arguments suggest that an efficient allocation of rights would be one in which the transactions and negotiation costs are minimized. In this case, the appropriate comparison involves the transactions cost to the individual of having his or her name removed from the list to the cost to the mailing list owner of soliciting permission from individuals to add them to the list.

When phrased in this way, it appears that the current practice of adding someone's name to a list unless they specifically request removal probably minimizes transactions costs. However, the rapid advances in information and communications technology may change this conclusion. The development of social institutions such as Laudon's market would also have a significant impact on transactions costs.

Summary

Privacy is becoming a very contentious public policy issue. The danger, in my opinion, is that Congress will rush into legislation without due consideration of the options. In particular, a poorly thought-out legislative solution would likely result in a very rigid framework that assigns individuals additional rights with respect to information about themselves, but does not allow for ways to sell such property rights in exchange for other considerations.

In my view, legislation about rights individuals have with respect to information about themselves should explicitly recognize that those rights can be "leased" to others for specific uses, but cannot be *resold* without explicit permission. This simple reform would lay the foundation for a more flexible and more useful policy about individual privacy.

In addition, it would enable business models that would potentially allow for reduced transactions costs and better matches between buyers and sellers.

Notes

Research supported in part by NSF Grant SES-93-20481. Thanks to Pam Samuelson for providing useful comments on an earlier draft. The author's home page and contact information are available at <http://www.sims.berkeley.edu/~hal>. An earlier version of this chapter was published on the Web in "Privacy and Self-Regulation in the Information Age," a report issued by the National Telecommunications and Information Administration in June 1997. See http://www.ntia.doc.gov/reports/privacy/privacy_rpt.htm

1. There are many other aspects of privacy that this chapter does not cover for lack of space – issues involving, for example, misrepresentation, unauthorized publicity, and so on.
2. Certain sorts of behavior have legislative protection, for example, lists of rental videos.
3. http://www.epic.org/privacy/intl/default.html
4. Educause.edu Electronic Publications (1996). Privacy versus Freedom of Information on the Web (11 August). Reproduced from Edupage archives, <http://www.educause.edu/pub/edupage/archives/96/edupage-0811.html#anchor8> (Associated Press August 8, 1996).
5. Educause.edu Electronic Publications (1996). Victoria Pulls the Plug on Web Site (30 September). Reproduced from Edupage archives, <http://www.educause.edu/pub/edupage/archives/96/edupage-9.30.96html> (Toronto Globe & Mail September 27, 1996, A30)
6. Economic efficiency is, of course, only one concern involved in assignment of property rights. Considerations of fairness, natural rights, etc., are also relevant.

References

Blattberg, R. C. and Deighton, J. 1991. Interactive Marketing: Exploiting the Age of Addressability. *Sloan Management Review* 33, no. 1 (fall): Xd14.

Camp, L. J., Micael, H., Bennet, Y., and Tygar, J. D. 1996. Anonymous Atomic Transactions. Technical report. Carnegie Mellon University.

Froomkin, A. and Michael, H. 1996. Flood Control on the Information Ocean: Living with Anonymity, Digital Cash, and Distributed Databases. Technical report. University of Miami School of Law.

Karnow, Curtis E. A. 1994. The Encrypted Self: Fleshing out the Rights of Electronic Personalities. Conference on "Computers, Freedom, and Privacy."

Laudon, K. C. 1996. Markets and Privacy. *Communications of the ACM* 39. no. 9 (*day, week, month, or season?*): Xd104.

Chapter 8
Cybercrimes vs. Cyberliberties[1]

Nadine Strossen

Introduction for the 2009 Edition

I originally wrote my chapter in 1999, when the Internet was a fairly new phenomenon, with which US policymakers and courts were just beginning to grapple. As with all new media, throughout history, too many policymakers and others initially viewed Internet communications as posing unique new dangers to community concerns, including personal safety and national security. Accordingly, government officials reacted to the advent of the Internet in the classic way that government officials have consistently reacted to new media – by restricting freedom of speech and privacy in communications using these new media. The original chapter discusses why such suppressive measures have not even been effective in promoting safety and security, much less necessary to do so.

Elected officials in the USA consistently have supported measures targeting Internet expression, and, true to America's Puritanical heritage, these measures have specifically singled out sexually oriented expression, seeking to shield children from viewing it. In contrast, the courts have consistently struck down such suppressive laws, concluding that the government could more effectively promote its child-protective goals through noncensorial approaches that would also respect adults' rights.

This new Introduction explains how all of the themes and conclusions of the original chapter remain valid despite intervening developments, including the 2001 terrorist attacks. It shows that the major points that the 1999 chapter made about one particular medium, at one particular historical point, concerning particular safety and security issues that were then at the forefront of public concern, apply more universally to other media, during other historical periods, and regarding other safety and security concerns. The Introduction supports this generalization by

N. Strossen
Professor of Law, New York Law School, New York, NY, USA
email: nadine.strossen@nyls.edu

W.H. Lehr and L.M. Pupillo (eds.), *Internet Policy and Economics*,
DOI 10.1007/978-1-4419-0038-8_8,

analyzing two sets of subsequent developments. First, it shows that post-911 surveillance measures that target communications, including Internet communications, violate freedom of speech and privacy without sufficient countervailing security benefits. Second, it shows that the government's continuing efforts to suppress online sexual expression, in order to protect children from seeing it, continue appropriately to be struck down by the courts as violating free speech rights without sufficient countervailing benefits.

Overview: Plus ça Change, Plus c'est la Même Chose[2]

Many policy and legal arguments since 2001 have posited a supposedly new post-911 paradigm for many issues, including issues concerning Internet regulation and the (non)protection of free speech and privacy rights in the Internet context.[3] However, the allegedly new terrorist dangers, and the allegedly increased justifications for Internet regulations that restrict free speech and privacy in the name of the War on Terror prove, on analysis, to be just the same old.[4]

Before President George W. Bush declared a War on Terror, other US Presidents had declared and maintained a War on Drugs and a War on Crime, invoking strikingly similar rationales. Indeed, even before these metaphorical wars of the past four decades, the USA had been engaged in a cold war, which also raised virtually identical issues about the appropriate balance between government power and individual rights.[5] The proponents of all of these metaphorical wars have maintained, first, that the USA as a nation, as well as all individuals in the USA, have been facing unprecedented threats to national security, the social order, and/or personal safety. Second, all of these advocates have maintained that, in order to counter the threats in question, government requires increased power, including increased surveillance power over communications, resulting in reduced free speech and privacy rights.

In all of these contexts, though, analysis shows that at least the second part of the common argument is overblown. Thus, even assuming for the sake of argument that the threats posed by terrorism, drugs, and crime are as great as maintained by the proponents of the various wars against them, these warriors still have not satisfied their burden of proving that the increased government powers they advocate actually are necessary to counter the posited threats. Worse yet, many of the new powers are not even effective to counter such threats, let alone necessary. Therefore, they fail to pass muster under the strict scrutiny test that governs measures infringing on fundamental constitutional rights, including free speech and privacy. Under that test, the government must show not only that the rights-restrictive measure is designed to promote a countervailing goal of compelling importance, such as national security or public safety. The government must also show that the challenged measure is narrowly tailored or necessary to promote that goal, and that there is no less restrictive alternative measure, which would also effectively promote the government's goal, with less cost to individual rights.[6]

In the War on Terror, along with other recent metaphorical wars, the increased powers the government has sought to engage in surveillance of Internet and other communications, far from being necessary to advance the government's goals, have to the contrary been criticized by pertinent experts as actually undermining the government's goals. Specifically concerning increased surveillance of Internet and other communications post-911, security and counterintelligence experts have maintained that the government's dragnet methods have deflected scarce resources from honing in on the communications of particular individuals regarding whom the government has some basis for suspicion. Moreover, these dragnet methods have deterred many communications that could provide information and insights that could actually aid the government's counterterrorism efforts.[7]

Although I initially wrote the chapter about Cybercrimes and Cyberliberties in 1999, substantially before the 2001 terrorist attacks, and although the US government (as well as governments in other countries[8]) has contended that those attacks warrant extensive new regulations of all communications, including on the Internet, the fundamental points and themes in that chapter remain fully applicable to the post-911 world. Both the government arguments in favor of regulation, and the counterarguments in favor of free speech and privacy, have remained essentially the same. The only changes have been the particular factual details that are cited to flesh out what are, at bottom, disagreements about matters of principle: how to strike the appropriate balance between, on the one hand, safety and security, and, on the other hand, liberty and privacy. Indeed, in rereading the 1999 chapter in order to prepare this new Introduction, I was struck by how many of the pertinent factual considerations and policy concerns that the government has stressed in our supposedly new post-911 world were also significant before the 2001 terrorist attacks. Even back in 1999, terrorism was of course already a major concern in the USA and many other countries. Accordingly, at the very beginning of the chapter, in its very first line, it recognizes that terrorism, along with crime, is a worldwide concern. Likewise, throughout the chapter, the analysis refers regularly and interchangeably to both crime and terrorism, in assessing competing claims about government regulation and individual freedom. In short, the following is one key takeaway point from the 1999 chapter, which is reinforced by considering the subsequent developments: enduring general themes unify all specific debates about whether restrictions on Internet free speech and privacy are justified for the asserted sake of safety and security.

The themes that I addressed in the 1999 chapter continue to be of general, ongoing relevance in another sense. Although that chapter's specific factual focus was on Internet regulations, it also applies to all communications media beyond the Internet. When I wrote the chapter, the Internet was still quite new in terms of public, political, and press awareness. Accordingly, it generated the same reactions that all new communications media have triggered, throughout history. Proponents of government power, as well as many people who are concerned about safety and security, maintain that the new medium raises unique new risks to these concerns, and therefore warrants unique new regulations. Over the course of the twentieth century, these claims were made successively about the telephone, movies, radio, broadcast television, cable and satellite television, video cassette recorders, and, most recently, the Internet. The arguments are more alike than different, and indeed parallel the arguments made in support of shutting down that assertedly dangerous new communications innovation introduced by Johannes Gutenberg in the 15th century – the printing press.

Since I am writing this new Introduction to the 1999 chapter almost a decade later, the Internet is no longer so new, and hence, following the historic pattern that has applied to other media, it is no longer regarded as uniquely dangerous. Instead, the Internet is largely considered to be just one of many communications media, all of which raise the same competing concerns regarding safety and liberty, weighing for and against regulations that restrict freedom and privacy of communications. This development, the recognition that the Internet has more in common with other communications media than otherwise, is manifested by the fact that the recent US communications regulations have not singled out the Internet.[9]

Instead, online communications have been included in the same general regulatory initiatives that also have embraced other communications media, and this has specifically been true for post-911 regulations that the government has advocated as countering terrorism, from the US PATRIOT Act[10] in 2001 to the Protect America Act in 2007.[11]

To sum up what I have said so far, major points that the 1999 chapter made about one particular medium, at one particular historical point, concerning particular safety and security issues that were then at the forefront of public and political consciousness, apply more universally to other media, during other historical periods, and regarding other safety and security concerns. This Introduction will bolster that overarching conclusion by summarizing the most important general points that the 1999 chapter made, and by citing some of the many intervening developments that demonstrate their continuing validity.

The 1999 chapter made two sets of major interrelated points, which have continuing relevance today:

1. Far from being inevitably antagonistic, safety and freedom are often mutually reinforcing. Many measures that are touted as promoting safety are in fact not even effective, let alone necessary, which is the standard that is required by both the US Constitution (as well as the constitutions of many other countries, along with international and regional human rights treaties) and common sense. These generalizations apply to measures that restrict either free speech or privacy online.
2. In addition to protecting safety in general, the US government's other most cited justification for suppressing Internet communications has been to protect children from the alleged adverse effects of exposure to sexually oriented expression, which has traditionally been viewed as especially suspect in American culture and law. Accordingly, it is not surprising that US politicians, of both major political parties, have overwhelmingly voted in favor of laws restricting online sexual expression for the sake of shielding children from it. In contrast, though, US judges have overwhelmingly ruled that these laws are

unconstitutional, and the judges furthermore have stressed that alternative measures, which are less restrictive of free speech and privacy, might well also be more effective in advancing the government's countervailing concerns.

This Introduction will highlight the continued pertinence of these two sets of points by briefly discussing two sets of subsequent developments. First, this Introduction will outline the mutually reinforcing relationship of safety and freedom in the context of government surveillance of communications, including Internet communications, as part of its post-911 War on Terror. Second, this Introduction will discuss the judicial rulings that have continued to strike down laws, which politicians continue to support, that suppress online sexual expression for the sake of shielding children.

Post-911 Surveillance Measures That Target Communications, Including Internet Communications, Violate Freedom of Speech and Privacy Without Sufficient Countervailing Security Benefits

Ever since the September 11, 2001, terrorist attacks, the ACLU has worked with ideologically diverse allies, including many national security and counterterrorism experts, in what we have called our "Safe and Free" campaign.[12] This name highlights, specifically in the post-911 context, the single most important overarching theme of the 1999 chapter: that safety and freedom, far from being inherently antithetical, are often positively interrelated. That theme applies to the government's entire arsenal in its War on Terror, but this Introduction will summarize its pertinence specifically to surveillance measures that target Internet communications, along with other communications.

Starting with the PATRIOT Act, which was enacted just 45 days after the terrorist acts, the US government has exercised increasing surveillance over all communications, including online communications, with measures that violate the fundamental Fourth Amendment[13] requirements of individualized suspicion and a judicial warrant. Among other things, the PATRIOT Act vastly expanded the government's power to issue National Security Letters (NSLs), demanding that Internet Service Providers (ISPs) turn over information about their customers' online communications, without any judicially issued warrants. The PATRIOT Act also imposed a sweeping gag order on any ISP that receives an NSL, barring the ISP from disclosing any information about this NSL to anyone, including the affected customers.[14] Sweeping and unchecked as these new powers were, we subsequently learned that the Bush Administration had secretly arrogated to itself even more wide-ranging powers to engage in dragnet, suspicionless surveillance of online (and other) communications, without any judicial warrant, using the supersecret National Security Agency (NSA), and also enlisting the telephone companies to turn over their customers' data en masse.[15] The NSA is supposed to be engaged in foreign intelligence gathering against suspected terrorists. However, as the *New York Times* revealed in December, 2005,[16] ever since 9/11, the NSA been spying on online and phone communications of completely unsuspected (and unsuspecting) American citizens.

In addition to violating the privacy principles that the Fourth Amendment protects, these dragnet communications surveillance measures also violate the freedom of expression principles that the First Amendment[17] protects. Individuals who have reason to fear that their communications will be subject to government spying engage in self-censorship, not using the Internet to discuss or research certain subjects. This chilling effect has especially wide-ranging repercussions when it affects journalists, scholars, and others who seek information to distribute to the public through their research and writings. For example, when their sources will not communicate with them via e-mail, reasonably fearing that the government may be spying on such communications, this violates not only the rights of the would-be parties to these online communications; furthermore, their government-induced self-censorship violates the free speech rights of all potential readers of the suppressed information. As the Supreme Court has stressed, the First Amendment protects the right to receive information and ideas, as well as the right to purvey them.[18] Far from being less important in a time of national security crisis, the right to receive information, including information about government policies, is especially important in such a context, so that We the People,[19] and our elected representatives, can make informed decisions about the especially pressing issues at stake.

Consistent with the foregoing principles, the American Civil Liberties Union ("ACLU) filed a lawsuit challenging the NSA's post-911 warrantless, suspicionless surveillance of Internet and other communications, maintaining that this domestic spying program violates both the Fourth Amendment and the First Amendment. The trial court judge in this case, *ACLU v NSA*, ruled in the ACLU's favor on both constitutional claims.[20] The appellate court panel, by a 2–1 vote, dismissed the complaint on technical, jurisdictional grounds, without addressing the merits of the claims.[21] Notably, the only appellate court judge who did address the merits of the case, having rejected the alleged jurisdictional bars to doing so, agreed with the ACLU and the lower court judge that this sweeping surveillance program was unconstitutional.[22]

The ACLU's clients in *ACLU v NSA* included respected, ideologically diverse journalists and scholars who were researching and writing about issues directly related to US counterintelligence policies, including the wars in Afghanistan and Iraq.[23] Therefore, not surprisingly, their sources had particular reasons to desist from online communications, leading to suppression of information that is especially important to everyone in the USA and, indeed, around the world. In short, the government's unwarranted, suspicionless surveillance of online communications through this NSA program was as bad for national security as for individual rights. This point was made as follows by one of the plaintiffs in *ACLU v NSA*, New York University Professor Barnett Rubin, a leading expert on Afghanistan. At the time *ACLU v NSA* was filed, Professor Rubin had been conducting interviews with key individuals in Afghanistan for a report he was doing for the Council on Foreign

Relations, making recommendations for furthering the USA's vital security interests in that strategically significant country.[24] As Prof. Rubin said,

> [F]or me to provide analysis and updates for the American public and officials who are concerned about Afghanistan, I need to be able to have confidential communications. My experience in Afghanistan convinces me that illegal programs such as warrantless NSA spying… actually undermine national security.[25]

Along with other constitutional rights and civil liberties, those protected by the Fourth Amendment are fully consistent with promoting national security and public safety. The mutually reinforcing relationship between safety and freedom is illustrated by the fundamental Fourth Amendment principle that is violated by so many post-911 programs that involve sweeping surveillance of online communications: The government may not invade anyone's freedom or privacy without individualized suspicion, a particular reason to believe that a particular person poses a threat.[26] In short, the Fourth Amendment bars dragnet surveillance measures that sweep in broad groups of people and their communications.[27]

Of course, the Fourth Amendment's individualized suspicion requirement protects individual liberty. Specifically, it protects each of us from government surveillance of our e-mails and Web surfing based on group stereotyping and guilt by association.[28] Moreover, this individualized suspicion requirement also promotes national security. It channels our government's resources – in other words, our precious tax dollars – in the most strategic, effective way toward those persons who actually pose a threat. Precisely for this reason, experts in national security and counterintelligence, as well as civil libertarians, have opposed many of the post-9/11 measures that involve mass surveillance, including mass surveillance of Internet and other communications.[29] In short, these measures are the worst of both worlds; they make all of us less free, yet they do not make any of us more safe.

As noted above, one important example of the many doubly flawed post-9/11 mass surveillance measures, which target Internet communications, is the NSA domestic spying program.[30] That program has been sweeping in countless e-mails and telephone calls of American citizens who are not suspected of any illegal activity, let alone terrorism.[31] Therefore, the program's harshest critics include FBI agents.[32] The agents complain about the huge amount of time they have been wasting in tracking down the thousands of completely innocent Americans whose electronic communications have been swept up in this NSA fishing expedition.[33]

This same dual flaw infects the even more sweeping secret surveillance program, affecting apparently essentially all Internet and telephone communications, which *USA Today* revealed in 2006,[34] and which the ACLU is also challenging across the country.[35] This massive communications surveillance program apparently[36] seeks to collect data about all telephone and online communications from all of the US telephone companies about all of their customers.[37] The government asserts that it is using these massive customer calling records for data mining. The government looks for patterns of calls according to certain mathematical formulas that, it says, might point to suspected terrorists.[38] However, this whole data-mining approach has been denounced as junk science by prominent experts in mathematics and computer science.[39] For example, this perspective was stressed by Jonathan David Farley, who is not only a mathematics professor at Harvard University, but also a science fellow at Stanford University's Center for International Security and Cooperation.[40] As he wrote: "[T]he National Security Agency's entire spying program seems to be based on a false assumption: that you can work out who might be a terrorist based on calling patterns. Guilt by association is not just bad law, it's bad mathematics."[41]

The NSA domestic spying and data-mining programs, as well as many other post-9/11 surveillance programs, are overly broad dragnets or fishing expeditions. Thus, by definition, they are doubly flawed: they sweep in too much information about too many innocent people, and they make it harder to hone in on the dangerous ones. As one ACLU critic of these surveillance programs memorably put it: "You don't look for a needle in a haystack by adding more hay to the [stack]!"[42]

The Government's Continuing Efforts to Suppress Sexual Expression, for the Sake of Shielding Children from it, Continue to Be Struck Down by the Courts as Violating Free-Speech Rights Without Sufficient Countervailing Benefits

As the 1999 chapter explained, after the Supreme Court unanimously struck down the first federal law censoring online expression, the Communications Decency Act (CDA),[43] in the landmark case of *ACLU v Reno*,[44] Congress promptly enacted a somewhat narrower law, targeting another category of online sexual expression, which it called the Child Online Protection Act, or COPA.[45] The ACLU promptly sought and obtained a court order enjoining the government from enforcing this law, on the ground that it violates fundamental free speech principles.[46] So far, there have been no fewer than seven court rulings on this ACLU challenge to COPA, including two by the US Supreme Court, and all seven rulings have refused to lift the injunction.[47]

The many judges who have ruled in this protracted litigation have espoused a range of reasons for the conclusion that COPA is unconstitutional, including that it is not sufficiently narrowly tailored to promote its goal of shielding children from certain online sexual material that is assumed to be harmful to minors.[48] In fact, these judges have concluded that COPA is not even effective in shielding minors from the material at issue, and that this goal could be more effectively promoted, instead, by blocking software that individual parents install on their own children's computers. Of course, such user-based blocking software, which is utilized only by particular individuals who opt to do so, is completely consistent with First Amendment principles. Therefore, in this context, as well as the post-911 context, the chapter's overarching conclusion is once again reaffirmed; protecting civil liberties online is fully consistent with government's countervailing concerns, far from being antithetical to them.

The second time the Supreme Court ruled on COPA, in 2004, the Court recognized that user-based blocking software was likely more effective than COPA's criminal bar as a means of restricting childrens' access to materials harmful to them.[49] Because the trial in the COPA case had taken place in 1999, the Supreme Court's 2004 ruling remanded the case to the trial court to reconsider that conclusion, in light of intervening technological developments. The second trial, on that remand, took place in the fall of 2006. Based on the extensive, updated evidentiary materials presented at that second trial, following the Supreme Court's remand, the trial court once again concluded that the government had failed to show that COPA is the least restrictive alternative for advancing Congress's interest in protecting minors from exposure to sexually explicit material on the World Wide Web.[50] Moreover, the court concluded that the government "failed to show that other alternatives are not at least as effective as COPA."[51] To the contrary, the court concluded that user-based blocking or filtering programs are actually more effective than COPA, for several reasons, including the following: filters block sexually explicit online material that is posted outside the USA, and individual parents can customize the settings of filters according to the ages of their children and what type of content those parents find objectionable.[52]

In sum, the courts that have ruled on COPA have repeatedly concluded that children's online safety, as well as adults' online free speech, are more effectively promoted not through censorship, but rather through alternative measures that enhance freedom of choice for all adults and parents. This same conclusion has also been reached by both of the two expert government commissions that have recently examined how best to shield children from online sexual material that their parents might deem inappropriate for them. One panel was authorized by Congress in the COPA statute itself,[53] and the other panel was convened by the prestigious National Research Council (NRC).[54] Both groups were very diverse, including leading antipornography activists as well as Internet experts.[55] The NRC panel was chaired by Richard Thornburgh, a conservative Republican who had served as US Attorney General under Presidents Reagan and Bush I. All members of both commissions rejected the proposition that online sexual material should be regulated to prevent minors from accessing it. Instead, both groups most strongly recommended social and educational strategies that teach children to make wise choices about using the Internet.[56] Of course, that alternative is completely consistent with free speech rights, including the free speech rights of children themselves,[57] as well as those of adults.

In addition to the two post-1999 Supreme Court decisions sustaining the ACLU's constitutional challenge to COPA, the Court has issued one other post-1999 decision ruling on one other federal law that suppresses certain Internet expression – the Children's Internet Protection Act (CIPA).[58] Consistent with the pattern that the 1999 chapter describes, this law, along with the CDA and COPA, singles out online sexual expression in particular, and also focuses on harms that are assumed to be caused to children in particular as a result of viewing such expression.[59] Again following the pattern that the 1999 chapter outlined, the courts that ruled on CIPA, including the Supreme Court, have continued consistently to limit government power to restrict adults' online free speech rights for the purported sake of shielding minors from exposure to online sexual expression.

In 2003, in *United States v American Library Association*,[60] the Supreme Court narrowly construed CIPA in order to restrict its interference with adults' online free speech and privacy rights. CIPA requires all public libraries that receive certain government funding, as a condition of that funding, to install blocking software on all library computer terminals, which is designed to block certain sexually oriented material. In a fragmented ruling, with no majority opinion, six Justices in total, for various reasons, rejected a facial challenge that the ACLU and the American Library Association (ALA) had brought to CIPA; in other words, the ACLU and the ALA sought to invalidate CIPA altogether, no matter how it was enforced. However, these six Justices rejected the facial challenge only after construing CIPA very narrowly, in a way that respected the free speech and privacy rights of adults who access the Internet at affected public libraries.

Specifically, in their three separate opinions, all of these Justices stressed that any time an adult library patron asked to have the blocking software turned off, the library staff had to do so automatically and promptly, without seeking any information from any such adult.[61] Moreover, a majority of the Justices stressed that if CIPA were ever enforced in a way that did infringe on the free speech or privacy rights of adult library patrons, then CIPA would be vulnerable to a constitutional challenge on an as-applied basis, invalidating any such enforcement.[62]

In fact, in 2006, the ACLU instituted an as-applied challenge to CIPA as it was enforced by certain libraries in Washington state, which did block adult patrons' access to various Internet sites, including sites that had no sexual content.[63]

Conclusion

Although I initially wrote my chapter in 1999, before the 2001 terrorist attacks, all of its themes and conclusions retain their force. Analysis of the post-911 measures for government surveillance of Internet communications reinforces the conclusion that we need not sacrifice online privacy and free speech in order to promote personal safety or national security. Likewise, the same general conclusion, that safety and freedom are compatible concerns, is also reinforced by the post-1999 judicial rulings about US statutes that suppress online sexual expression in order to protect children from seeing it. These rulings further reaffirm that measures suppressing Internet free speech and privacy are the worst of both worlds; they do curtail individual liberty, but they do not effectively advance countervailing safety or security goals.

The Thomas Jefferson insight that I quoted in the 1999 chapter remains enduringly prescient today, two centuries after he uttered it: "A society that will trade a little liberty for a little order will deserve neither and will lose both."[64]

Original Chapter: Introduction

Cyberspace is an inherently global medium. Cybercrime and terrorism are worldwide concerns. Preserving human rights in cyberspace is also an international concern.

This chapter reviews legal developments in the USA, which has had more legislation and litigation in this area than has any other country. Our courts' rulings, of course, have been grounded on US law – in particular, the free-speech guarantee of the First Amendment to our Constitution and our constitutional right of privacy. Those same freedoms, however, are also guaranteed under international human rights law, under regional human rights instruments – including the European Convention on Human Rights – and under the domestic law of nations around the world.[65] Therefore, the principles that have guided legal developments in the USA should be relevant in the British Isles and elsewhere, just as developments in Britain and in other parts of the world are relevant in the USA.

Overview of Interrelationship Between Cybercrime and Cyberliberties

The interrelationship between cybercrime and cyberliberties is a broad subject that encompasses two major subtopics. The first subtopic is the extent to which the exercise of certain liberties – notably, free expression – may be criminalized online even if it would be lawful in the traditional print media. The second subtopic is the extent to which online liberties – notably, privacy – may be restricted to facilitate punishment of established crimes, such as trafficking in child pornography or engaging in information terrorism. In other words, the first subtopic concerns whether government may restrict our cyberliberties in order to create new crimes, peculiar to cyberspace; the second subtopic concerns whether government may restrict our cyberliberties in order to prosecute existing crimes, common to all media, more effectively.

In both contexts, many officials argue that we have to make trade-offs between individual rights and public safety. In fact, though, this alleged tension is oversimplified and misleading. In terms of advancing public safety, measures that stifle cyberliberties are often ineffective at best and counterproductive at worst. This doubly flawed nature of laws limiting cyberliberties shows the sadly prophetic nature of a statement that Thomas Jefferson made to James Madison more than 200 years ago. When these two American founders were corresponding about the Bill of Rights to the US Constitution, Jefferson warned: "A society that will trade a little liberty for a little order will deserve neither and will lose both."[66] This statement is right on the mark, for several reasons, concerning the current debates about cybercrimes and cyberliberties. First, claims about the allegedly unique dangers of online expression are exaggerated. Second, the types of criminal laws and enforcement strategies that have worked effectively in other media are also effective in cyberspace. Third, far from harming minors, much of the online expression that has been targeted for censorship is beneficial for them.

For these reasons, even those who specialize in protecting young people from sexual exploitation and violence – indeed, especially those experts – oppose Internet censorship. This is true, for example, of Ernie Allen, director of the National Center for Missing & Exploited Children in the USA, which works closely with the Federal Bureau of Investigation and local police agencies around our country. Mr. Allen and his colleagues understand that the political obsession with suppressing ideas and images that allegedly are harmful to children's minds is a dangerous distraction and diversion from constructive efforts to protect actual children from tangible harm.[67]

In short, cybercensorship does no more good for the safety and welfare of young people than it does for the free-speech rights of everyone. I say "everyone" advisedly, as young people have free speech rights of their own.[68]

The same false tension between liberty and security also makes too much of the political rhetoric about protecting online privacy through such measures as strong encryption or cryptography and anonymous communications. To be sure, law enforcement would be aided to some extent if officials could gain access easily to online communications, just as law enforcement would receive some benefits if officials could readily spy on all communications of any type. But such pervasive surveillance would violate internationally respected, fundamental privacy rights.[69] The consensus of the international community is that this violation would be too high a price to pay for reducing crime. After all, what would be the point of limiting our fellow citizens' interference with our personal security, only at the price of increasing police officers' interference with the very same security?[70]

This point was eloquently stated by a great former justice of the US Supreme Court, Louis Brandeis, who was one of the architects of the legal right to privacy even before he ascended to the high Court[71]:

> Decency, security and liberty alike demand that government officials shall be subjected to the same rules of conduct that are commands to the citizen.... Our Government is the potent, the omnipresent teacher.... Crime is contagious. If the Government becomes a lawbreaker it breeds contempt for law.... To declare that in the administration of the criminal law the end justifies the means... that the Government may commit crimes in order to secure the conviction of a private criminal - would bring terrible retribution.[72]

Just as weakened privacy protections would let government officials access online communications by ordinary, law-abiding citizens, these same weakened protections would also enhance access to online communications by cybercriminals and terrorists who will not comply with government restrictions on encryption. To the contrary, criminals and terrorists will take all available measures, including illegal measures, to secure their own communications. Meanwhile, thanks to legal limits on encryption, cybercriminals will prey more easily on law-abiding individuals and businesses, and vital infrastructures will be more vulnerable to cyberterrorists.

For these reasons, even some government officials have joined with cyberlibertarians in opposing limits on encryption. They concur that, on balance, such limits do more harm than good to public safety.[73]

In broad overview, the relationship between cyberliberties and crime control is not inherently antagonistic but, rather, is often mutually reinforcing. In many respects, law and public policy are developing in a way that is consistent with this perspective. US courts consistently have struck down new laws that seek to criminalize expression online that would be legal in other media. Many judges who have ruled on such laws have agreed with the American Civil Liberties Union (ACLU) and other cyberlibertarians that the laws are not well designed for protecting children, which is their asserted goal. These judges include the entire US Supreme Court, ruling in the landmark 1997 case that struck down the first federal Internet censorship law in the USA, the CDA,[74] in *Reno v ACLU*.[75]

Now we have to call that case *ACLU v Reno I*, since the US federal government subsequently enacted its second cybercensorship law, the so-called Child Online Protection Act or COPA,[76] which at the time of this writing is being fought in a case called *ACLU v Reno II*.[77] It is not surprising that few politicians had the political courage to oppose a law with a name like the "Child Online Protection Act." Fortunately, though, the only judge to rule on the law to date has agreed with us that it not only is unconstitutional but also is unwise and misnamed, as it does not really protect children. Indeed, he concluded his opinion on this note:

> Perhaps we do the minors of this country harm if First Amendment protections, which they will with age inherit fully, are chipped away in the name of their protection.[78]

When we turn from online free speech to privacy, the US courts have been likewise supportive of our arguments that restricting cyberliberties cannot be justified in terms of the alleged countervailing law enforcement concerns. For example, in *ACLU v Miller*,[79] we successfully challenged a state law that prohibited anonymous and pseudonymous online communications. There have, though, been fewer rulings concerning privacy than concerning free speech in the online context. Rulings concerning privacy have been issued only by lower-level courts, and they have not been as consistently supportive of the cyberliberties positions.[80]

In the USA, the battle over online privacy and encryption is being waged mostly in the legislative and executive branches of government, rather than in the courts. The Clinton Administration steadily opposed strong encryption, but many members of Congress, from both major political parties, were on the other side.

Thus far, at least, the US government is quite isolated in the international community in this respect, as most other countries allow strong encryption.[81] There is certainly a preference for strong encryption in Europe, which in general has stronger legal protections for privacy of communications and data than we have in the USA[82] The Clinton Administration, however, worked hard to export its antiprivacy, antiencryption stance around the world,[83] and it did gain support from some officials in Britain. It is essential, therefore, to understand why this stance is as inimical to public safety as it is to personal privacy.

Criminalizing Sexually Oriented Online Expression

With this general picture of the relationship between cyberliberties and cybercrime, let us next fill in some details, starting with the area where we have had the most legislation and litigation in the USA. This is also an area of great concern in other countries, namely, criminalizing online expression that is sexually oriented.[84]

From the moment that cyberspace first hit the public radar screen in the USA, we immediately saw political and media hysteria about "cyberporn" and efforts to censor online expression of a sexual nature. This reaction was not surprising. Despite Americans' general commitment to free speech, sexually oriented expression in any medium has been suspect throughout our history. That is because of our Puritanical heritage, which we share, of course, with the British Isles. One of America's most popular humorists, Garrison Keillor, put it this way:

My ancestors were Puritans from England [who] arrived in America in 1648 in the hope of finding greater restrictions than were permissible under English law at the time.[85]

Consistent with this long-standing American tradition, we have seen many efforts throughout the USA to stifle online sexual expression. This has transpired at all levels of government, from the US Congress and the Clinton Administration to local school boards and library boards.[86] From a free-speech perspective, that is the bad news about sexually oriented expression online. But there is good news, too. While elected officials mostly have supported censorship of sexually oriented online material, the courts, as I have indicated, have provided a welcome contrast. So far, the ACLU has brought constitutional challenges to seven new laws that censor sexually oriented material online: the two federal statutes I already mentioned,[87] four state laws (in New York,[88] Virginia,[89] New Mexico,[90] and Michigan[91]), and one local law (in Loudoun County, Virginia[92]). And so far, with only one recent exception – which I do not think is too significant for cyberliberties, as I will explain in a moment – we have won every single one of these challenges.

Moreover, these decisions affirming freedom of cyberspeech have been joined in by 19 different judges who span a broad ideological spectrum. These are judges who were appointed by the last six US Presidents, four Republicans, and two Democrats, going all the way back to Richard Nixon. In short, the ACLU position on online free speech is essentially the position that is now enshrined in First Amendment law.

The one recent setback is an intermediate appellate court ruling on a Virginia state law that restricts government employees' access to sexually oriented online material.[93] The US Supreme Court has held that the government, when it acts as employer, may impose more limits on its employees' expression than the government, when it acts as sovereign, may impose on its citizens' expression.[94] Nevertheless, the lower court agreed with us that Virginia's law violates even the reduced free-speech rights of government employees.[95] The intermediate appellate court subsequently overturned that decision in February, 1999, on the broad rationale that government employees, when they act primarily in their role as employees, have no free-speech rights concerning any communications in any medium.[96] This court maintained that it was not imposing special restrictions on expression in cyberspace as opposed to other media; rather, it was imposing special restrictions on expression by government employees, regardless of the medium. We think this ruling is wrong, and we hope to overturn it on further appeal. In any event, though, it really has no special impact specifically on cyberlaw or cyberliberties.

In contrast, our two most recent victories in cybercensorship cases do have broad positive implications for online free speech, and I would like to describe them. First, let me tell you a bit more about our lower court victory in February, 1999, in *ACLU v Reno II*, against the second federal cybercensorship law, COPA. In response to the Supreme Court's decision striking down the CDA in *ACLU I*,[97] Congress wrote a somewhat less sweeping law the second time around. The CDA had criminalized any online expression that is "patently offensive"[98] or "indecent."[99] In contrast, the Child Online Protection Act (COPA) outlaws any online communication "for commercial purposes"[100] that includes any material that is harmful to minors.[101]

Both of COPA's critical terms are defined broadly. First, a communication is "for commercial purposes" if it is made "as a regular course of… trade or business, with the objective of earning a profit," even if no profit is actually made.[102] Therefore, COPA applies to many not-for-profit Web sites that provide information completely free, including the ACLU's own Web site. Second, material is "harmful to minors" if it satisfies US law's three-part obscenity definition specifically with respect to minors, namely, if it appeals to the prurient interest in sex, is patently offensive, and lacks serious value from a minor's perspective.[103]

I should note that the ACLU opposes the obscenity exception that the US Supreme Court has carved out of the First Amendment (over the dissenting votes of many respected justices).[104] However, we have not used our cybercensorship cases as occasions for challenging that exception. In other words, we have not challenged these new laws to the extent that they simply transplant to cyberspace existing free-speech exceptions that have been upheld in other media, in particular, obscenity, child pornography, and solicitation of a minor for sexual purposes. Rather, what we have actively opposed in these new laws is their creation of new, broader categories of expression that are unprotected specifically online, even though it would be constitutionally protected in traditional print media.

With that perspective, let me turn back to *ACLU v Reno II*. On February 1, 1999, a federal judge, Lowell Reed, granted our motion for a preliminary injunction.[105] He enjoined the government from enforcing COPA pending the trial on the merits. Judge Reed held that we had shown the necessary "likelihood of success" on the merits of our claim that COPA violates the First Amendment for many of the same reasons that CDA did. Since COPA regulates expression that is protected "at least as to adults,"[106] Judge Reed ruled, it is presumptively unconstitutional unless the government can satisfy the demanding "strict scrutiny" test. It has to show both that the law's purpose is to promote an interest of "compelling" importance and that the law is narrowly tailored to promote that purpose; in other words, that there are no "less restrictive alternative" measures that would be less burdensome on free speech.[107]

Judge Reed concluded that the government does have a compelling interest in shielding minors even from materials that are not obscene by adult standards.[108] However, he also concluded that the government was unlikely to be able to show that COPA is the least restrictive means of achieving this goal.[109] He noted, for example, that the evidence before him "reveals that blocking or filtering technology may be at least as successful as COPA would be in restricting minors' access to harmful material online without imposing the burden on constitutionally protected speech that COPA imposes on adult users or Web site operators."[110] The government has appealed from Judge Reed's ruling.[111] Quite likely, this case will go all the way to the US Supreme Court that has issued only one decision on the "harmful to minors" doctrine, and that was more than 30 years ago.[112]

Now let me turn to a second victory, in another important cyberspeech case, which also is still working its way through the court system at the time of this writing. This case is called *Mainstream Loudoun v Loudoun County Library*,[113] and it is so far the only court ruling on the burgeoning controversy over filtering and blocking software.

Ever since it became clear that the CDA and other direct censorial measures are facing constitutional difficulties, advocates of suppressing online sexual expression stepped up their promotion of rating and filtering systems, which also would bar access to the same expression. The ACLU has issued two reports explaining many reasons why all these systems are problematic.[114] For one thing – in terms of blocking all the material it purports to, and only that material – the filtering software is inevitably both underinclusive and overinclusive. Therefore, while individual Internet users certainly have the right to install software on their own computers that blocks out material they consider contrary to their values, there is still a problem. Almost all manufacturers of blocking software refuse to disclose either the sites they block or the criteria they use to determine which sites they will block. Consequently, the manufacturers are imposing their value choices on their customers. Manufacturers are not facilitating the customers' exercise of their own freedom of choice. In short, this is really more of a consumer protection problem than a free-speech problem.

There is a serious free-speech problem, however, when the filtering software is installed not as a matter of choice by individual users but, rather, by government officials who control the computers in public institutions. Across the USA, officials are busily installing or advocating blocking software on computers in public libraries, schools, and universities.[115] Individual choice thereby is stripped from the many members of the public whose only access to the Internet is through such computers. For them, the installation of filtering software on, say, library computers has the same censorial impact as the removal of books from library shelves.

Book banning, in fact, is precisely the analogy that was invoked by the only court that has ruled on this issue to date. In November, 1998, federal judge Leonie Brinkema upheld a First Amendment challenge to mandatory filtering software that had been installed in the public libraries of Loudoun County, Virginia.[116] Pursuant to a "Policy on Internet Sexual Harassment," library officials required software to block "child pornography and obscene material," as well as material deemed "harmful to juveniles" under state law.[117]

As an aside – but an important one – I want to note the distorted, overbroad concept of sexual harassment that is reflected in this policy, along with too many others. The policy assumes that the presence of sexually oriented expression on library computer terminals ipso facto constitutes illegal sexual harassment. But that assumption is patently incorrect. As the US Supreme Court has held, expression does not give rise to a sexual harassment claim merely because a person at whom it is directed considers it offensive.[118]

Even beyond their misguided concept of sexual harassment, library officials also implemented their policy in a way that violated online First Amendment rights, and that was the focus of Judge Brinkema's ruling. Specifically, the library installed a commercial software product called "X-Stop." Judge Brinkema held that the filtering requirement operated as a presumptively unconstitutional "prior restraint" on expression. Therefore, it had to withstand the same type of strict judicial scrutiny that also has been applied to other censorial laws, such as CDA and COPA.[119]

Judge Brinkema assumed for the sake of argument that the government's asserted interests – namely, its interests in minimizing access to obscenity and child pornography and in avoiding the creation of a sexually hostile environment – were of compelling importance.[120] She concluded, however, that the blocking policy was unconstitutional on several independently sufficient grounds: (1) it is not necessary to further the government's asserted interests, (2) it "is not narrowly tailored," (3) it limits adult patrons to accessing only material that is fit for minors, (4) it "provides inadequate standards for restricting access," and (5) "it provides inadequate procedural safeguards to ensure prompt judicial review."[121]

One particularly interesting feature of Judge Brinkema's analysis is her catalog of "less restrictive means" that Loudoun County could have used to pursue its asserted interests: installing privacy screens, charging library staff with casual monitoring of Internet use, and installing filtering software only on some Internet terminals and limiting minors to those terminals, and installing filtering software that could be turned off when an adult is using the terminal.[122] Significantly, Judge Brinkema cautioned that while all of the foregoing alternatives are less restrictive than the challenged mandatory filtering policy, she did not "find that any of them would necessarily be constitutional," since that question was not before her.[123] Loudoun County officials decided not to appeal from Judge Brinkema's ruling.[124] Of course, the constitutional questions involved will not be settled until the US Supreme Court rules on them in another filtering controversy.[125]

Debates About Online Privacy and Cryptography

This section discusses further the second major aspect of the cyberliberties/cybercrime debate – the controversy about online privacy and encryption or cryptography. Advocates of restricting encryption argue that, as the price for barring criminals and terrorists from using effective cryptography, we must also bar law-abiding citizens and businesses from doing so. This rationale was debunked effectively by Brian Gladman in "Cyber-Crime and Information Terrorism," an excellent report that was issued in September, 1998:

> Many things are valuable to criminals and terrorists but this alone does not provide a reason for imposing controls.... [C]riminals find cars useful but society doesn't control the supply of cars because of this.[126]

In light of this passage, it is ironic to note that when the automobile was first invented, law enforcement officials did seek to restrict its use, precisely because they did fear that it would facilitate criminal activities.[127] Today that argument seems ludicrous but, at bottom, it is precisely the same as the one now being offered in an attempt to justify restrictions on cryptography.

This is the argument the Clinton Administration made. They insisted that the only kind of encryption technology that should be available is "key recovery" or "key escrow" cryptography. Yet this type of encryption is inherently insecure, as it is expressly designed to give covert access to the plaintext of encrypted data to a third party, in particular, the government.

Although some government officials contend that there is a conflict between cyberliberties and cybercrime or cyberterrorism, that in fact is not so. To the contrary, this situation vividly illustrates Thomas Jefferson's previously quoted observation: "Liberty and security concerns work in tandem, rather than in tension, with each other. Indeed, it is particularly apt, in the cryptography context, to refer to Jefferson's communications with Madison; when these two American founders corresponded prior to the signing of the Declaration of Independence, they encoded all their messages. They used eighteenth-century-style encryption!"[128]

Notwithstanding the Clinton Administration's adamant official position, individual officers and agencies in the US government have broken ranks. One important example is a high-level government committee, the National Research Council (NRC) committee on cryptography. In its 1996 report, this committee concluded that strong encryption is essential for promoting law enforcement and national security:

If cryptography can protect the trade secrets and proprietary information of businesses and thereby reduce economic espionage (which it can), it also supports in a most important manner the job of law enforcement. If cryptography can help protect nationally critical information systems and networks against unauthorized penetration (which it can), it also supports the national security of the USA.[129]

Accordingly, even though this NRC report recognized that restricting encryption would strengthen some law enforcement efforts, it nevertheless concluded the following:

On balance, the advantages of more widespread use of cryptography outweigh the disadvantages.[130]

Some of the reasons for this conclusion were outlined as follows in a September, 1998, GILC report that focused specifically on the precise type of cryptography regulation that the USA has enforced and advocated, that is, export restrictions:

> [E]xport controls on cryptography hurt law-abiding companies and citizens without having any significant impact on the ability of criminals, terrorists or belligerent nations to obtain any cryptographic products they wish.
>
> [E]xport restrictions imposed by the major cryptography-exporting states limit the ability of other nations to defend themselves against electronic warfare attacks on vital infrastructure.
>
> [F]ailure to protect the free use and distribution of cryptographic software will jeopardize the life and freedom of human rights activists, journalists and political activists all over the world.
>
> [A]ny restriction on the use of cryptographic programs will be unenforceable in practice, since the basic mathematical and algorithmic methods for strong encryption are widely published and can easily be implemented in software by any person skilled in the art.
>
> [T]he increasingly common use of public networks to electronically distribute such products in intangible form reinforces the unenforceability of export controls.[131]

For these reasons, restrictions on encryption are not even effective, let alone necessary, in countering cybercrime. On this ground alone, such restrictions should be rejected. But there are also additional grounds for this conclusion.

For one thing, the government cannot show that there is in fact a substantial danger of the specific type of crime that is claimed most urgently to warrant restrictions on cryptography, namely, information terrorism. Fortunately, claims about this potential problem turn out to be greatly overblown. This was shown, for example, by a recent study, published in the Fall 1998 issue of the Internet publication, *Issues in Science and Technology Online*. Its title effectively summarizes its conclusion: "An Electronic Pearl Harbor? Not Likely."

The study was written by George Smith, an expert on computer crime, security, and information warfare.[132] He dismissed government and media descriptions of the dangers of cyberterrorism as "myths,"[133] "hoaxes,"[134] and "the electronic ghost stories of our time."[135] Although the Smith study focused on the USA, it is no doubt relevant for other countries also. Here is its conclusion:

> The government's evidence about US vulnerability to cyber attack is shaky at best.... Although the media are full of scary-sounding stories about violated military Web sites and broken security on public and corporate networks, the menacing scenarios have remained just that – only scenarios.... [An examination of the] sketchy information that the government has thus far provided.... casts a great deal of doubt on the claims.[136]

Precisely the same conclusion was reached in a report by a commission appointed by President Clinton on "Critical Infrastructure Protection."[137] The Commission was charged with analyzing the danger that information terrorists could pose to our nation's infrastructure – communications lines, power grids, and transportation networks. The Commission consisted primarily of military and intelligence officials and therefore was presumed to be especially sympathetic toward government claims of threats to law enforcement and national security. Yet even this group was forced to acknowledge that there was "no evidence of an impending cyber attack which could have a debilitating effect on the nation's critical infrastructure."[138]

Nonetheless, that recognition did not deter the Commission from seizing upon the fear of cyberterrorism to press for government measures – including key recovery encryption – that constrict individual rights. Indeed, the Commission was so eager to leverage public concerns about infoterrorism into heightened government surveillance over the public that it disregarded the countervailing dangers that key recovery encryption poses to the very infrastructure that the Commission was created to protect![139] Brian Gladman described those dangers well in "Cyber-Crime and Information Terrorism," the report from which I quoted earlier:

> Increasingly, the economies of the developed (and developing) nations are dependent on networked computing resources. Irrespective of whether it is communications, electrical power generation, road, rail or air transport, stock exchanges, banks, finance houses, agriculture, hospitals or a host of other infrastructures, all now depend on regular and continuous information exchanges between networked computer systems for their continuing safe operation. In the absence of effective cryptographic protection the computer systems that keep these infrastructures operating are wide open to attacks by terrorist and criminal organisations using only modest resources. Cryptographic export controls are preventing the protection of these civil infrastructures and rendering them easy and tempting targets for international terrorists and criminals. Far from impeding crime and terrorism, therefore, controls on cryptography are having precisely the opposite impact.[140]

These same dangers had been heralded in "The Risks of Key Recovery, Key Escrow, and Trusted Third Party Encryption," a May, 1997, report by a group of authors who call themselves "an Ad Hoc Group of Cryptographers and Computer Scientists":

> Any key recovery infrastructure, by its very nature, introduces a new and vulnerable path to the unauthorized recovery of data where one did not otherwise exist. This.... creates new concentrations of decryption information that are high-value targets for criminals or other attackers.... The key recovery infrastructure will tend to create extremely valuable targets, more likely to be worth the cost and risk of attack.[141]

In sum, not only are claims about the dangers of cyberterrorism exaggerated but also the proposed countermeasures – notably, restrictions on cryptography – far from being necessary to respond to any such dangers, are not even effective; to the contrary, they are counterproductive. A number of government reports present precisely the same conclusions. In September, 1999, for example, a European Parliament report called for rejecting encryption controls, including those advocated by the USA.[142] Significantly, this report was issued in the wake of increasing evidence of unjustified surveillance by law enforcement agencies in various European countries. Indeed, the vast majority of governments that have considered the issue have opposed restrictions on encryption.[143] This pattern was documented by a comprehensive report that GILC issued in February, 1998, entitled *Cryptography and Liberty 1998*. This report surveyed the cryptography policies of all countries in the world, based on direct communications with their governments. It concluded that, in most countries, cryptography may be freely used, manufactured, and sold without restriction:

> For those [countries] that have considered the topics, interests in electronic commerce and privacy appear to outweigh the concerns expressed by law enforcement.[144]

Conclusion

Everyone who values human life and human rights must, of course, be vigilant against the fear, insecurity, and manipulation caused by terrorists and other criminals. But we must also be vigilant against the fear, insecurity, and manipulation caused by those who seek to fight against criminals.

In a classic 1927 opinion, the great US Supreme Court Justice Louis Brandeis cautioned against ceding our hard-won freedoms to even well-intentioned government agents. Tellingly, that opinion warned against electronic surveillance and restrictions on free speech and privacy with respect to the then-newest communication technology – the telephone – despite claims about the urgent need to fight against telephonic crime.

Justice Brandeis's stirring, prophetic words apply fully to electronic surveillance and restrictions on free speech and privacy with respect to the now-newest communication technology – cyberspace – despite claims about the urgent need to fight against cybercrimes and information terrorism. As Justice Brandeis warned:

> Experience should teach us to be most on our guard to protect liberty when the government's purposes are beneficent.... The greatest dangers to liberty lurk in insidious encroachment by men of zeal, well-meaning but without understanding.[145]

Notes

1. This new introduction was completed in May, 2008. For assistance with research and endnotes, the author gratefully acknowledges her Chief Aide, Steven Cunningham (NYLS ' 99), who bears both credit and responsibility for the endnotes. Valuable research assistance was also provided by Graig Craver (NYLS ' 09).
2. The more things change, the more they stay the same.
3. *See*, for example, Richard A. Posner, *Not a Suicide Pact: The Constitution in a Time of National Emergency (Inalienable Rights)* (New York: Oxford University Press, 2006).
4. *See*, for example, James Cole and Jules Lobel, *Less Safe, Less Free: Why America Is Losing the War on Terror* (New York: New Press, 2007).
5. *See*, for example, "A Bill to Repeal Certain Cold War Legislation and for Other Purposes," S. 236, introduced January 17, 1991 (102nd Congress) by Senator Daniel Patrick Moynihan (D-NY).
6. Erwin Chemerinsky, *Constitutional Law: Principles and Policies*, 694–695 (New York: Aspen, 3rd edn., 2006).
7. Richard A. Clarke, "Bush Legacy: Setting a Standard in Fear-Mongering," *Philadelphia Inquirer*, February 8, 2008; Bruce Schneier, *Beyond Fear* (New York: Springer Press, 2004).
8. *See*, for example, "Application No. 2947/06: Ismoilov and Others v. Russia Intervention," Submitted by Human Rights Watch and AIRE Centre (New York: Human Rights Watch, 2007); "UK: Counter the Threat or Counterproductive?" Commentary on Proposed Counterterrorism Measures (New York: Human Rights Watch, 2007); Judith Sunderland, "In the Name of Prevention Insufficient Safeguards in National Security Removals" (New York: Human Rights Watch, 2007) (France); Joanne Mariner, "Double Jeopardy CIA: Renditions to Jordan" (New York: Human Rights Watch, 2008); Joanne Mariner, "Ghost Prisoner: Two Years in Secret CIA Detention" (New York: Human Rights Watch, 2007) (Israel), *all available at*: http://www.hrw.org/doc/?t'ct_pub

9. This Introduction discusses only nationwide regulations, enacted by the US government. Accordingly, the statement in this sentence applies only to such regulations. In contrast, at the state level, some recent regulations have specifically singled out the Internet. It should be noted, though, that courts have struck down many such state regulations on various constitutional and statutory grounds, including on the ground that the US Constitution and/or US statutes preempt state regulation. *See*, for example, H. Russell Frisby, Jr. and David A. Irwin, "The First Great Telecom Debate of the 21st Century," *15 CommLaw Conspectus 373* (2007); Transcript: "The Federalist Society Presents its 2006 Telecommunications Federalism Conference: Intro and Opening Remarks," *B.C. Intell. Prop. & Tech. F. 165* (2007); *Ctr. for Democracy and Tech. v. Pappert*, 337 F. Supp. 2d 606 (E.D. Pa. 2004) (striking down Pennsylvania Internet censorship law as inconsistent with the First Amendment and Dormant Commerce Clause); 47 U.S.C. §230 (preempting state laws imposing liability on Internet intermediaries for material supplied by users); *Voicenet Communs. Inc. v. Corbett*, No. 04–1318, 2006 US Dist LEXIS 61916 (E.D. Pa. 2006) (applying §230 to preempt application of state anti-pornography law to Internet service provider).
10. Pub. Law No. 107–56, 115 Stat 272; Title I-§105; Title II-§§201, 202, 204, 209, 210, 211, 212, 214, 215, 216, 217, 220, 225 Title VIII §814, Title X §1003 (October 26, 2001) *Uniting and Strengthening America by Providing Appropriate Tools Required to Intercept and Obstruct Terrorism Act*.
11. Pub.L. No. 110–055_1, 121 Stat 552, *enacted* 50 U.S.C. §1805(a)-(c) *amended* 50 U.S.C. §1803 (August 5, 2007) *Clarification of Electronic Surveillance of Persons Outside the United States*.
12. Nadine Strossen, Safety and Freedom: Common Concerns for Conservatives, Libertarians, and Civil Libertarians, *29 Harv. J.L. & Pub. Pol'y 73 (2005)*; ACLU Safe and Free Campaign website: http://www.aclu.org/safefree/index.htm
13. US Const, Amend. IV (The right of the people to be secure in their persons, houses, papers, and effects, against unreasonable searches and seizures, shall not be violated, and no Warrants shall issue, but upon probable cause, supported by Oath or affirmation, and particularly describing the place to be searched, and the persons or things to be seized).
14. Pub.L. No. 107–56, 115 Stat. 272 (October 26, 2001) *USA PATRIOT Act*, NSL parts codified in 18 U.S.C. §§2709, 2709 was originally enacted as part of Title II of the Electronic Communication Privacy Act of 1986, Pub.L. No. 99–508, '201, 100 Stat. 1848, 1867–1868 (1986). Congress then passed the US Patriot Improvement and Reauthorization Act of 2005, Pub.L. No. 109–177, 120 Stat. 192 (March 9, 2006). The Reauthorization Act included substantial changes to §2709 and added several provisions relating to judicial review of NSLs which were codified in 18 U.S.C. a 3511 Congress made further changes to §2709 in the US Patriot Act Additional Reauthorizing Amendments Act of 2006, Pub.L. No. 109–178, 120 Stat. 278 (March 9, 2006).This act amended §2709(c)(4), which requires NSL recipients to inform the FBI of anyone to whom they disclosed having received the NSL, with the exception of counsel, and it added §2709(f), which excludes libraries from the definition of wire or electronic communications service providers. *Doe v. Gonzales*, 500 F. Supp. 2d 379, 384–387.
15. Leslie Cauley, "NSA has massive database of Americans' phone calls," *USA Today*, May 11, 2006; John Markoff, "Questions Raised for Phone Giants in Spy Data Furor," *New York Times*, May 13, 2006.
16. James Risen and Eric Lichtblau, "Bush Lets U.S. Spy on Callers Without Courts," *New York Times*, December 16, 2005.
17. US Const, Amend. I (Congress shall make no law … abridging the freedom of speech, or of the press…).
18. *Stanley v. Georgia*, 394 US 557, 564 (1969).
19. US Const, Preamble (We the People of the United States, in Order to form a more perfect Union, establish Justice, insure domestic Tranquility, provide for the common defense, promote the general Welfare, and secure the Blessings of Liberty to ourselves and our Posterity, do ordain and establish this Constitution for the United States of America).

20. *ACLU v. NSA*, 438 F. Supp. 2d 754 (E.D. Mich. 2006), *stay granted*, 467 F.3d 590 (6th Cir. 2006), *vacated and remanded*, 493 F.3d 644 (6th Cir. 2007), *cert. denied*, 128 S. Ct. 1334 (2008).
21. *ACLU v. NSA*, 493 F.3d 644.
22. *ACLU v. NSA*, 493 F.3d at 693 (Gilman, dissenting).
23. *ACLU v. NSA* Complaint filed January 17, 2006 in US District Court for the Eastern District of Michigan, Southern Division at pages 2, 44, 46, 4, 50. *Available at*: http://www.aclu.org/pdfs/safefree/nsacomplaint.011706.pdf
24. Barnett A. Rubin, *Afghanistan's Uncertain Transition from Turmoil to Normalcy* (New York: Council on Foreign Relations Press, April 2006).
25. ACLU Press Release, "Federal Court Strikes Down NSA Warrantless Surveillance Program," August 17, 2006. *Available at*: www.aclu.org/safeandfree/nsaspying/26489prs20060817.html (last accessed May 15, 2008).
26. *See* US CONST, AMEND. IV; *Michigan Dept. of State Police v. Sitz*, 496 US 444, 449–450 (1990).
27. *See*, for example, *Davis v. Mississippi*, 394 US 721, 723–725 (1969) (suspects were wrongfully detained by police merely because of the color of their skin).
28. Ibid, 726.
29. *See*, for example, ACLU Press Release, "Applauds Local Police Departments for Refusing to Join in Justice Department Dragnet" (March 4, 2002), *available at*: http://www.aclu.org/police/gen/14530res20020304.html
30. *See*, for example, *ACLU v. NSA*, 438 F. Supp. 2d 754.
31. *See*, for example, *ACLU v. NSA*, 438 F. Supp. 2d at 773–775.
32. *See*, for example, Lowell Bergman et al., "Spy Agency Data After Sept. 11 Led F.B.I. to Dead Ends," *New York Times*, January 17, 2006.
33. Ibid (FBI officials repeatedly complained to the spy agency that the unfiltered information was swamping investigators and said that the torrent of tips led them to few potential terrorists inside the country they did not know of from other sources and diverted agents from counterterrorism work they viewed as more productive.)
34. Leslie Cauley, "NSA Has Massive Database of Americans' Phone Calls," *USA Today*, May 11, 2006.
35. *See generally ACLU v. NSA*, 438 F. Supp. 2d at 754; *Doe v. Gonzales*, 386 F. Supp. 2d. 66 (D. Conn. 2005); ACLU, Safe and Free: Secrecy, *available at*: http://www.aclu.org/safefree/secrecy/index.html
36. I include the qualifying word "apparently" since the clandestine nature of this program as well as conflicting government statements about it in the wake of the USA Today disclosure have obscured its precise nature. *See* "A Note to Our Readers," *USA Today*, June 30, 2006; Frank Ahrens and Howard Kurtz, "USA Today Says It Can't Prove Key Points in Phone Records Story," *Star-Ledger* (Newark, New Jersey), July 2, 2006.
37. Cauley, *supra* note 34.
38. *See*, for example, *Elec. Privacy Info. Ctr. v. Dep't of Def.*, 355 F. Supp. 2d 98, 99 (D.D.C. 2004).
39. *See* Computer Professionals for Social Responsibility Press Release, "CPSR Signs ACLU Letter Supporting 132," October 23, 2005, *available at*: http://www.cpsr.org/issues/privacy/support132; *see also* Jonathan David Farley, "The N.S.A.'s Math Problem," *New York Times*, May 16, 2006.
40. Ibid.
41. Ibid.
42. Barry Steinhardt, ACLU Press Release, "Statement of Barry Steinhardt, Director Technology and Civil Liberty Program, American Civil Liberties Union, On Government Data Mining, Before the: Technology, Information Policy, Intergovernmental Subcommittee of the House of Representatives Committee on Government Reform" on May 20, 2003. *Available at*: http://www.aclu.org/safefree/general/17262leg20030520.html
43. 47 U.S.C. §223 (1996).

44. 521 US 844 (1997).
45. 47 U.S.C. §231 (1998).
46. *ACLU v. Reno*, 31 F. Supp. 2d 473 (E.D.Pa. 1999).
47. These rulings, listed in chronological order, are: *ACLU v. Gonzales*, 478 F. Supp. 2d 775 (E.D.Pa. 2007); *Ashcroft v. ACLU*, 542 US 656 (2004); *ACLU v. Ashcroft*, 322 F.3d 240 (3rd Cir. 2003); Ashcroft v. ACLU, 535 US 564 (2002); *ACLU v. Reno*, 217 F.3d 162 (3rd Cir. 2000); *ACLU v. Reno*, 31 F. Supp. 2d 473 (E.D.Pa. 1999); *ACLU v. Reno*, 1998 WL 813423 (E.D.Pa. 1998).
48. *See*, for example, *ACLU v. Ashcroft*, 322 F.3d 240 (3rd Cir. 2003); *ACLU v. Gonzales*, 478 F. Supp. 2d 775 (E.D.Pa. 2007); *ACLU v. Reno*, 31 F. Supp. 2d 473 (E.D.Pa. 1999).
49. *Ashcroft v. ACLU*, 542 US 656, 667 (2004).
50. *ACLU v. Gonzales*, 478 F. Supp. 2d 775, 813–814 (E.D. Pa. 2007).
51. Ibid, 814–816.
52. Ibid, 814–815.
53. 47 U.S.C. §231 (2000) (Established Commission on Online Child Protection).
54. Dick Thornburgh and Herbert S. Lin, eds. *National Resource Council, Youth Pornography, and the Internet* (New York: National Academy Press, 2002).
55. John Schwartz, "Support is Growing in Congress for Internet Filters in Schools," *New York Times*, October 20, 2000.
56. National Research Council Press Release: "Youth Pornography, and the Internet." *Available at*: http://www8.nationalacademies.org/onpinews/newsitem.aspx?RecordID'10261
57. The Supreme Court has repeatedly held that minors, as well as adults, have free speech rights. *See*, for example, *Tinker v. Des Moines Ind. Comm. School Dist.*, 393 US 503 (1969).
58. 47 U.S.C. §254 (2000).
59. Since 1999, the Supreme Court also has issued two decisions that I will briefly note here, but not discuss in the text, since they address two US statutes that are only indirectly relevant to the issues considered in this new Introduction and the 1999 chapter. These two cases are: *U.S. v. Williams* 2008 WL 2078503 (2008) [Concerning the Prosecutorial Remedies and Other Tools to end the Exploitation of Children Today Act,18 U.S.C '2252(A)(a)(3)(b)] and *Free Speech Coalition v. Ashcroft* 535 US 234 (2002) [concerning the Child Pornography Prevention Act, 18 U.S.C. §§2256(8)(A), 2256(8)(B), 2256 (8)(C), 2256 (8)(D)]. Both cases are beyond the scope of this Introduction for two reasons. First, the laws at issue did not single out the Internet, but rather, targeted all expression with the prohibited content, in any medium. Second, these laws did no seek to protect children from viewing sexually oriented expression, but rather, they sought to protect children from being used to produce child pornography. It should be noted, however, that both statutes, as well as both Supreme Court decisions, protected adults' rights to view even virtual child pornography, sexually explicit images that look like child pornography, but that are produced without using actual minors. In that significant respect, both cases are consistent with the general speech-protective pattern of the judicial rulings that the 1999 chapter and the new Introduction discuss.
60. 539 US 194 (2003).
61. 539 US 194, 209 (plurality opinion), 214 (Kennedy, J., concurring), 220 (Breyer, J., concurring).
62. Ibid, 215 (Kennedy, J., concurring), 220 (Breyer, J., concurring), 233 (Souter, J., dissenting).
63. As of May, 2008, this lawsuit was still pending, with no ruling yet on the merits. *See Bradburn v. North Central Regional Library District* Complaint filed November 16, 2006 in US District Court Eastern District of Washington. Both *available at*: http://www.aclu-wa.org/detail.cfm?id'557; ACLU Press Release, *ACLU Suit Seeks Access to Information on Internet for Library Patrons* (November 16, 2006, updated April 23, 2008).
64. *Williams v. Garrett*, 722 F. Supp. 254, 256 (W.D. Va. 1989) (quoting Thomas Jefferson).
65. *See*, for example, Global Internet Liberty Campaign, *Regardless of Frontiers: Protecting the Human Right to Freedom of Expression on the Global Internet*, 1998; Global Internet Liberty Campaign, *Privacy and Human Rights: An International Survey of Privacy Laws and Practice*, 1998.

66. *Williams v. Garrett*, 722 F. Supp. 254, 256 (W.D. Va. 1989) (quoting Thomas Jefferson).
67. *See* Nadine Strossen and Ernie Allen, "Megan's Law and the Protection of the Child in the Online Age," *American Criminal Law Review*, 35, no. 4 (summer 1998): 1319–1341. In a related vein, Professor Frederick Schauer of Harvard University testified against the Child Pornography Prevention Act of 1996, a federal law punishing anyone who possesses any work that depicts someone who appears to be a minor engaged in "sexually explicit conduct." Schauer stated that the law would "wind up hurting rather than helping the cause of prosecuting the... individuals who exploit children by diverting resources away from actual prosecution of child molesters." (*See* Nadine Strossen, "Bang the Tin Drum No More," Speakout.com, July 17, 1997 http://www.speakout.com/activisim/opinions/3669–1.html.)
68. *See Erznoznik v. City of Jacksonville*, 422 U.S. 205, 212 (1975) ([M]inors are entitled to a significant measure of First Amendment protection.); *Tinker v. Des Moines Indep. Community Sch. Dist.*, 393 U.S. 503, 506 (1969) (First Amendment rights... are available to... students...); United Nations Children's Fund (1989) *Convention on the Rights of the Child. See* Article 13 under "Convention Full Text" tab from http://www.unicef.org/crc/crc.htm>: "The child shall have the right to freedom of expression; this right shall include freedom to seek, receive and impart information and ideas of all kinds, regardless of frontiers, either orally, in writing or in print, in the form of art, or through any other media of the child's choice."
69. *See* Electronic Privacy Information Center, *Cryptography and Liberty 1999: An International Survey of Encryption Policy* (1999), http://www2.epic.org/reports/crypto1999.html, 8.
70. The concept of the right to privacy as personal security against unwarranted intrusion by others is embodied in many legal guarantees of that right, including the Fourth Amendment to the US Constitution, which provides, in pertinent part: "The right of the people to be secure in their persons, houses, papers, and effects, against unreasonable searches and seizures, shall not be violated..." Indeed, many individuals feel particularly threatened by governmental intrusions.
71. *See* S.D. Warren and L.D. Brandeis, "The Right to Privacy," *Harvard Law Review*, 4 (1890) 193.
72. *See Olmstead v. United States*, 277 U.S. 438, 485 (1928) (Brandeis, J. dissenting), overruled by *Katz v. United States*, 389 U.S. 347 (1967).
73. *See* National Research Council, *Cryptography's Role in Securing the Information Society*, eds. Kenneth W. Dam and Herbert S. Lin (Washington, DC: National Academy Press, 1996), http://www.nap.edu/readingroom/books/crisis/.
74. *See* 47 U.S.C. Section 223 (a, d) (1999).
75. *See Reno v. American Civil Liberties Union*, 521 U.S. 844 (1997).
76. *See* 47 U.S.C. Section 231 (1999).
77. *See American Civil Liberties Union v. Reno*, 31 F. Supp. 2d 473 (E.D. Pa. 1999).
78. Id, at 498.
79. *See American Civil Liberties Union v. Miller*, 977 F. Supp. 1228 (N.D. Ga. 1997).
80. *Bernstein v. U.S.*, 974 F. Supp. 1288 (N.D. Ca. 1997), *aff'd*, 176 F. Supp. 3d 1132 (9th Cir. May 6, 1999) (holding that encryption regulations were an unconstitutional prior restraint in violation of the First Amendment). But cf. *Junger v. Dale*, 8 F. Supp. 2d 708, 715 (N.D. Oh. 1998) (holding that although encryption source code may occasionally be expressive, its export is not protected conduct under the First Amendment); *Karn v. US Dept. of State*, 925 F. Supp. 1 (D.D.C. 1996) (rejecting First Amendment challenge to encryption export regulations). In mid-September 1999, the Clinton Administration announced that it will relax encryption export controls. *See* J. Clausing, "In a Reversal, White House Will End Data-Encryption Export Curbs," *New York Times*, September 17, 1999. However, even with the Clinton Administration's recent pronouncement, civil libertarians continue to point out the problems with encryption regulations – namely, that export control laws on encryption are unconstitutional prior restraints on speech, and that the new proposed regulations apply only to commercial, not academic, work; *see* Electronic Frontier Foundation, "Latest Governmental Encryption Scheme Still Unconstitutional: EFF-Sponsored Legal Challenge Will Proceed," September 16, 1999, http://www.eff.org/91699_crypto_release.html. In 1999, the Ninth Circuit withdrew the three-judge panel decision in *Bernstein* and ordered the case to be reheard *en banc*. *Bernstein v. U.S.*, No. 97–16686, 1999 US App. LEXIS 24324 (9th Cir. September 30, 1999).

81. *See* Global Internet Liberty Campaign, Wayne Madsen et al., "Cryptography and Liberty 1998: An International Survey of Encryption Policy," February 1998, http://www.gilc.org/crypto/crypto-survey.html, 5.
82. Ibid.
83. Ibid, 6.
84. *See* Y. Akdeniz and N. Strossen, "Obscene and Indecent Speech," in *The Internet, Law and Society*, eds. C. Walker, Y. Akdeniz, and D. Wall (Essex: Addison Wesley Longman, 2000).
85. *See* Garrison Keillor, Statement to the Senate Subcommittee on Education, March 29, 1990 (Testimony on NEA Grant Funding and Restrictions) 136 Cong. Rec. E. 993 (1990).
86. *See* American Civil Liberties Union Freedom Network, "Cyber-Liberties," http://www.aclu.org/issues/cyber/hmcl.html.
87. *See Reno v. American Civil Liberties Union*, 521 U.S. 844 (1997); *American Civil Liberties Union v. Reno*, 31 F. Supp. 2d 473 (E.D. Pa. 1999).
88. *See American Library Assn v. Pataki*, 969 F. Supp. 160 (S.D.N.Y. 1997).
89. *See Urofsky v. Allen*, 995 F. Supp. 634 (E.D. Va. 1998), overruled by *Urofsky v. Gilmore*, 167 F. 3d 191 (4th Cir. 1999).
90. *See American Civil Liberties Union v. Johnson*, 4 F. Supp. 2d 1029 (D.N.M. 1998).
91. *See Cyberspace v. Engler*, 55 F. Supp. 2d 737 (E.D. Mich. 1999).
92. *See Mainstream Loudoun v. Loudoun County Library*, 24 F. Supp. 2d 552 (E.D. Va. 1998).
93. *See Urfosky v. Gilmore*, 167 F. 3d 191 (4th Cir. 1999).
94. *See Waters v. Churchill*, 511 U.S. 661, 674–675 (1994); *Pickery v. Board of Educ.*, 391 U.S. 563, 568 (1968).
95. *See Urofsky v. Allen*, 995 F. Supp. 634 (E.D. Va. 1998).
96. *See Urofsky v. Gilmore*, 167 F. 3d 191, 196 (4th Cir. 1999).
97. *See Reno v. American Civil Liberties Union*, 521 U.S. 844 (1997).
98. *See* 47 U.S.C. Section 223(d)(1)(B).
99. *See* 47 U.S.C. Section 223(a)(1)(B)(ii).
100. *See* 47 U.S.C. Section 231(a)(1).
101. Id.
102. *See* 47 U.S.C. Section 231(e)(2)(B).
103. *See* 47 U.S.C. Section 231(e)(6).
104. *See* Nadine Strossen, *Defending Pornography: Free Speech, Sex, and the Fight for Women's Rights* (New York: Scribner, 1995; reprint New York: New York University Press, 2000), 57–58.
105. *See American Civil Liberties Union v. Reno*, 31 F. Supp. 2d 473 (E.D. Pa. 1999).
106. Id, 492.
107. *See* E. Chemerinsky, *Constitutional Law: Principles and Policies* (New York: Aspen Law & Business, 1997), 416.
108. *See American Civil Liberties Union v. Reno*, 31 F. Supp. 2d 473, 495 (E.D. Pa. 1999).
109. Id, 497.
110. Id.
111. *See* American Civil Liberties Union, "Internet Censorship Battle Moves to Appeals Court," 1999, http://www.aclu.org/features/f101698a.html. *Link actually goes to*: ACLU Freedom Network, "ACLU v. Reno II Victory! Appeals Court Rejects Congress' Second Attempt at Cyber-Censorship," June 22, 2000, http://www.aclu.org/features/f101698a.html.
112. *See Ginsberg v. New York*, 390 U.S. 629 (1968).
113. *See Mainstream Loudoun v. Loudoun County Library*, 24 F. Supp. 2d 552 (E.D. Va. 1998).
114. *See* American Civil Liberties Union, "Fahrenheit 451.2: Is Cyberspace Burning?" 1997, http://www.aclu.org/issues/cyber/burning.html; also American Civil Liberties Union, "Censorship in a Box," 1998, http://www.aclu.org/issues/cyber/box.html.
115. *See* American Civil Liberties Union, "Censorship in A Box," 1998 http://www.aclu.org/issues/cyber/box.html, 9–10.
116. *See Mainstream Loudoun v. Loudoun County Library*, 24 F. Supp. 2d 552 (E.D. Va. 1998).
117. Id, 567.

118. *See Harris v. Forklift Sys. Inc.*, 510 U.S. 17, 21 (1993); and Nadine. Strossen, *Defending Pornography: Free Speech, Sex, and the Fight for Women's Rights* (New York: Scribner, 1995; reprint New York: New York University Press, 2000), 119–140.
119. *See Mainstream Loudoun v. Loudoun County Library*, 24 F. Supp. 2d 552, 564–565 (E.D. Va. 1998).
120. Id, 564.
121. Id, 570.
122. Id, 567.
123. Id.
124. *See* D. Hedgpeth, "Libraries Abandon Court Fight; Board Won't Appeal Internet Policy Rulings," *Washington Post*, April 22, 1999.
125. For detailed information on all of these cases, including the parties' litigation papers and the courts' rulings, *see* the ACLU's Web site: http://www.aclu.org/issues/cyber/hmcl.html.
126. *See* Brian Gladman, "Wassenaar Controls, Cyber-Crime and Information Terrorism," Cyber-Rights and Cyber-Liberties (UK), September 1998, http://www.cyber-rights.org/crypto/wassenaar.htm, 4–5.
127. *See* National Public Radio, "Feds Say E-Mail Scrambler is a Weapon," National Public Radio Morning Edition, April 14, 1995.
128. *See* J. Fraser, "The Use of Encrypted, Coded and Secret Communications is an 'Ancient Liberty' Protected by the United States Constitution," *Virginia Journal of Law and Technology*, 2 (1997): 25, n.123.
129. *See* National Research Council, *Cryptography's Role in Securing the Information Society*, eds. Kenneth W. Dam and Herbert S. Lin, 1996, http://www.nap.edu/readingroom/books/crisis/, 24.
130. Ibid, 27.
131. *See* Global Internet Liberty Campaign, "Cryptography is a Defensive Tool, Not a Weapon," September 14, 1998, http://www.gilc.org/crypto/wassenaar/gilc-statement-998.html, 2.
132. *See* George Smith, "An Electronic Pearl Harbor? Not Likely," *Issues in Science and Technology Online*, Fall 1998, http://www.nap.edu/issues/15.1/smith.htm.
133. Ibid, 1.
134. Ibid, 2.
135. Ibid, 9.
136. Ibid, 1.
137. *See* The President's Commission on Critical Infrastructure Protection (Report Summary), "Critical Foundations: Thinking Differently," 1997, http://www.info-sec.com/pccip/web/summary.html.
138. *See* Andy Oram, "A Sacrifice to the War Against Cyber Terrorism," 1997, http://www.oreilly.com/people/staff/andyo/ar/terror_pub.html (quoting the report issued by the President's Commission on Critical Infrastructure Protection on October 13, 1997 and presented by its Chairman Robert T. Marsh, before a Congressional Committee on November 5, 1997).
139. *See* Electronic Privacy Information Center (White Paper), "The Clinton Administration's Policy on Critical Infrastructure Protection: Presidential Decision Directive 63," May 22, 1998, http://www.epic.org/security/infowar/cip_white_paper.html.
140. *See* Brian Gladman, "Wassenaar Controls, Cyber-Crime and Information Terrorism," Cyber-Rights and Cyber-Liberties (UK), September 1998, http://www.cyber-rights.org/crypto/wassenaar.htm, 4–5.
141. *See* Ad Hoc Group of Cryptographers and Computer Scientists, "The Risks of Key Recovery, Key Escrow, and Trusted Third Party Encryption," September 1998, http://www.cdt.org/crypto/risks98>, 15–16.
142. *See* Omega Foundation, "An Appraisal of the Technologies of Political Control," September 1998, http://www.jya.com/stoa-atpc-so.htm.
143. *See* Global Internet Liberty Campaign, "Cryptography and Liberty 1998," February 1998, http://www.gilc.org/crypto/crypto-survey.html *See* also Electronic Privacy Information

Center, *Cryptography and Liberty 1999: An International Survey of Encryption Policy*, 1999, http://www2.epic.org/reports/crypto1999.html.

144. *See* Global Internet Liberty Campaign, *Cryptography and Liberty 1998*, February 1998, http://www.gilc.org/crypto/crypto-survey.html, 7.

145. *See Olmstead v. United States*, 277 U.S. 438, 479 (1928) (Brandeis, J. dissenting), overruled by *Katz v. United States*, 389 U.S. 347 (1967).

Acknowledgments An alternate version of this chapter was printed in the *International Review of Law, Computers & Technology*, 14, no. 1 (March 2000): 11–24. For research assistance with this chapter, including drafting the endnotes, Professor Strossen gratefully acknowledges her chief aide, Amy L. Tenney, and her research assistant, Cesar de Castro. The endnotes were added through the efforts of Professor Strossen's staff, who thereby have earned both the credit and the responsibility for them (which Professor Strossen has not reviewed, and for which she disclaims both credit and responsibility).

Part V
Economics Challenge

Chapter 9
Implications of Electronic Commerce for Fiscal Policy

Austan Goolsbee

Introduction

Partly as the result of historical circumstance, most people in the USA are not paying sales taxes on their purchases over the Internet. As a result, state and local officials are quite agitated that the rise of the Internet will severely erode the state and local tax base. Their fear, as spelled out by Newman (1995), is that "state and local government finances are becoming road kill on the information superhighway." Although sales taxes on physical goods have received most of the attention, other tax issues such as the taxation of Internet access and international taxation of Internet commerce are also important.

In the last 2 years, a debate over taxes and the Internet has raged at the highest levels. In 1998, Congress passed the somewhat misleadingly titled Internet Tax Freedom Act. Contrary to popular impression, this act did *not* place a moratorium on sales taxes on Internet purchases – only on discriminatory taxes and on Internet access taxes. The act did create a commission to study the sales-tax issues, but the commission was unable to reach a consensus (Advisory Commission, 2000). Congress has since proposed extending the Tax Freedom Act temporarily, but the major issues have not been resolved.

In this chapter, I will consider both sides of the relationship between electronic commerce and fiscal policy. For the impact of electronic commerce on fiscal policy, I will pay particular attention to the potential sales-tax revenue losses. The data suggest that the potential losses are actually modest over the next several years. I will also consider the reverse relationship – how fiscal policy affects Internet commerce. Here the evidence suggests that taxes have a sizable effect. I point out, though, that this only supports special treatment if there is some positive externality. Without one, the tax system will lead to excessive online buying to avoid taxes. I will then deal the neglected issue of taxes and Internet access, which can create large deadweight costs both because demand may be price-sensitive and because

A. Goolsbee
Professor of Economics, University of Chicago, Graduate School of Business, Chicago, IL, USA
email: goolsbee@gsb.uchicago.edu

W.H. Lehr and L.M. Pupillo (eds.), *Internet Policy and Economics*,
DOI 10.1007/978-1-4419-0038-8_9,

taxes can slow the spread of new technologies. Finally, I offer some discussion of the international context of taxes and the Internet and the international temptations to raise rates on E-commerce.

Taxes and Internet Commerce

The current rules for taxation of Internet commerce evolved from the rules on out-of-state catalog sellers. Many people mistakenly believe that state sales tax does not apply to out-of-state transactions. In fact, such taxes *do* apply, but are largely unenforceable except in rather specific circumstances.

The normal burden of collection for sales taxes resides with merchants. When a customer buys something at a bookstore, for example, the merchant collects and pays the sales tax to the state. The Supreme Court has ruled that a state has no jurisdiction to require an out-of-state merchant with no employees or other physical presence in a state – known as "nexus" – to collect the tax.[1] In other words, when Seattle-based Amazon.com sells a book to someone in California, the state of California cannot require the out-of-state retailer to add California sales tax to the purchase. In places where the merchant does have nexus, the state can make such a requirement. Amazon does collect sales tax on sales to state of Washington customers.

The story does not end there, however. Every state with a sales tax also has a "use" tax of the same rate, and this use tax applies to exactly those goods bought out of state where sales taxes aren't collected by the merchant. The use tax is levied *on the consumer*. California customers of Amazon are legally supposed to pay California use tax on their purchase. The enforcement costs of pursuing the revenues from these numerous small and undocumented transactions have proved prohibitive in most circumstances and so compliance rates, though unknown, are extremely low except in certain situations. Use tax compliance is very high for goods that must be registered (like automobiles) as well as for taxable business purchases (e.g., computers in many states) because larger companies are systematically audited for use tax compliance.

The Internet Tax Freedom Act of 1998 imposed two moratoria: one on new and discriminatory taxes on the Internet and the other on applying sales or other taxes to monthly Internet access fees (grandfathering existing state taxes). But neither of these provisions created a moratorium on sales taxes or use taxes because such taxes are neither new nor discriminatory. They have always been on the books and apply equally to all purchases. The issue is that use taxes simply haven't been enforced, making purchases effectively tax-free.

The Implications of Internet Commerce for Tax Collections

Since sales taxes account for about 33% of state revenues, it is easy to understand the fear politicians have of E-commerce. Some politicians have tended toward alarmism, arguing that in the near future revenue losses due to Internet commerce may exceed $20 billion, but most of these claims are not based on actual data (Graham, 1999).

Table 9.1 Current and projected online commerce(in millions dollars)

Type of good	1999 estimate	2004 forecast
Total Sales	20,252	184,481
Little revenue loss	*8,965*	*71,928*
Automobiles	-	16,567
Leisure travel	7,798	32,097
Event tickets	300	3,929
Food	513	16,863
Flowers	354	2,472
Partial revenue loss	*3,204*	*24,211*
Computer hardware	1,964	12,541
Computer software	1,240	11,670
Full revenue loss	*8,080*	*96,624*
Books	1,202	3,279
Music	848	4,286
Videos	326	1,743
Apparel	1,620	27,128
Greetings and special gifts	301	2,087
Household goods	250	5,755
Toys and recreation	595	15,039
Consumer electronics	1,205	11,670
Housewares	446	5,908
Health and beauty	509	10,335
Miscellaneous	778	9,394

Note: Not all numbers sum because of rounding within groups
Source: Forrester (Williams et al., 1999)

Any legitimate estimate of future revenue losses must begin with a forecast of Internet sales, the most comprehensive of which comes from Forrester Research. Table 9.1 presents Forrester's estimates of retail commerce in 1999 and their forecast for 2004 by sector (Williams et al., 1999). Forrester foresees consumer spending online rising dramatically for the next 5 years.

One cannot simply multiply total sales by the average sales-tax rate to get the amount of revenue loss caused by the Internet. For several of the categories, state sales tax does not apply – for example, leisure travel and event tickets. Moreover, several of the categories such as automobiles, groceries/food, and flowers are likely either to generate nexus or else are exempt from taxation. Sales in these cases do not lose tax revenue. They are listed together as the first group of products in Table 9.1.

For the second group of products, computers and computer software, the growth of Internet sales has largely cannibalized the mail-order sales of the same merchants. Dell Online, for example, reduced sales of Dell's catalog rather than the sales of retail computer stores (see the discussion of Goolsbee, 2000a). For purposes of estimating sales-tax revenue losses, I make the conservative guess that half of computer hardware and software sales online would have been bought from catalogs rather than in stores. In reality, the share is likely to be higher, at least for computer hardware.

The third group of products in Table 9.1 are those where Internet sales from out-of-state purchasers might plausibly involve the direct loss of tax revenue. Adding the total for these sectors (8.080) to half of the online computer sales (1.602), the total tax-losing online sales in 1999 were just under $9.7 billion. With an average sales-tax rate across states of 6.33% (Goolsbee, 2000b), the implied loss of tax revenue is $612.8 million or 0.3% of the total sales-tax revenue of $203 billion (US GAO, 2000). Similar calculations are presented in Goolsbee and Zittrain (1999), Cline and Neubig (1999), McQuivey and DeMoulin (2000), and US GAO (2000).

Although current tax-revenue losses are not large, future losses could be more of a concern. Doing the same calculation for 2004, for example, the total sales base becomes about $109 billion and the lost revenue rises to about $6.88 billion. Assuming average growth in off-line sales of 5% annually, the possible loss of tax revenue from the Internet amounts to 2.6% of projected 2004 sales-tax revenue – larger but still modest. If this calculation is projected further into the future, it likely will be more than a decade before the total revenue loss arising from E-commerce reaches, say, 10% of sales-tax revenues. In the discussion of taxing Internet sales, it is worth remembering that current estimates put the tax revenue loss from out-of-state catalog sales at around $6 billion, about ten times larger than the revenue loss calculated above from Internet commerce (US GAO, 2000).

Even these estimates of lost sales-tax revenues from E-commerce are probably biased upward. First, this calculates that there are no behavioral responses to taxation. If raising taxes on Internet commerce leads people to buy fewer books, for example, rather than just to divert their purchases back to retail bookstores, the revenue losses here will be overstated. Second, some fraction of online spending even of the third category of goods takes place in the state of the merchant, in which case nexus applies and the retailer can be required to collect the sales tax. In the Forrester Technographics 1999 data, for example, used in Goolsbee (2000c), about 7% of Dell customers were in Texas, where Dell is located. In general, people in California have much higher rates of online purchase; they make up 15% of online buyers but only about 9.5% of nonbuyers, as well as a major share of Internet businesses.

The main wild card for estimating revenue loss is what fraction of online business-to-business purchases may avoid paying use tax. Online business-to-business sales are almost ten times larger than online retail sales, and many states tax numerous business purchases such as computers. Since the majority of online business-to-business sales are carried out by very large firms who are audited for their use tax, my view is that the underpayment is pretty low. However, this view is controversial; for example, Bruce and Fox (2000) estimate tax revenue losses of up to $11 billion by 2003 with as much as 70% coming from lost revenue from business-to-business sales.[2]

Generally, though, economists are skeptical about the wisdom of *any* sales tax on business purchases. These are intermediate goods. Sales taxes on business purchases will have a cascading effect, since the same output (not value-added) gets taxed repeatedly as it moves through the chain of production, and then taxed again when sold to consumers. A number of distortions will arise as a result, such as an incentive to produce products in-house rather than to buy from other producers. As Varian (2000) points out in his discussion of Internet taxation, the current system of use taxes enforced on businesses and not on consumers is precisely the opposite of what economic theory suggests. If businesses could use the Internet to avoid paying use taxes, this might be lost tax revenue that makes society better off, although any efficiency gains must be balanced against the distortion created by shifting one type of business commerce to another.

Overall, the revenue loss from the Internet is likely to be small. Even so, governments still might want to collect the tax if the cost of compliance is low. The main costs of compliance seem to be collecting rate information for the several thousand jurisdictions around the country and filling out the paper work. The fact that there are many different jurisdictions with different tax rates may not be too serious a problem in a world of cheap software and databases. The more difficult compliance issues revolve around differences in the sales-tax base, with some states exempting various items that other states tax. For example, some states tax clothing, some do not, and some tax clothing with various exceptions, such as only purchases over $500, or no tax except on fur and formal wear.

It is important to remember that the states could make taxing interstate commerce much easier if they would act to simplify or normalize their tax bases and rates. McLure (forthcoming) argues that equalizing the bases and setting one rate per state could serve as the basis for a grand political bargain. Thus far, however, few states have expressed a willingness to give up their discretionary powers, even though it would seem to be leaving money on the table. Estimates of the cost of compliance vary considerably, but one key factor is whether tax will be collected on very small merchants whose compliance cost is high and sales are low. Since about three-quarters of online retail are sold by 50 firms, the idea of exempting small firms from such a tax would only reduce tax revenue slightly (Boston Consulting Group, 1998). The most important issue for compliance is likely to be ensuring that businesses can find tax rates and bases in a simple way and that they will not be legally at risk so long as they use the official database.

The Impact of Tax Policy on Electronic Commerce

Although electronic commerce appears to have had little impact on fiscal policy, the same cannot be said for the role of fiscal policy on E-commerce. The evidence suggests that people are sensitive to local tax rates when deciding whether to buy over the Internet. I show that in places where sales taxes are higher (i.e., the relative price of buying online is lower), individuals are significantly more likely to have bought online (controlling for individual characteristics) (Goolsbee, 2000b). Moreover, this effect is unlikely to result from a spurious correlation of tax rates and technological sophistication, since those people in jurisdictions with higher tax rates do not appear more likely to use the Internet more frequently, nor to own computers, nor to differ systematically on other measures of technological sophistication. They are only more likely to buy things online. Further, taxes effects are found with products where sales tax is relevant, such as books, and not found in products where taxes aren't relevant, such as mutual funds and stocks. On the basis of these data, enforcing sales/use taxes on out-of-state purchases would reduce the number of online buyers by as much as 24%.

This sensitivity of purchases to taxation has since been corroborated in other studies. In 2000, I use updated data from 1999 and find a smaller but still sizable elasticity of E-commerce (Goolsbee, 2000c). Brynjolfsson and Smith (2000) use data from individuals' behavior at comparison shopping sites and find that individuals strongly favor booksellers outside their own state, where they do not have to pay taxes. Nonacademic survey data have also tended to suggest that taxes matter, though such studies do not control for other factors.[3]

Of course, the fact that applying taxes would reduce Internet commerce does not imply that such commerce should not be taxed.[4] There is clearly an economic distortion created from diverting commerce from retail stores to online venues simply for the purpose of avoiding taxes. To justify lower tax rates for E-commerce requires some positive externality or some especially high cost of compliance.

Plenty of candidates for such externalities have been nominated. There may be a network externality argument against penalizing Internet commerce at an early stage of development because current growth exerts a positive impact on future growth (Goolsbee and Zittrain, 1999; Goolsbee and Klenow, 1999; Zodrow, 2000). Some make arguments that forbidding Internet taxation could reduce the market power of local retailers or limit the overall spending and size of state government (Trandel, 1992; Becker, 2000). But there are some counterbalancing reasons that weigh against lower E-commerce tax rates, too. I find that that recent adopters are much less sensitive to taxation than the early adopters were, but that as shoppers gain experience, their tax sensitivity rises dramatically as they learn how to game the system (Goolsbee, 2000c). Others argue that imposing taxes before an industry is established is the only politically feasible way to get such taxes passed.

My view is that most arguments regarding externalities are based on politics, not on economics. They are not the types of issues that are amenable to testing given our data about the Internet, so they become matters of opinion. Moreover, even if the size (or direction) of the perceived externalities were known, the policy prescription would be unclear. Would a positive externality justify a complete sales-tax exemption as opposed to some lower (but positive) sales-tax rate, or would it warrant some altogether different policy intervention? The strictly empirical questions are both easier to answer and more convincing than these questions.

The Forgotten Issue of Taxing Internet Access

A largely neglected issue arising from the Internet Tax Freedom Act was the moratorium on taxes that forbade states from applying sales taxes to monthly Internet fees. I believe that this issue is extremely important and will move to the front burner as high-priced broadband connections become more prevalent.

For perspective, total spending on Internet access was almost $10 billion in 1999 (Kasrel et al., 1999). If all states applied sales tax to these charges and there were no behavioral responses, the $630 million of tax revenue collected would exceed the revenue loss from lost sales tax online. Imposing such access taxes is likely to be a tempting target once the moratorium expires, especially since the average annual income of Internet users exceeds $60,000.

However, taxing Internet access may create considerable deadweight loss. First of all, work on Internet usage seems to indicate that it is highly price-sensitive (Varian, 1999; Goolsbee, 2000d). High elasticities mean large distortions. But since almost all Internet service providers charge flat monthly fees rather than per-hour charges, applying taxes to access fees is not likely to have much impact on the hours of use. They may still influence the decision of whether to get access at all.

The impact of taxes on the decision to adopt new technology can make these deadweight losses even larger. If there are fixed costs associated with expanding broadband service to a city, anything that reduces profitability runs the risk of delaying or even preventing diffusion. In this case, as discussed in Romer (1994), the deadweight loss of the policy will be the entire consumer and producer surplus that would have existed if the tax had not existed and the technology had spread (minus the fixed cost that need not be incurred, of course).[5]

Goolsbee (2000d) finds that allowing states to apply sales taxes to Internet access fees could significantly delay the spread of broadband in a number of smaller-sized markets, leading to dynamic losses more than twice as large as in conventional deadweight loss calculations and losses that would be a multiple of the revenue generated by the tax. However, this evidence is based on reported willingness-to-pay data and it would be useful to find whether similar results hold with better information. The impact of taxation on innovation is a fruitful topic for further research.

International Implications

The taxation of Internet commerce has received considerable attention internationally, especially in Europe. However, Europe does not have anything like the revenue-loss issues faced in the USA. European countries typically apply a value-added tax (VAT) to purchases coming from other countries through customs. Further, for goods originating within the European Union, VAT is paid at each stage of production, so it is much less an issue revenue-wise, even if the final sale were to avoid paying tax (Nordhaus, 2000). Europe has recently expanded efforts to tax E-commerce, including an attempt to tax services bought online and downloaded digital goods such as online music. This type of tax provision is likely to be extraordinarily difficult to enforce, and of extremely little revenue consequence in the medium run even if enforcement were possible. Digital goods are a tiny fraction of online purchases and will continue to be small for many years.

Although there is no academic evidence examining how much taxes contribute to the widely varying levels of E-commerce internationally, the anecdotal evidence is consistent with at least some effect. In the USA, buying online saves consumers something like 6% relative to buying in stores. In Europe, VAT rates are more like 18% and there is no savings in buying online. In Europe – even in countries such as Sweden where online penetration is as high as in the USA – the share of online users who have ever purchased something online is less than half the US level, and total European E-commerce is less than one-seventh of the US level (Nordan et al., 2000). Also, most countries in Europe have high charges and taxes on Internet access and simultaneously much lower online penetration than does the USA.

European officials will face a powerful temptation when it comes to taxing Internet commerce. The majority of online merchants are located in the USA. There will be increasing pressure to put special taxes on E-commerce that will disproportionately affect US merchants competing with domestic retailers. Thus far, no special E-commerce taxes exist. However, the question of future international taxes on E-commerce remains very much up in the air. We have already seen a United Nations proposal to tax e-mail in developed countries to pay for computer access in developing nations. The US agenda in this area at the World Trade Organization is to argue for an agenda of no special taxes on Internet commerce. It will be interesting to see whether other nations find this position persuasive.

Conclusion

As a final thought regarding the domestic taxation of the Internet, the losses of tax revenue due to E-commerce are likely to be small in the short run and rise over time. Conversely, any positive externalities for the economy as a whole arising from electronic commerce and the spread of Internet access are likely to be largest in the short run and diminish as the Internet becomes an established retail channel (Goolsbee and Zittrain, 1999). In such circumstances, choosing not to enforce online sales taxes aggressively for a few years, followed by equal treatment once the Internet is established, may be a desirable outcome s well as being a plausible political compromise.

Notes

An earlier version of this chapter was printed as the "The Implication of Electronic Commerce for Fiscal Policy (and Vice Versa) in the winter 2001 issue of *Journal of Economic Perspectives*, volume 15, number 1, pages 13–24.

1. The key cases are *National Bellas Hess*, 386 US 753 [1967] and *Quill*, 504 US 298 [1992]. For more detailed discussions of the law, *see* Hellerstein (1997a), Prem et al. (1999), and US GAO (2000).
2. The report by US GAO (2000) outlines the importance of the underlying assumptions in this difference of opinion. If use-tax noncompliance among businesses is pervasive, the revenue loss from Internet sales could reach 5% of sales-tax revenue by 2003. If compliance is high, the forecast revenue loss is lower by a factor of five.
3. A survey of 7,000 people conducted by Bizrate.com indicated that nearly half of people claim they would not have made their last online purchase if they had been required to pay sales tax on it (Pastore, 1999). A survey of 1,600 people by Jupiter Communications indicated that 29%

of people would consider rejecting an online purchase of less than $50 if they had to pay sales tax and 41% would reject the online purchase if the item costs more than a $100 (Tedeschi, 2000).

4. There are excellent discussions of E-commerce tax plans in Hellerstein (1997a, 1997b, 1997c, 1999), McLure (1997a, 1997b, 1999a, 1999b), Fox and Murray (1997), Eads et al. (1997), Prem et al. (1999), and Varian (2000).
5. Hausman (1997, 1998) makes similar arguments regarding the deadweight losses of taxes and regulatory delays in telecommunications industries.

References

Advisory Commission on Electronic Commerce. 2000. Report to Congress. < www.ecommerce-commission.org/acec_report.pdf>.

Advisory Council on Intergovernmental Relations. 1986. State and Local Taxation of Out-of-State Mail Order Sales. Washington, DC: Government Printing Office.

Becker, Gary. 2000. The Hidden Impact of not Taxing E-Commerce. Business Week (28 February).

Bell, Steven, Stan Dolberg, Shah Cheema, and Jeremy Sharrard. 1998. Resizing Online Business Trade. The Forrester Report 2, no. 5 (November).

Bernhoff, Josh, Shelley Morrisette, and Kenneth Clemmer. 1998. Technographics Service Explained. The Forrester Report (January).

Boston Consulting Group. 1998. The State of Internet Retailing. Mimeo. (November).

Boston, Globe. 1998. Governors Fear Tax Loss from Internet. December 31.

Bruce, Donald, and William Fox. 2000. E-Commerce in the Context of Declining State Sales Tax Bases. Mimeo. University of Tennessee Center for Business and Economic Research (April).

Brynjolfsson, Erik, and Michael Smith. 2000. The Great Equalizer? Consumer Choice at Internet Shopbots. Mimeo. M.I.T. Sloan School (July).

Cline, William, and Thomas Neubig. 1999. The Sky Is not Falling: Why State and Local Revenues Were not Significantly Impacted by the Internet in 1998. Ernst and Young, Economics Consulting and Quantitative Analysis (June).

Eads, James, Harley Duncan, Walter Hellerstein, Andrea Ireland, Paul Mines, and Bruce Reid. 1997. National Tax Association Communications and Electronic Commerce Tax Project Report No. 1 of the Drafting Committee. State Tax Notes 13: 1255. Doc 97-30985.

Fox, William, and Matthew Murray. 1997. The Sales Tax and Electronic Commerce: So What's New? National Tax Journal 50, no. 3: 573–592.

Goolsbee, Austan. 2000a. Competition in the Computer Industry: Retail Versus Online. Mimeo. University of Chicago, GSB.

Goolsbee, Austan. 2000b. In a World Without Borders: The Impact of Taxes on Internet Commerce. Quarterly Journal of Economics 115, no. 2 (May): 561–576.

Goolsbee, Austan. 2000c. Tax Sensitivity, Internet Commerce, and the Generation Gap. Tax Policy and the Economy, volume 14, 45–65, edited by James Poterba. Cambridge, Mass.: MIT Press.

Goolsbee, Austan. 2000d. The Value of Broadband and the Deadweight Loss of Taxing New Technologies. Mimeo. University of Chicago, GSB.

Goolsbee, Austan, and Jonathan Zittrain. 1999. Evaluating the Costs and Benefits of Taxing Internet Commerce. National Tax Journal 52, no. 3 (September): 413–428.

Goolsbee, Austan, and Peter Klenow. 1999. Evidence on Learning and Network Externalities in the Diffusion of Home Computers. NBER WP#7329.

Graham ,Senator Robert. 1999. Should the Internet Be Taxed? Communities Hurt if the Web Isn't Taxed. Roll Call, 22 February.

Hausman, Jerry. 1997. Valuing the Effect of Regulation on New Services in Telecommunications. Brookings Papers on Economic Activity; Microeconomics, 1–38.

Hausman Jerry. 1998. Taxation by Telecommunications Regulation. Tax Policy and the Economy, Chapter 12, edited by James Poterba. Cambridge, Mass.: MIT Press.

Hellerstein, Walter. 1997a. Telecommunications and Electronic Commerce: Overview and Appraisal. State Tax Notes 12, no. 7: 519–526.

Hellerstein, Walter. 1997b. Transactions Taxes and Electronic Commerce: Designing State Taxes That Work in an Interstate Environment. National Tax Journal 50, no. 3: 593–606.

Hellerstein, Walter. 1997c. State Taxation of Electronic Commerce: Preliminary Thoughts on Model Uniform Legislation. Presented at the Symposium on Multi-Jurisdictional Taxation of Electronic Commerce at Harvard Law School, Cambridge, Mass. State Tax Notes 12, no. 17 (5 April): 1315–1324.

Kasrel, Bruce, Christopher Mines, and Karen Kopikis. 1999 From Dial-Up to Broadband. The Forrester Report (April).

McLure, Charles. 1997a. Electronic Commerce, State Sales Taxation, and Intergovernmental Fiscal Relations. National Tax Journal 50, no. 4: 731–750.

McLure, Charles. 1997b. Taxation of Electronic Commerce: Economic Objectives, Technological Constraints, and Tax Law. Tax Law Review 52, no. 3 (Spring).

McLure, Charles. 1999a. Achieving Neutrality Between Electronic and Nonelectronic Commerce. State Tax Notes 17, no. 3 (July): 193–197.

McLure, Charles. 1999b. Electronic Commerce and the State Retail Sales Tax: A Challenge to American Federalism. International Tax and Public Finance 6, no.2 (May): 193–224.

McQuivey, James, and Gillian DeMoulin. 2000. States Lose Half a Billion in Taxes to Web Retail. Technographics Brief. Forrester, Cambridge, Mass. (24 February).

Newman, Nathan. 1995. Prop 13 Meets the Internet: How State and Local Government Finances Are Becoming Road Kill on the Information Superhighway. Mimeo. Center for Community Economic Research, University of California, Berkeley.

Nordan, Matthew, Cliff Condon, Abigail Leland, and Wouter Aghina. 2000. Retail's Pan-European Future. The Forrester Report (April).

Nordhaus, William. 2000. E-Commerce and Taxation. Mimeo. Yale University (9 June).

Pastore, Michael. 1999. Sales Tax Would Hurt E-Commerce. Internetnews.com (19 September).

Prem, Richard, et al. 1999. Establishing a Framework to Evaluate E-Commerce Tax Policy Options. Report of Deloitte and Touche and University of California at Berkeley (December).

Romer, Paul. 1994. New Goods, Old Theory, and the Welfare Costs of Trade Restrictions. Journal of Development Economics 43: 5–38.

Tedeschi, Bob. 2000. Some Retailers Go Against the Grain in Integrating Their Online Operations. New York Times (5 June).

Trandel, Gregory. 1992. Evading the Use Tax on Cross-Border Sales: Pricing and Welfare Effects. Journal of Public Economics 35: 333–354.

US Bureau of the Census. Monthly Retail Sales. Various Issues. Bureau of the Census. Washington, DC.

US General Accounting Office (GAO). 2000. Sales Taxes: Electronic Commerce Growth Presents Challenges: Revenue Losses Are Uncertain. Report to Congressional Requesters (June). GAO/GGD/OCE-00-165.

Varian, Hal. 1999. Estimating the Demand for Bandwidth. Mimeo, University of California (August).

Varian, Hal. 2000. Taxation of Electronic Commerce. Mimeo. University of California (March).

Williams, Seema, David Cooperstein, David Weisman, and Thalika Oum. 1999. Post-Web Retail. The Forrester Report (September).

Zodrow, George. 2000. Network Externalities and Preferential Taxation of E-Commerce. Mimeo. Rice University.

Chapter 10
Spectrum Allocation and the Internet

Bruce M. Owen and Gregory L. Rosston

Introduction

The Internet is transforming communications around the world, even with the downturn in the technology market that we saw at the start of this century. This transformation permeates all forms of communications, but its success at realizing maximum consumer benefits depends, at least in part, on the flexibility of communications regulation. Regulation must not constrain firms responding to competitive incentives.

Five years ago, the Internet was just beginning. It is mentioned by name only ten times in the 128-page Telecommunications Act of 1996. Allowing firms to react to dramatic opportunities such as those the Internet has created in just 5 years is critical for smooth functioning of the market system and maximization of consumer benefits.

Given the high cost of connecting homes and businesses by installing additional wires, the most promising avenue for new capacity – and new competition – is through the use of spectrum. Regulators traditionally have placed strict limits on the uses to which each portion of the spectrum can be put. Flexible use and a concern for antitrust and competition principles can help to realize greater benefits from wireless communications.

This chapter focuses on spectrum policy and how changes in spectrum policy can affect the development of wireless communications. In some cases, wireless Internet access may be the perfect solution, but in other cases, setting up rules specifically to promote wireless Internet access may be the wrong answer for consumers. Section 1 provides a brief review of the evolution of spectrum policy. Section 2 looks at the role of spectrum in communications. Section 3 lays out the fundamentals for increased flexibility in spectrum regulation, and my concluding section presents hopes for the future.

B.M. Owen (✉)
Gordon Cain Senior Fellow, Standford Institude for Economic Policy Research, and Morris M. Doyle Professor in Public Policy, Standard University, Stanford, CA, USA
email: BruceOwen@stanford.edu

W.H. Lehr and L.M. Pupillo (eds.), *Internet Policy and Economics*,
DOI 10.1007/978-1-4419-0038-8_10,

A Bit of Spectrum History

Marconi, despite his aristocratic background, was a promoter. His great contribution was not just to invent a commercially useful form of wireless telegraphy, but also to sell the new medium to a skeptical marketplace.

Early radios and receivers were cumbersome and cranky; they required constant fiddling and tinkering with the components, and they spoke in the Morse code of telegraphy. In light of these features of the new technology, Marconi saw his best chance for commercial success in selling his radio services either as a substitute for wires, or for situations where wires were impossible, as between ships at sea.

While Marconi might have sought to develop radio as a broadcast service, he had ample reason to concentrate his promotional energies on wireless telegraphy. Among the areas for development, one of the most dramatic uses of radio was in improving response to distress calls from sinking ships. While the Titanic was equipped with a radio, for example, nearby ships that might have heard her distress calls either did not have radios or did not man their radio rooms regularly. The Titanic disaster enabled Marconi to persuade the USA and other governments to require radios in large ships and to require that the radios be manned constantly. Marconi thus may have been the biggest beneficiary of the sinking of the Titanic (until Leonardo Di Caprio).

Then, World War I followed close on the heels of the legitimization of radio as a rescue tool. Radio became a military technology, and the American Marconi Company was commandeered by the War Department.

So radio, as a serious technology, got its start in rescuing the rescuing of crews of sinking ships and in communication among military units. Its first commercial uses were as a wireless telegraph rather than as a wireless newspaper, or as the young David Sarnoff (later the founder of RCA) is said to have put it, as a wireless music box.

By the time the first commercial broadcasters came along in the 1920s, the government and the public for 20 years had thought of radio in the same way they thought of public roads.[1] In this climate of opinion, it is not surprising that both government and the public regarded the radio spectrum as a public resource whose administration should be centralized in federal hands. From this somewhat accidental beginning, all the central assumptions of modern radio spectrum allocation principles were born.

Broadcasting (first radio and then television) later came to supplant wireless telegraphy as the most important use of the radio spectrum – economically, socially, and politically. But the same principles, based on the same assumptions, were applied to broadcasting that had been applied to wireless telegraphy. The result has been a disaster for American consumers – exactly how big a disaster we will never know, for we cannot predict fully the consequences of the path not taken.

Although its impact on us can be felt and seen, the electromagnetic spectrum is intangible and is mysterious to many people. For centuries the existence and nature of the "aether" was hotly debated by philosophers and scientists. By the nineteenth century, its properties were better understood. The modern theory of electromagnetism has its roots in quantum mechanics – the nature and interactions of fundamental subatomic components. This covers everything from shortwave ham radio transmitters to the stars above. If you turn the transmitter power on and off at short intervals, you can radiate "dots and dashes" (or zeros and ones – the lowly telegraph was a digital transmission medium!). In other words, you can modulate the signal. To receive such a signal, you must have a receiver that can detect the oscillations and turn them into audible or visible form, just as you use a stethoscope to listen to a beating heart.

The theory of electromagnetic transmission will strike most readers as intimidating – clearly a subject best left to scientists, engineers, and expert government agencies. Nevertheless, the right to make such transmissions should be sufficiently well defined, as a legal matter, to be bought and sold in commercial markets, and most consumers would be considerably better off if it were. Just like any resource, the capacity to communicate via electromagnetism (which we call simply "spectrum") should be allocated to whatever use is most valuable to society. There is nothing unique about spectrum that makes it an exception to this rule.

Spectrum policy in the USA has gone through various phases since Marconi provided the commercial impetus for radio transmission. The Federal government got involved in the early days through the efforts of Herbert Hoover. But, as Hazlett (2001) explains, that was just the start of a long process of missteps in spectrum management aimed primarily at enriching incumbents and conferring power on the government in exchange.

Later, the government issued a set of principles to govern its early spectrum allocations for mobile radio.[2] Using these principles, the Federal Communications Commission (FCC) used a command and control allocation system to determine the best use for each specific block of spectrum and assign users to these blocks. Much of the decision-making allegedly was done on a technical basis to prevent destructive interference, but the result was to protect specific user groups' access to spectrum by prohibiting access by others. Specific frequencies, for example, were set aside for ice delivery companies.

Technological change both in the radio industry and in other industries (e.g., the refrigerator industry) increased the cost of these inefficient static allocations. Spectrum became less valuable in industries that had allocations and more valuable in other industries. In addition, possibly because of advances in complementary products such as computers and microprocessors, overall demand for mobile applications has mushroomed, increasing the value of spectrum.

At the same time, technology has advanced so that more spectrum is usable for communications, and specifically for mobile communications. Prior to the 1970s, mobile uses were limited to frequencies below 800 MHz. Cellular providers, specialized mobile radio (SMR), and personal communications services (PCS) all use frequencies above that level because technological innovations have increased the range of usable frequencies. Digital technology and cellular applications have also increased spectrum capacity by squeezing more data into a given amount of spectrum. Both advances have effectively increased the supply of usable spectrum.

Advances in technology and changes in the nature of demand, among other things, have recently led the Commission to adopt a somewhat more flexible regulatory framework for spectrum allocation.[3] One example is the use of auctions to award licenses to particular users.

Selling the spectrum is hardly a new idea. The Nobel Prize winning economist Ronald Coase analyzed the concept of spectrum markets at length half a century ago.[4] But the idea was treated with derision by government officials because it challenged the basic assumptions and self-interested arguments upon which all communication policy has been based since Marconi's day: that the spectrum is a uniquely scarce and valuable resource; that government regulation is required in order to ensure that transmissions do not interfere with each other; that market allocation is inconsistent with vital military and civilian emergency service needs; that spectrum if marketed would be hoarded and left unused by wealthy individuals or commercial interests, or that such interests would monopolize the spectrum in order to control public opinion and exclude competing viewpoints; that spectrum would not be available to deserving groups such as minorities and religious or educational organizations, but would instead be wasted in frivolous uses; and that without federal standards transmitters and receivers would be incompatible.[5] Ronald Coase's ideas made little progress at first against this conventional wisdom – much of it enshrined in legislation and elevated by the courts to the level of Constitutional principle, and all of it dead wrong.

So what is different now? Lord Keynes said that policymakers were often in thrall to some defunct economist. Coase's ideas have been gradually – glacially – accepted in the world of communications policy. Nowadays, few serious policy analysts or policymakers doubt that markets can do a better job of spectrum allocation than bureaucrats can do. The policymakers are no longer under the spell of defunct assumptions. Instead, they are under the influence of only the powerful special economic interests they themselves created. Similarly, the courts seem to have awakened to the bankruptcy of the basic assumptions of communications law, especially in broadcasting. In the slow and dignified manner required of courts abandoning their own finely argued precedents, judges have been changing the law. And while it cannot fairly be said that our elected representatives in Congress have understood that the ancient foundations of communications policy are built on sand, they certainly have understood that considerable revenues can be raised by spectrum auctions to benefit the federal fisc.

All of these changes make the business of spectrum allocation ripe for reform. But the key factor that could trigger significant change is the appearance of a set of economic interests potentially powerful enough to challenge and perhaps dislodge the powerful broadcaster lobby. The new boys on the block are the developers of the next generation of devices that use wireless transmission to connect to the Internet, and the associated software industries. As it happens, they need vast quantities of spectrum to support their dreams of Dick Tracy video wrist watches, and the chunk of spectrum that would suit them best is presently, and quite wastefully, devoted to television broadcasting.

As a result, in the next few years, we are quite likely to witness a political struggle in which the titans of Silicon Valley and their allies take on the titans of broadcasting.

This is an opportune moment for the proponents of spectrum markets. In the old days, the wireless Internet crowd would have attempted to persuade the FCC to take some frequencies away from the broadcasters' exclusive use and to turn them over – for free – to exclusive wireless use. Such a transfer is no longer politically possible. The wireless interests can get their spectrum only if the government auctions it off or permits the broadcasters to sell it off. Achieving this outcome means the final abandonment of the old wrongheaded assumptions of spectrum policy. It also presents us with a unique opportunity to shape the future of spectrum policy in the USA in ways that benefit the public rather than the old – or the new – special interests.

Given the preceding developments, support for the allocation of spectrum by marketplace forces rather than by central planning will come as no surprise. While it is likely that the current spectrum devoted to broadcasting would make a greater contribution to economic welfare in other uses, it is unclear what those uses are. The creation of spectrum markets in order to support the claims of "third-generation" (3G) wireless technologies would be as unwise as the mistakes in the past. Silicon Valley should succeed because its success would mean the creation of spectrum markets and efficient, market-driven use of spectrum, not spectrum use by government fiat or political power.

Economic Issues Relevant to Spectrum-Based Communications

Most communications use spectrum regardless of whether they transmit voice, video, or data messages. Some spectrum transmissions occur within wires, and other transmissions occur over the air. Even the light waves found in fiber-optic cables are a form of high-frequency spectrum. But spectrum is simply an input that is used to transmit information, the ultimate product that consumers desire. Consumers generally do not care if their communications travel by fiber, microwave, or satellite, as long as they get to the destination in the same amount of time.

Throughout the last hundred years, companies have developed various ways to transmit information using spectrum and have vastly increased the carrying capacity and reliability of transmissions. Innovations have increased the carrying capacity of spectrum both inside wires and over the air. Transmissions have moved from analog to digital, from single high-powered systems to low-powered cellular systems, and from copper wire to fiber-optic cable.

Future transmissions will make use of different innovations that will continue this path. They will reduce the cost per bit transmitted, increase the carrying capacity of the spectrum in use, expand the range of usable spectrum, and increase the quality of transmissions. At the same time, innovations in computing and changes in consumer demand patterns – partially exogenously and partially in response to the lower prices and higher quality – will lead to an increase in the quantity of bandwidth demanded. This may lead to the predictable and familiar cries that we are in a bandwidth shortage.

There are some economic principles that are often discussed when assessing spectrum policy issues, but these economic concerns are by no means unique to spectrum.

However, laying out the ideas makes it clearer how they play in the spectrum debates – especially with respect to spectrum flexibility.

Externalities: Interference Concerns

The fundamental difference between communications enclosed in wires or cables and over-the-air communications is the extent of interference and the ability to reuse spectrum. Interference can still be a problem within wires, or when wires are bundled together, but those concerns have been much less of an issue as the owner of the wires has generally had the incentive and ability to internalize the interference concerns.

On the wireless side, it is a different story. Because there are many different users and the potential for interference is greater, interference concerns have played prominently in the debates about spectrum policy in the USA through the last 80 years. The threat of interference has often served to promote other agendas that have not led to efficient spectrum use. Many parties have used the political process and the specter of chaos in the aether to prevent competition and to keep new users from entering the market.

Path Dependence

Luckily, spectrum cannot be destroyed. Past decisions thus do not necessarily forever relegate spectrum to inefficient usage. Poor past decisions are not the equivalent of cutting down old-growth forests. Used spectrum is identical to new spectrum – there is no change to its physical properties. However, past decisions do affect the nature and availability of complementary products such as radios and transmitters. Because of the possibility of path dependence and network effects, past decisions can affect the future course and ultimate efficiency of spectrum usage. It is not clear in any spectrum allocation decision, however, what the "right" path is.

When one path is taken, a set of complementary investments will be undertaken and money will be sunk in complementary equipment. For example, when a system adopts GSM technology, radio base stations and handset investments will be sunk, whereas the tower sites and towers are not nearly so irreversibly committed, as they can be used, at least to some extent, for other technologies (depending on specific locations). But the presence of sunk investment raises the bar for choosing a different technology. Rather than simply being better than the existing technology, the new technology has to be sufficiently better so as to make it worthwhile to discard the sunk investment. This means that there may be some additional cost to picking the "wrong" technology or even to the adoption of "correct" earlier technology. For example, the widespread adoption of 2G handsets in the USA may make it more difficult for 3G services to achieve marketplace acceptance.

Spectrum as a Scarce Resource

Although it cannot be used up or altered, spectrum is, like most other things in the economy, a scarce resource. This means that use by one party can preclude use by others, or at least affect the usefulness to others. While sharing of spectrum is possible, and advanced techniques may increase the usability of spectrum by different parties at the same time, it is impossible to make unlimited spectrum-based transmission capacity available to all at the same time. This limitation holds despite significant advances that may arise from spread spectrum, ultrawideband, or software-defined radio. Although these technologies hold the promise to increase capacity greatly, they do not eliminate contention for the spectrum.[6]

Spectrum is, and is likely to remain, scarce. This fundamental capacity constraint has serious implications for wireless Internet access. Internet services typically require relatively large amounts of transmission capacity relative to voice services. Existing allocations do not provide sufficient spectrum for such uses. As a result, companies will invest in ways to increase the capacity of the limited spectrum at their disposal – through investments such as multiple tower sites and low-power radios, as well as through advanced technology that allows compression of data.

Companies make investments when they expect a profitable return. Much of communications investment is made upfront, and then the marginal operating cost of the network is quite small. For example, satellite communications requires development and deployment of a satellite before any traffic can be carried. Building a geostationary communications satellite and putting it into orbit can easily cost $200 million. Similar upfront infrastructure investments are required for wireline and wireless networks, although they are more scalable than satellite systems. Because of the high upfront sunk costs, a firm must have a reasonable expectation that it will be able to charge for the use of its services to recoup the investment.[7]

If a firm has no assurance that it will be able to charge for its services because it has no assurance that it will have a product to sell, it will be less likely to undertake the investment. Even if advances in spectrum-sharing techniques such as ultrawideband come to fruition, there still will be contention for the use of spectrum. If there is no contention, then the investment in infrastructure may be worth very little – the shadow price of spectrum capacity should be zero. In either case, the lack of a property right might reduce substantially the incentive to invest in wireless networks to increase capacity.

Importance of Economic Issues

This section has looked at three economic issues that are important to the analysis of spectrum flexibility: interference, path dependence, and scarcity. Each of these issues has played a major role in spectrum policy in the past and is sure to be raised by parties with vested interests to affect the direction of policy change in the future, and especially to oppose increased flexibility. Nevertheless, these issues actually are not critical to most arguments in favor of flexibility.

Spectrum Flexibility

To realize the full potential of the spectrum for Internet or other services, the FCC will have to adopt a more flexible approach toward spectrum management. The FCC should adopt an explicit spectrum-management philosophy that essentially abdicates most of the historical functions of the agency.[8] The FCC should not "manage" the spectrum. Instead, the FCC should set up rules that ensure a reasonable way to resolve interference disputes, possibly in an expert court. The government generally should rely on the antitrust authorities (or at least antitrust reasoning) to prevent anticompetitive aggregation of spectrum resources, and should endeavor to get as much spectrum as possible into the market.

The current system contains artificial restrictions on ownership, services, and technology. This leads to distortions in investment and innovation and a waste of spectrum. Right now, for example, there is an important debate about where we will get spectrum for the vaunted 3G services.[9] This occurs because all of the international allocations for advanced wireless services are already in use or are allocated for other services in the USA. One area of spectrum is currently being used by wireless cable operators, schools, and religious institutions. These groups, particularly churches, have vigorously protested any forced reallocation of "their" spectrum for new advanced services. To an economist, the solution is simple – let them sell their spectrum licenses to the wanna-be 3G providers. As it stands, it appears that incumbent spectrum licensees have little choice but to use the political process to retain the benefits of their current licenses. But markets work much better than political compromises in resolving such problems. Eliminating the political process from the negotiation will reduce wasteful expenditures and, more important, speed transfers of spectrum to more beneficial uses.

Flexibility and Windfalls

Current spectrum licensees should be granted maximum flexibility in how they use their current assignments. Ice delivery companies, for example, should be free to use their spectrum assignment for some more promising purpose. Such freedom may prove to be a windfall for some licensees who gain additional flexibility to provide valuable services they previously could not provide. Windfalls may incite envy or outrage.

Primarily, concerns fall into two camps – equity and revenue. Some (those whose economic interests are hurt) will argue that granting additional rights to incumbent licensees would be unfair. The other complaint will be that these licensees should not get valuable additional rights for free in an era of auctions – instead, the windfall should go to the government.

Auctioning initial licenses is clearly the right answer when it can be done quickly and easily. But when an auction would have only a single bidder, which is likely to occur when the bidding is for additional rights for an existing license, an auction may be pointless. First, if there is truly only a single party that could use the grant of additional flexibility, an auction should produce a price of zero. But the Commission may decide to put a reserve price on the additional rights in order to raise revenue. If the reserve price were so low that it did not cause any bidder not to participate, then the auction would simply result in a transfer and cause no harm. If the price is set high enough that some bidders do not participate, then the additional flexibility rights will lie fallow, even though they have a zero opportunity cost. Consumers will lose the benefit of the additional services that could be provided with additional flexibility. Knowing this may cause bidders to hold back on their bidding even if the reserve price is below their valuation, because they might expect the Commission to reauction the rights with a lower reserve price. In addition, if additional flexibility would cause licensees to become more effective competitors, it may pay potential rivals to bid on the flexibility rights as a blocking tactic.[10]

Additional flexibility is not guaranteed to cause huge windfalls, even if on the surface it would appear to do so. The primary impact would be to give the opportunity for incumbent licenses to provide more services to consumers, leading to increased consumer welfare.[11] But for each licensee liberated to provide additional or more valuable services, there would be other licensees similarly freed to compete. Some licensees might even end up worse off on balance as a result of the increased competition. It would therefore be a serious mistake for policymakers to become preoccupied with the need to extract assumed windfall gains from licensees.

Flexibility Recommendations

The FCC should grant flexibility to existing licensees in at least four dimensions: services, technology, implementation, and scope. This way, spectrum will be able to provide the services that consumers demand. One possibility is that wireless Internet access will be an appropriate use for spectrum. But flexibility will prevent an outcome in which either too much or too little spectrum is dedicated to this use.

In addition, the FCC should move forward with its proposal to facilitate secondary markets for spectrum.[12] Secondary markets can be thought of in two ways: leasing or resale. Many providers have spectrum licenses and are using the spectrum according to its assigned use, but the spectrum would be more valuable if used in other ways. Others may not need to use the spectrum for a year or two or would like to hold spectrum as insurance against future spectrum needs. In the interim, they could benefit from their spectrum by allowing others to use it rather than letting it sit idle. Both leasing and resale of spectrum should be permitted. However, the FCC should not mandate how these transactions should work.

There are many regulations from the command and control era that will need to be changed to allow a more flexible market for spectrum. For example, the rules that are used to determine whether a licensee is in "control" of the operations will have to be changed to allow dynamic reassignment of channels for extremely short-term spectrum sharing.

Service Flexibility

Licensees (and unlicensed users) should have substantial service flexibility. This means that they should be able to use spectrum to provide whatever services they think will satisfy consumer demand. The Commission has already moved to provide service flexibility in some areas, with useful results. For example, PCS licensees have relatively broad flexibility for the services they can provide.[13] At the same time, the Commission has attempted to increase the flexibility regarding the services that existing licensees can provide. The Commission allowed Nextel to incorporate cellular like service into its former dispatch systems and soon afterward allowed cellular carriers to provide dispatch services, which had previously been banned. By allowing each of these providers additional flexibility, the FCC has expanded the range of services that SMR and cellular providers can offer, but also has allowed better use of spectrum resources to meet consumer demand. Competition has been permitted to increase in areas where it can provide the greatest benefits. Had spectrum been limited to specific uses as in the old regime, neither provider could respond to scarcity in the other service, nor could any provider easily offer bundled services.

This trend toward more flexible service provision should continue, but there are roadblocks. Incumbent operators may pressure the Commission to limit the ability of other spectrum users to compete. Such limits would harm consumers by denying them the benefits of competition and ensuring that spectrum is not used in the most efficient manner. Some argue that the Commission has a legal obligation and duty to allocate spectrum for specific services. But in fact there is actually substantial leeway to define services broadly as the Commission did in PCS and other services. It is important to avoid the trap of artificially constricting spectrum use.

In a recent ruling, the Commission set up band-manager licenses in the frequency range that is designed to protect public safety transmissions from interference in the 700 MHz band. The Commission mandated that the licensees, with either 2 or 4 MHz of spectrum, lease at least half of their spectrum to unaffiliated third parties. The Commission justified this requirement in their order by stating that the band manager concept was an experiment and they wanted to see if it would work. By mandating that it will be done, there is much less of an experiment, and it may be at great cost, as many beneficial applications requiring 2 or 4 MHz may now be precluded as a result of the rule. Rather than mandating the resale or leasing of spectrum, the rules should allow and facilitate them. That way, if it is efficient, it would have a chance to happen. With only 2 or 4 MHz of spectrum, there is no competitive concern, given the relatively large amount of spectrum capable of providing the relevant services.

Technical Flexibility

Users should have broad technical flexibility. They should be able to choose the technology they think will best allow them to provide the service and quality that customers will demand.[14] Technical flexibility means that users can design and redesign their systems without the need for delay or regulatory uncertainty. This way, experimentation is less costly and firms will be better able to find the spectrum-efficient, low-cost, and consumer-friendly technologies best suited for their markets. For example, PCS providers in the USA have chosen different technologies; this allowed them to provide different quality service and to tailor their choices to the markets they serve.

European governments recently garnered headlines on account of the unexpectedly large sums they received in auctions for licenses for 3G wireless systems. The idea of getting the spectrum into the hands of operators with incentives to serve customers was very good. However, these licenses were issued with a requirement that could ultimately reduce the public benefit substantially – the licenses require the actual deployment of 3G UMTS-based wireless systems.

There are many different technology and quality-of-service choices. With four or five new licensees, it is far too restrictive for the government to mandate that all five have to provide top-of-the-line high-quality service. 3G promises great advances in quality and choice of services. But the new systems will also be very expensive. In order to pay for the development, deployment, and operation of the systems, operators may be expecting large numbers of subscribers and relatively high prices for the services they offer. But there might be a different way. It might be better to allow some networks to offer lower quality services at lower prices. Even though one might argue that Rolls Royce offers the best automobile, we do not require all automakers to offer a Rolls Royce. Some consumers want Yugos and Chevys. Some carriers foresee that there may not be sufficient demand for five networks of 3G wireless technology. As a result, they are contemplating offering so-called 2.5G services. They should not be prevented from doing this.

Technical flexibility may increase the cost of global roaming. It may require some customers to adopt dual-mode phones or even multiple handsets. The question to be addressed is whether this cost is outweighed by the benefits of having more tailored systems in the home countries. That calculus depends on the number of people who roam, the value they place on seamless connection or the cost penalty for multimode handsets, and the change in system to achieve compatibility. It might be that the cost to adopt a compatible system is low, so that achieving worldwide roaming might be a low cost to home consumers. It also might be the case that few people demand worldwide roaming, place a low value on it, or that the extra cost of handsets is small so that home consumers face no penalty. Markets do well in balancing these trade-offs because the firms who get it right earn more profits. Governments have no basis but guesswork for making such decisions.

Aggregation Flexibility

The FCC is very involved in the initial grants of licenses. This is because much of the spectrum is not currently allocated to anyone. Before releasing spectrum to the market, the Commission has to determine the spectrum block size and geographic scope of the licenses it will issue. New Zealand initially thought that it would be a good idea to try "postage stamp"-sized licenses so that users could aggregate licenses covering the geographic area and spectrum blocks they wanted. The USA faced an analogous choice when it decided on the initial size of homestead grants in the Oklahoma Land Rush of 1893. These also turned out to be too small in some places and too large in others.

Unfortunately, auction technology has not progressed far enough to make this type of licensing scheme feasible. To protect against the "exposure" problem requires some sort of package-bidding option for bidders. The exposure problem occurs when bidders have a higher value for a package than the sum of the values for the individual licenses. But with a large number of licenses and hence potential packages, the computational complexity can be much more difficult.[15]

For smaller numbers of licenses, package bidding appears to be promising. Package bidding allows competition between bidders with different preferences and lead to an efficient allocation of licenses. Without a package-bidding procedure, inefficient allocation of licenses can occur because some bidders may hold back in the fear that they will overbid for licenses that would be worth their bid price only if a complete package is assembled because of the exposure problem.

Spectrum caps may be useful during the course of an auction. When there are multiple bidders for licenses, it may be the case that acquisition of spectrum by multiple licensees would cause competitive concern. An appropriately determined spectrum cap could avoid the necessity of choosing between two identical purchasers and forcing one to divest its newly acquired licenses. In addition, because an auction relies on certainty and commitment to bids, setting a bright-line standard would ensure that all bids were legitimate. A temporary spectrum cap of this sort makes sense, of course, only if it is determined on the basis of the usual analytical techniques of antitrust.

However, at the conclusion of an auction, the case for bright-line spectrum caps becomes much less clear. The best argument appears to be that it could ensure a competitive market structure. However, there is no reason to suppose that a spectrum cap is superior to standard antitrust enforcement from this perspective. Moreover, there are costs to a bright-line test as well. It may be the case, for example, that a licensee wants to develop a new technology that requires more spectrum than the cap would allow. If a single firm acquired more spectrum than the cap allows, it might not cause competitive concern, and it might allow a firm to become a much more vigorous competitor.

Subsequent to auction, users should have the flexibility to determine which geographic areas they wish to serve and how much spectrum they should use to serve those areas. Users should be free to aggregate or disaggregate spectrum or geographic areas to suit their business needs. When there is a concern about a company controlling too much of the spectrum on the market, the first response should be to try to increase the available supply. Only where it is impossible to create sufficient competition, and where the Department of Justice and the Federal Trade Commission are incapable of promoting a competitive market, should the FCC prevent the free trading of spectrum – and then only after a careful weighing of the effects on consumers.

Implementation Flexibility

Finally, licensees should have implementation flexibility. Currently, many countries assign licenses with associated "buildout" requirements. Buildout requirements are sometimes tied to technical requirements and other times simply mandate that "service" be provided. These provisions mandate that a licensee construct systems that cover minimum or specific geographic areas or a certain number of people in order to maintain the license.

At any point in time, the best use of spectrum may be to not use it (even though, as discussed above it will not wear out). Spectrum is useless by itself. Transmitting information requires radios and receivers. The cost of using these for a short period of time may outweigh the benefits from using spectrum during a period when a licensee is waiting to undertake a different business plan. It is possible, for example, that a licensee is waiting to develop technology or for a market to develop. If the licensee expects that market or technology to develop in a relatively short period, it might pay to leave the spectrum fallow for some time. As long as the licensee does not have a dominant position in spectrum related services (services for which a specific block of spectrum is uniquely useful) and the ability to prevent other spectrum from providing services, the licensee cannot benefit at consumer expense from withholding spectrum from the market.

A buildout requirement does nothing to ameliorate the problem of a licensee that has a dominant position in a particular service; instead, it may cause socially wasteful expenditure simply to meet a requirement to retain a license. The licensee can meet a buildout requirement by providing a noncompetitive service. It will satisfy the buildout requirement, but do nothing to increase competition for the service.

Unlicensed Flexibility and Other Unlicensed Issues

Flexibility should also be given to unlicensed spectrum users. Unlicensed bands have led to a great variety of different services, from automatic garage door openers to two-way walkie-talkies and now to the burgeoning wireless data connections of Bluetooth and IEEE 802.11.[16] All of these wireless innovations are important, and some unlicensed application may be the "next big thing." But it is also important to remember that dedicating spectrum to unlicensed uses comes at a cost – the opportunity cost of the spectrum in some licensed use, or some other unlicensed use that is precluded because of the particular rules adopted.

Benkler (1998), Lessig (2001), and others have argued that the spectrum should be allocated much more in the form of a commons without licenses. However, it is unclear what, if any, market failure in a licensed allocation system they or other advocate of unlicensed spectrum seek to address. For example, many device manufacturers have come together to agree on standards for IEEE 802.11b; if voluntary agreements on technical standards are feasible, so should agreement be possible on the acquisition of wireless spectrum licenses.

Despite the skepticism with which we view increased unlicensed spectrum, there is unlicensed spectrum already in the public domain, and the Commission should also attempt to make that as productive as possible. Rules for unlicensed use must allow users to live together and to avoid at least some interference concerns. While unlicensed spectrum can be open to all, generally the government has set specific protocols to minimize interference. These protocols may include power limitations or transmission guidance. As a result of these rules, there is bound to be some constraint on the uses to which unlicensed spectrum can be put, and some possibility for interference or contention among users.

Unfortunately, there is no way to set rules for using unlicensed spectrum to eliminate spectrum scarcity. If it were possible to allow unlimited transmissions, then we would have no problem and would not worry about spectrum allocation. But, whenever one party transmits, it creates some possibility of interference with other transmissions. When interference gets high enough to cause some other user's service to degrade, there is a scarcity, even with unlicensed services; hence, the necessity for rules regarding transmission protocols, power limits, and other restrictions. But within the protocol rules, wherever possible, the Commission – or whatever governing body is responsible – should give maximum flexibility.

Global Compatibility

Some spectrum-based services are very localized and some are global. Even spectrum decisions for local services may implicate global competition because of the economics of equipment manufacturing. Having technically compatible equipment for a specific band may increase competition among manufacturers of that technology and may also permit economies of scale in manufacturing. At the same time, mandating compatibility may foreclose other beneficial avenues for innovation or competition.

Some frequent business travelers would prefer to be able to use their wireless phones everywhere on the globe. Uniform global standards also would permit economies of scale in equipment manufacturing. Despite the benefits from a coordinated worldwide system, there are also costs to such a system. The costs may exceed the benefits. There is no reason to assume that market decisions will not sort out these trade-offs in a way that maximizes net consumer benefits. Farrell and Topper (1998) discuss the trade-offs for a mandated system of standards. They point out that there are many private incentives to adopt standards to achieve the same economies of scale, which implies that government-imposed uniformity may be quite costly to consumers.

Broadband wireless deployment (3G) may depend very much on the different infrastructure needs of different countries. In the USA, Internet access has been adopted extremely rapidly on a narrowband basis. Some of this is likely due to the traditional USA pricing of local telephone service, which is based on a flat monthly fee for unlimited usage. USA consumers clearly prefer this to metering of usage, even when metering would save them money.[17] As a result, consumers can use Internet service for long periods without incurring large bills, increasing the attractiveness of the service.

Metered local service is more common outside the USA, dampening the demand for Internet access. Because of the possibility of high bills for high usage, some customers do not sign up at all, and others curtail their usage.

Finally, in some countries, the wireline infrastructure is sufficiently poor that many customers do not have access even to narrowband dial-up access. Without the ability to get access, it is obvious why online subscription rates are low.

The need for wireless access may be very different in these three environments. And wireless licensing and standards policy might be a very blunt instrument for determining appropriate wireless access in different environments. A single unified worldwide policy would have to balance the needs of consumers in these and other environments. Even then, as in all social welfare optimizations, the policy objective is subject to debate – should we maximize total social welfare? This might end up setting global wireless policy that makes consumers in the USA and Europe very well off, while the rest of the world has to make do with a set of standards inappropriate for their needs.

Once again, flexibility would allow the benefits of compatibility along with a chance to tailor spectrum to the needs and desires of consumers in each market. For example, it is unlikely that a country like Ghana will be willing to pick a unique standard for wireless access because it will be difficult to get equipment manufacturers to provide equipment on a small scale. However, licensees in Ghana have the correct incentives to balance the availability of equipment of various types with the needs of Ghanian consumers, and thus to determine whether they need state-of-the-art 3G systems, 2.5G systems, 2G systems, or some combination of systems.

Without flexibility, some countries will be stuck with an operating standard that is too rudimentary for their needs while at the same time others may view this: Yugo" as a "Rolls Royce" – far too pricey for the incomes and needs of their consumers. Global flexibility may increase welfare much more than increased economies of scale in manufacturing and ease of international roaming that results from mandated international compatibility. The marketplace should make this trade-off, not the government.

Moving to the Future

Flexible spectrum use will not guarantee the future of Dick Tracy video watches. But it will make such products appear more rapidly in some areas and more cheaply in others. It also will increase the amount of spectrum deployed for broadband services where customers demand that type of service, while allocating spectrum for less-advanced services in areas where customers do not demand advanced services.

There are battles looming for reallocation of spectrum among over-the-air television broadcasters, religious and educational interests, the Defense Department, and interests trying to get access either to spectrum or to more spectrum. These battles will turn on whether the government continues to dictate spectrum use or allows market forces to reallocate spectrum efficiently. The government might be able to facilitate trades in spectrum licenses by easing the regulatory burdens on licensees.

However, these battles are small and specific. For reforms to have real and long-lasting effect, the government should take the steps outlined above – increasing service, implementation, and technical flexibility while at the same time removing ownership and control requirements. The guiding light in spectrum policy for the government should be to prevent anticompetitive aggregation of spectrum and to provide adjudication for interference complaints. Then the market will allocate spectrum to the services that consumers demand. If that is mobile broadband, we will likely see mobile broadband providers under a flexible regime. If there is not a demand for this, then licensees will not waste the resources to build systems simply to comply with the terms of their licenses. Instead they will build systems suitable to the demands of their customers.

Notes

1. Hazlett (2001) provides an excellent history and analysis of spectrum policy decisions in the USA.
2. *See* Federal Communications Commission (1945).
3. Unfortunately, this movement has hardly been a runaway freight train down a straight track. The Commission has made many deviations from this, including some recent decisions in which they specifically blocked flexibility. *See* Rosston (2001).
4. *See* Coase (1959).
5. *See* Hazlett (2001).
6. Spread spectrum technologies make use of a wide band of spectrum with low signal levels and filters on the receiving end to focus on the signal. As the number of users sharing the spectrum increases, the "noise" level increases and the signal can degrade.
7. There may be other ways to recoup the investment such as charging for ancillary services, but they essentially still tie back to recouping the infrastructure investment.
8. *See* Comments of 37 Concerned Economists (February 7, 2001).
9. "3G" or third-generation mobile services encompass broadband mobile devices, such as cell phones that also permit web surfing.
10. *See* Gilbert and Newberry (1982).

11. *See* Hausman (1997).
12. *See* Federal Communications Commission (2000).
13. Note that the one service that PCS licensees are not permitted to provide is broadcast service. There is no reason for this prohibition other than the protection of incumbent broadcasters. Presumably incumbents were able to use political clout to get this prohibition inserted, even though the likelihood of broadcast use on PCS frequencies is relatively low.
14. Obviously, health and safety standards are important to consider.
15. The number of possible packages is equal to $2N$ ñ 1 where N is the number of licenses.
16. These are two different unlicensed wireless protocols that have been adopted by a number of different equipment manufacturers.
17. This section is not meant as a comment on the efficiency of current embedded wireline systems in different countries, but merely the impact of wireless policy on broadband access.

References

Benkler Y. 1998. Overcoming Agoraphobia: Building the Commons of the Digitally Networked Environment. Harvard Journal of Law & Technology 11: 287. <http://www.law.nyu.edu/benklery/agoraphobia.pdf>.

Coase R. 1959. The Federal Communications Commission. *2* J.L. & Econ. 1.

Comments of 37 Concerned Economists. 2001. In the Matter of Promoting Efficient Use of Spectrum Through Elimination of Barriers to the Development of Secondary Markets (February 7).

Farrell J., and Topper M. 1998. Economic White Paper on National Third Generation Wireless Standards. Cornerstone Research Staff Working Paper.

Federal Communications Commission. 1945. Allocation of Frequencies to the Various Classes of Non-Governmental Services in the Radio Spectrum from 10 Kilocycles to 30,000,000 Kilocycles. Docket No. 6651. Report of Proposed Allocation from 25,000 Kilocycles to 30,000,000 Kilocycles at 18–20 (released January 15, 1945).

Federal Communications Commission. 2000. In the Matter of Principles for Promoting the Efficient Use of Spectrum by Encouraging the Development of Secondary Markets (released December 1, 2000).

Gilbert R., and Newberry D. 1982. Preemptive Patenting and the Persistence of Monopoly. *72* Am. Econ. Rev. 514 (June).

Hazlett T. 2001. The Wireless Craze, The Unlimited Bandwidth Myth, The Spectrum Auction Faux Pas, and the Punchline to Ronald Coase's "Big Joke": An Essay on Airwave Allocation Policy. AEI-Brookings Joint Center for Regulatory Studies. Working Paper 01–02 (January). Harvard Journal of Law & Technology (Spring).

Hausman J. 1997. Valuing the Effect of Regulation on New Services in Telecommunications. Brookings Papers on Economic Activity: Microeconomics.

Lessig L. 2001. The Future of Ideas. New York: Random House.

Rosston G. 2001. The Long and Winding Road: The FCC Paves the Path with Good Intentions. SIEPR Policy Paper No. 01–008, <http://siepr.stanford.edu/papers/pdf/01–08.html>.

Chapter 11
The Role of Unlicensed in Spectrum Reform

William H. Lehr

Introduction

In many countries, there is a growing consensus among industry participants, academics, and policymakers that traditional models for managing radio frequency spectrum are badly outdated.[1] The existing management regime is premised on century-old radio technology. Under the traditional approach, regulators allocate narrow frequency bands to specific uses and users under restrictive licenses that constrain the choice of technology, business model, and ability to redeploy the spectrum to higher value uses or to make use of new technologies. This approach has resulted in acute spectrum scarcity. This scarcity is largely *artificial* in that it results from an outmoded regulatory regime, rather than because of any technical or market capacity constraints.

This artificial scarcity distorts the opportunity cost of spectrum. New technologies and uses face excessively high costs for accessing spectrum. Spectrum is available either not at all or only after the payment of high auction fees. Meanwhile, incumbents (e.g., government users and over-the-air broadcasters) face excessively low opportunity costs for the spectrum they control, which provides them little incentive to invest in enhancing spectral efficiency. Appropriate regulatory reform can eliminate this *artificial* scarcity which ought to result in more efficient spectrum use and lower prices for spectrum overall.[2]

Economists are generally agreed that substituting market forces for direct government management of spectrum use (the so-called legacy "command and control" model) will enhance efficiency and promote innovation.[3] There are two basic regulatory models for reforming spectrum management to be more responsive to market forces: the "flexible licensed" and the "unlicensed" models.[4] Most economists who have focused on the issue favor the "flexible licensed" model for the spectrum that is currently perceived to be the most valuable, and hence most "scarce." This is the lower frequency spectrum below 3 GHz (and even more valuable, below 1 GHz).[5] Policymakers at the FCC and Ofcom have concurred in

W.H. Lehr
Research Associate, Computer Science and Artificial Intelligence Laboratory (CSAIL), Massachusetts Institute of Technology, Cambridge, MA, USA
e-mail: wlehr@mit.edu

W.H. Lehr and L.M. Pupillo (eds.), *Internet Policy and Economics*,
DOI 10.1007/978-1-4419-0038-8_11,

this view and current plans emphasize a flexible licensed approach for this lower frequency spectrum.[6]

This essay makes the counter case for why the unlicensed model is *also* important and should be relied on to manage a greater share of the high-value, lower frequency spectrum. Because it is neither desirable nor politically feasible[7] to advocate adopting the unlicensed model *instead* of the flexible licensed model, this chapter makes the case for unlicensed spectrum in a world where it is assumed that the majority of high-value spectrum is managed via flexible licensing. It explains why an overreliance on the "flexible licensed" model – reflected in a failure to provide for additional "unlicensed" use in lower frequency spectrum – will hamper progress toward eliminating artificial spectrum scarcity. This, in turn, will hamper the evolution of wireless technology and markets, and limit progress toward effective regulatory reform.

The balance of the essay is organized into three sections. In the next section, I explain key differences and commonalities in the licensed and unlicensed approaches. The following section then focuses on why the unlicensed model offers important benefits for regulatory reform. The final section concludes and discusses challenges with expanding the unlicensed use further.

Flexible Licensed and Unlicensed Spectrum Management Explained

Although there is a growing consensus that transitioning from the legacy regulatory model, caricaturized as "command and control," toward market-based spectrum management is desirable, there is no general agreement as to how this should be accomplished.[8] The two principal approaches under consideration are the "flexible licensed" and "unlicensed" models. The "flexible licensed" model is sometimes referred to as the "market mechanism," "exclusive use," or "property rights" approach; whereas the latter is sometimes referred to as the "license-exempt," "open," "free," or "commons" approach.

A False Dichotomy

These short-hand labels are intended to emphasize alleged distinguishing features, but as with most such labels, they conflate multiple issues that suggest an overly simplistic and misleading dichotomy. On the one hand, the licensed/property rights model is portrayed as more consistent with a market approach that treats spectrum as a scarce resource that is amenable to being traded in secondary markets once property rights are assigned. This is intended to contrast with the unlicensed/open/commons model which views spectrum as belonging to everyone, and hence, not amenable to such an assignment of property rights or trading. According to this stylized perspective, the "licensed" model recognizes that spectrum is "scarce," and that its allocation would be more efficient if it were first "auctioned" and then traded in "markets." In contrast, the "unlicensed" approach views whatever spectrum scarcity exists as wholly artificial, and therefore, access should be free to all, with the government establishing the framework to manage such access.

With this simplistic caricature of the debate, it is not surprising that most economists and current mainstream regulatory policy – which favors transitioning to markets wherever possible – favor the licensed approach for the most valuable spectrum. This is unfortunate because the dichotomy described above is more apparent than real.

First, both models represent a transition to increased reliance on market forces, but neither model eliminates regulation of the airwaves. In the case of a licensing regime, it is anticipated that policymakers will assign flexible and tradable spectrum use rights to licensees, eliminating the many constraints that characterize and encumber the current licensing regime. However, how to define such rights optimally is far from clear. Additionally, policymakers need to foster the emergence of secondary markets if the transition to a flexible licensing regime is to deliver the promised efficiency enhancements. Regulatory reform takes time and while it may not be possible to precisely foresee what the eventual outcome will be, we can be sure that the actual outcome will deviate from the theoretical ideal. Finally, there is the expectation that courts will substitute for administrative agencies in enforcing license property rights, but there is no a priori reason to believe that this will result in lower costs (greater immunity from influence costs).[9]

The view that unlicensed might be less deregulatory is ironic since an open access/unlicensed regime is much more deregulatory, at least in principle. Although it is unlikely that unlicensed spectrum would be managed without any regulation to limit interference, the protocol or rules could be chosen by users or industry (e.g., via industry standardization) and so need not require ongoing government management of the technology choices for how spectrum is accessed. Both the flexible licensing and unlicensed regimes will require ongoing regulation while at the same time offering greater scope for market forces.

Second, while the licensed approach only makes sense if one believes that spectrum will continue to be scarce, that is, have a nonzero opportunity cost, support for the unlicensed approach does not require belief that all scarcity will be eliminated. Indeed, the choice of regulatory regime cannot eliminate real spectrum scarcity that may arise whenever there are more contending potential uses than mutually can be accommodated. When congestion arises in unlicensed spectrum, there needs to be a mechanism for dealing with it – but it is not true that licenses offer the unique best mechanism for allocating scarce spectrum in all situations. Congestion imposes an externality (e.g., in the form of lower quality performance) that has a real opportunity cost that influences behavior in ways similar to (if not identical to) the ways in which a market-clearing price for licensed spectrum would be expected to operate. There are lots of cases where society chooses alternative (nonprice-based) mechanisms to allocate scarce resources (e.g., ambulances, public goods) and the "Tragedy of the Commons" often does not arise with collective resource management.

Third, auctions may (or may not) play a role in the transition to either licensed or unlicensed spectrum. Certainly, the hope for both models is that the transition will help reduce artificial spectrum scarcity and so dramatically reduce spectrum opportunity costs. Thus, if reform is successful, the expected proceeds from any auction should be substantially lower. This makes it both less necessary to allocate spectrum via auction and less costly to acquire unlicensed spectrum via auction.[10] Indeed, while auctions may be important as part of the transition mechanism to market-based management, allocating additional spectrum for unlicensed could be incorporated in this framework (e.g., as a transition mechanism).[11] Indeed, with the realization of effective reform, auctions will be less necessary to ensure efficient assignment (i.e., secondary market trading of licensed spectrum can achieve this) and to ensure fair sharing of the benefits from spectrum access (e.g., unlicensed and licensed coexisting and lower opportunity costs overall mean allocation of windfalls is less of an issue).

In summary therefore, both the flexible licensed and unlicensed regimes are deregulatory – without eliminating regulation, are consistent with scarcity – while anticipating that artificial scarcity will be greatly diminished, and are consistent with markets managing flexible use of the spectrum.

The Real Difference Between Licensed and Unlicensed Use

The essential difference between the two regimes is that flexible licensing assigns an "exclusive use" property right to the licensee to transmit; whereas the unlicensed regime assigns a nonexclusive right to all potential users to transmit. The principle motivation for the exclusive use right is to protect the licensee's use of the spectrum from other, potentially interfering transmitters. By making this property right/license tradable and by eliminating constraints on how the licensee uses the spectrum (what services are offered or what technology is used), a flexible licensing regime induces the licensee to internalize the opportunity cost of spectrum scarcity.

In contrast, in the unlicensed/open use model, no potential user has an exclusive right to transmit. In a theoretically perfect world without transaction or adjustment costs, the unlicensed model may appear to offer less powerful incentives to use spectrum efficiently. However, in the imperfect world, we actually inhabit with incomplete markets and where there are transaction and switching costs, concerns about market power and ongoing regulation remain a reality, it is unlikely that social opportunity costs of spectrum use will be fully internalized by a flexible, exclusive-use licensee. An economic comparison of the licensed and unlicensed models is much more complex than suggested above.

First, the flexible licensing approach represents an incremental improvement over the existing regime which already uses licenses to manage the majority of commercial spectrum. In contrast, the unlicensed model represents a more radical form of reform. In light of the inherent bias in political processes in favor of the status quo, this induces an inherent bias in favor of flexible licensing over the unlicensed model. The former is closer to what we have always done and what industry and policymakers understand.

Second, under the flexible licensing regime, the licensee can exclude other users even if there is no real spectrum scarcity.[12] That is, the licensee can choose to use its control of the license to induce artificial scarcity whenever that is consistent with its private interests (even when social welfare would be enhanced by allowing excluded users access). Certainly, in the past, a key feature of spectrum policy has been its use in shaping industry structure by limiting access to specific licensees. Hazlett (2001) documents the role of over-the-air broadcasters in the USA in opposing the allocation of additional broadcasting licenses, and thereby slowing the adoption of technologies like UHF television and FM radio. Similarly, mobile carriers in some markets have opposed the allocation of additional 3G licenses, fearing the implications of excess competition. Although it is certainly the hope that major reform, including the promotion of secondary markets, will preclude the market power that makes such abuses both feasible and likely, this hope may be only imperfectly realized. If market power remains an issue, then the risk will remain that exclusive licenses will be used to enforce ongoing artificial scarcity.

Third, the two models do imply different industry economics. The flexible licensing approach favors the network-centric service provider model, whereas the unlicensed approach favors the equipment-centric end-user model. The former implies more centralized management of spectrum while the latter is more distributed and decentralized. Which is better may depend on the circumstances and ones perspective. It is certainly no accident that most communication and broadcasting services are supported via businesses with a service-provider model (i.e., an integrated network that is owned and managed by single business entity is used to deliver services). This structure facilitates making coordinated decisions about management of the network and the spectrum that is used. This may facilitate the internalization of externalities over a wider region (e.g., when a provider offers wireless services over a metro-sized area) and if the network and frequency used are cospecialized (e.g., when the technology used is not frequency agile). New smart radio systems, however, make it increasingly feasible to decouple frequencies and radio networks and to manage interference in a decentralized fashion. With unlicensed spectrum, it is possible to build up a network from end-user equipment that can be linked in an ad hoc, wireless mesh. This supports viral, edge-based growth and offers an interesting alternative to the service-provider-based model that has traditionally dominated telecommunication services, including wireless services.

Models for Unlicensed Access: Primary Versus Secondary Use Underlays and Overlays

Certainly, the flexible licensing regime represents an improvement over the current regime of inflexible licensing. As an incremental improvement, for a regulatory economist, it seems hard to oppose.[13] Likewise, the complete abandonment of licensing in favor of unlicensed access for all spectra seems far too radical a departure from existing practice to be either desirable or politically feasible. However, this latter approach is not even under consideration. Rather, mainstream spectrum reformers are advocating a mixed approach that makes use of both the licensed and unlicensed models.[14]

While explicitly recommending a role for unlicensed, the mainstream reformers have relegated unlicensed to a secondary and more marginal role for the highest value, lower frequency spectrum. There are a number of good reasons for this outcome, which are worth considering, but they do not tell the whole story (as I explain in the next section). There are two basic approaches for implementing unlicensed access: primary or dedicated access and secondary access. There are two types of secondary access: underlays and overlays.

Underlay access allows secondary use of the spectrum by transmitters that operate at low-power levels, in the noise floor of licensed spectrum. An example of such an underlay technology is Ultrawideband that spreads the signal over a very wide bandwidth to limit the power emitted in any particular frequency band. The requirement to operate at low-power limits the range of underlay devices. This fits well with the view that a "commons" management scheme is well-suited to managing spectrum use conflicts/interference among a few users/transmitters in a locally concentrated area (e.g., within a home). There is a compelling need today for high-bandwidth wireless services to substitute for cabling (e.g., among stereo components) or to support WLANs. While it is certainly true that unlicensed has an important role to play in such situations, the converse is not universally true. While some wide area applications or providers may prefer the protection against interference afforded by an exclusive license, this is not necessary to ensure coordination and adequate interference protection.

The second type of secondary-use "easement" is overlay access. An overlay device is allowed to transmit when the primary-use licensee is not using the spectrum. This could be defined in the spatial domain (e.g., rural areas that a broadcaster is not currently serving) or time domain (e.g., when the primary licensee is not transmitting using "listen-before-talking" technology). The unlicensed overlay devices would use appropriate sensing technology to determine when the spectrum is free to transmit. Collectively, the devices that are able to modify their operation dynamically in response to local radio frequency conditions are referred to as "cognitive radios."[15]

As noted earlier, most mainstream policymakers advocate allocating most of the high-value, lower frequency spectrum to exclusive-use licensed primary users, with only minimal (if any) expansion of primary (dedicated) spectrum for unlicensed use. An important rationale for this approach is that unlicensed needs can be adequately met by secondary access via either overlays or underlays.[16] There is an obvious appeal to this approach since all transmitters in primary (dedicated) unlicensed spectrum are *secondary* users since no one has a right to exclude any other qualified user. In contrast, with licensed spectrum, the licensee with the exclusive right clearly has a primary claim to the spectrum.

While appealing, there are several problems with this view. First, the attempt to define overlays or underlays represents an attempt to circumscribe exclusive spectrum licenses to limit their scope, so that the licenses only protect against destructive interference. By its very nature, this exercise requires ongoing government regulation of the technology because today's "white space" is tomorrow's operating region for the licensee. Further encumbering the licenses will hamper the emergence of secondary markets and will retain regulatory constraints that the move to flexible licensing is intended to eliminate. Second, in part because of the valid concern just mentioned and in part because of a resistance to any reduction in existing rights, there is strong opposition to the creation of such secondary-use access rights for unlicensed devices. It might be easier to mobilize support for an additional allocation of dedicated unlicensed spectrum than for underlay or overlay rights. Third, ultrawideband and cognitive radio technologies are still under development and their technical and commercial viabilities remain speculative. While it seems likely that these technologies will be important, licensees have valid concerns that sharing licensed spectrum with these will cause interference and management problems that might be better addressed by segregating these access models.

In the next section, I explain why unlicensed access model is important and should be regarded as appropriate for more than (in addition to) secondary access.

Benefits of Unlicensed Spectrum Model

As noted earlier, the move to flexible licensing is more consistent with a smooth evolution of regulatory policy from a model of centralized command and control to management by markets. However, sole reliance on this model (or relegating unlicensed users to only secondary access) would be a mistake. In this section, I discuss three important reasons for why the unlicensed model is attractive and likely to be increasingly important in the future.

More Consistent with Trajectory of Technology and Market Trends

While the past may belong to a world of exclusive-use licenses, the future belongs increasingly to unlicensed. The unlicensed model is more consistent with the trajectory of technology and with market trends.

First, the trajectory of technological innovation in wireless services has made frequencies more substitutable. It is much easier to accommodate divergent uses in the same frequency band or to support the same uses at different frequency bands. Innovations in signal processing, antenna design, and modulation schemes have significantly increased the information carrying capacity of existing spectrum. Collectively, these innovations have made spectrum less scarce.

While scarcity remains an issue, it is reasonable to suppose that the acute (largely artificial) scarcity that has characterized spectrum in recent years and underlies the high prices paid for spectrum at auction will be greatly reduced by appropriate reform. Such reform should and is likely to include a substantial increase in the amount of commercial spectrum managed via flexible licenses that can be traded on secondary markets. In this future world, maximizing spectral efficiency may no longer be as important as other considerations in the choice of management regime. For example, it may be more important to provide low-cost entry for new services or technologies, or to minimize spectrum transaction costs. As spectrum scarcity declines, the opportunity cost of spectrum declines and the relative importance of any transaction costs becomes more important. Ceteris paribus, the reduction in scarcity makes unlicensed more attractive.

Second, technology has been evolving so as to decouple wireless services from specific frequency bands. Intelligence is moving into all components of radio systems. Smart radio systems enable more robust, lower power, higher data rate communications over longer distances. Smart receivers increase options for managing interference, empowering more decentralized and distributed models for spectrum management. Software radios able to support multiple protocols and capable of dynamically shifting frequencies reduce the extent to which services and much of network infrastructure (e.g., towers and wired connections to base stations) are cospecialized with particular frequencies.

Third, the transition to wireless broadband will increase the dynamic range of bandwidth requirements that will need to be supported. This will increase the opportunity cost associated with retaining the excess bandwidth needed to support high peak-to-average data rate traffic, increasing the benefits from sharing access to spectrum across multiple service providers.

Fourth, and finally, providing for more unlicensed is consistent with the growth of a more complex and heterogeneous wireless landscape. The future will not be composed of a single wireless network or technology. Rather there are likely to be multiple types of networks operating at a variety of geographic ranges, offering a range of capabilities, and implemented using many protocols and architectures. In this multiprotocol chaos, systems will adapt to become more tolerant of this sort of world. The transition to smart radio systems is more consistent with unlicensed and with the emergence of this heterogeneous wireless future.

Helps Promote Competition and Innovation

Allocating additional spectrum for unlicensed use also helps promote competition by making it easier for new services, networks, and architectures to deploy. Unlicensed facilitates the distributed and decentralized growth of equipment or edge-based networking technologies such as ad hoc or mesh networks. Islands of connectivity can be created by end-users and then linked together to virally grow alternative infrastructure. This could be an important source for last-mile competition for access services.

Exclusive licenses create the potential for artificial scarcity which might be used to foreclose new technologies or competition that threatens incumbent providers. As long as spectrum is scarce (and the presumption of such scarcity is used to justify the need for exclusive licensing in the first place), such ex ante foreclosure remains a risk. Additionally, there is a risk of ex post foreclosure. Technologies or services which turn out to be more successful than originally anticipated are liable to expropriation by a spectrum licensee if it turns out that the technology/service turns out not to be frequency agile. Control of the spectrum might be used to expropriate the value of customer premise equipment. Consider whether WiFi would have been as successful if purchasers of equipment faced uncertain future charges from third-party spectrum licensees to operate WLAN base stations. While it is both possible and likely that equipment makers can purchase spectrum also, unlicensed will remain an important option to foster small scale and experimental entry.

Unlicensed will also foster adoption of interference-tolerant, intelligent radio systems. To the extent operation in unlicensed spectrum suffers from congestion, the systems that will thrive there will be ones that are more interference tolerant. This may include both uses that simply care less about interference protection and so do not wish to pay for the added benefits afforded by operation under in exclusive licensed spectrum, or embody technologies that make it feasible to operate in uncertain and fluctuating congestion environments. Technologies that survive when there is a risk of a "Tragedy of the Commons" are those that either do not care or can ameliorate its impacts.

Helps Future-Proof Policy

Providing for unlicensed access both via more dedicated unlicensed and through targeted easements to allow unlicensed secondary access via underlays and overlays helps future-proof policy.

The future of wireless services and technology is too uncertain to determine what services should exist in which frequency bands. The structure of the communications industry is too uncertain to determine which business models or market structures will best support future networking needs.

If the debate over licensed versus unlicensed spectrum does nothing else, it demonstrates that there is consensus that the two models imply different regulatory and industry economics (even if disagreements continue as to which is better). The availability of unlicensed spectrum provides a safety valve for competitive entry and business models that may be less successful in flexible licensed spectrum. Some of these may choose to migrate to licensed spectrum when they grow up. Because spectrum at different frequencies has very different physical properties (e.g., antenna size, propagation properties, line of sight requirements), it is important to adequately provide for *both* unlicensed and licensed spectrum models in the higher value, lower frequency spectrum to ensure that the choice of regulatory model does not bias the evolution of the wireless future.

Conclusions

While there is growing consensus in many countries that there is a need to transition from command and control models for spectrum management to more market-based modes, implementing reform is providing very difficult. Holders of exclusive licenses do not want to see their rights circumscribed by the granting of new secondary-use easements. They do not want to be forced to pay more for spectrum they already occupy or to face competition from competitors able to exploit any new allocation of lower cost commercial spectrum. Entrants and consumer advocates are concerned that the incumbents may benefit unfairly if flexibility is provided for their exclusive licenses without compensation. All parties are bargaining over the allocation of surplus, the windfall gains, that are anticipated by the transition to a more efficient spectrum management regime. Not surprisingly, managing the transition to a new regime is difficult. Allocating additional spectrum to *both* flexible licensed *and* unlicensed uses can make this easier by helping to co-opt the opposition.

The future of wireless services will be for spectrum to be shared more intensively than it is today in most bands (with the exception of mobile service bands which in many markets are already at capacity). However, even with mobile services, it is reasonable to expect that it will be advantageous to share access to 3G spectrum, rather than allocate all of the spectra needed for each potential provider to support the full spectrum of anticipated services. These carriers may wish to manage their collective 3G spectrum as a private commons (i.e., shared access among a closed user community). Whether spectrum is shared via private or public commons, unlicensed has a role to play in helping to develop the necessary technologies and business models.

If we fail to allocate additional spectrum for unlicensed use in the highest value, lower frequency spectrum, we will never know what might have been. If we are successful in expanding commercial access to flexible use licensed spectrum but not of unlicensed, we will simply never observe what sorts of technologies or business models might have developed. We will have locked in only those equilibria that are possible in a world of exclusively licensed spectrum. No one will be able to measure the value of technologies that never develop or come to market. Because this world is closer to the status quo we have today, and is premised on a high marginal cost for incremental spectrum, if this model continues to result in significant artificial scarcity, it will appear as if the arguments in favor of licensed spectrum were correct.

The success of WiFi in recent years should caution policymakers against foreclosing alternative business models. WiFi operates in the 2.4 GHz band that was considered garbage spectrum because it was already so encumbered with noise (e.g., microwave ovens). The global growth of WiFi equipment markets, networks, and services has been exponential; and while it still accounts for substantially less activity than is associated with mobile wireless services and may not be suitable for building basic access infrastructure (i.e., not "carrier-grade"), it has had a profound impact on the trajectory of all wireless services. It has caused industry participants all along the value chain to rethink wireless futures. Mobile carriers are now looking at ways to incorporate WiFi access into their 3G architectures and new types of service providers (e.g., WISPs and power companies) are using WiFi as part of their last-mile alternative infrastructure plans.[17] To ensure that this sort of innovation continues and to realize the benefits of significant spectrum management reform, it is important that the role for unlicensed access models be expanded.

Notes

1. *See* Kolodzy (2002) or Ofcom (2004).
2. Eliminating artificial constraints on spectrum which currently block entry of new wireless technologies and services (and constrain the expansion of existing ones like mobile services) will expand total demand also, so it is not possible to predict a priori what the future equilibrium marginal price for spectrum will be. However, there are many technical innovations that have yet to be widely adopted that could greatly expand the capacity of wireless systems (e.g., smart radios systems, new modulation, and signal processing techniques). Reforms that encourage the adoption of such technologies will also expand the "marginal supply" of accessible spectrum.
3. *See* Comments of 37 Concerned Economists (2001).
4. I refer to "flexible licensing" to distinguish the new model from the legacy model that also uses spectrum licenses to manage access.
5. For leading economists supporting the "flexible licensed" model, *see* Cave (2002), Faulhaber and Farber (2002), Hazlett (2001), or Kwerel and Williams (2002). Among the economists, exceptions include Lehr (2004) and Noam (1995). Support for the unlicensed model has been lead by engineers and lawyers [*see*, e.g., Benkler (2002), Lessig (2001), Reed (2002), and Werbach (2003)].
6. *See* Kolodzy (2002) or Ofcom (2004).
7. There are still many issues (technical, business, and policy) associated with adopting an unlicensed management approach that need to be worked out and movement to unlicensed as the sole approach would represent far too dramatic a departure from the status quo for it to even be politically feasible.
8. I refer to the labeling of spectrum management models as "caricatures" because the simple taxonomy overstates the complexity in rules, and understates the significant progress that the FCC and other regulatory bodies have made in reforming rules for at least certain bands over time. For example, the PCS mobile telephone bands in the USA were first licenses to be auctioned. They allow licensees flexible choices with respect to the technology adopted, the services offered, and other features regarding how the spectrum is used.
9. Indeed, if spectrum courts are specialized administrative courts (which seems plausible), then they may be only marginally different from expert agencies with regards to their vulnerability to influence costs.
10. As long as there are active secondary markets for spectrum and prices on those markets are not excessive, spectrum can be efficiently assigned regardless of whether it was originally auctioned or not.
11. As in the "Big Bang" auction suggested by Kwerel and Williams (2002), Ikeda and Ye (2003) suggest a mechanism of spectrum buyouts to transition to open spectrum.
12. Real spectrum scarcity arises when it would not be socially efficient to allow additional transmitters to share the spectrum. This may occur either for technical reasons (i.e., given the current state of technology, allowing the excluded transmitters would result in destructive interference) or for economic reasons (i.e., while it is technically feasible to allow the transmitters to share the spectrum, the total benefit would exceed the total cost of making the necessary technical adjustments).
13. *See* Comments by 37 Concerned Economists (2001).

14. Most countries still rely heavily on the legacy command and control model for managing spectrum, and if considering reform, are following a much more incremental approach. Among the countries that have adopted major reform agendas, the USA (*see* Kolodzy, 2002) and UK (*see* Ofcom, 2004) are representative. The more radical approach of a complete transition to flexible licensing/property rights is relatively rare, with Guatemala an oft-cited example (*see* Hazlett, 2002), and no country as transitioned to a complete "unlicensed" model.
15. *See* Lehr et al. (2003) for discussion of cognitive or software radios.
16. *See* Farber and Faulhaber (2002).
17. *See* Lehr et al. (2004) and Lehr and McKnight (2003).

References

Benkler, Yochai, "Some Economics of Wireless Communications," *16 Harvard Journal of Law and Technology* 25 (2002).

Cave, Martin, "Review of Radio Spectrum Management," Independent Review Report prepared for Department of Trade and Industry, United Kingdom, March 2002 (available from. http://www.ofcom.org.uk/static/archive/ra/spectrum-review/index.htm).

Comments of 37 Concerned Economists, In the Matter of Promoting Efficient use of Spectrum through Elimination of Barriers to the Development of Secondary Markets, Before the Federal Communications Commission, WT Docket No. 00–230, February 7, 2001.

Faulhaber, Gerald R. and David Farber, "Spectrum Management: Property Rights, Markets, and the Commons," AEI-Brookings Joint Center, Working Paper 02–12, December 2002.

Hazlett, Thomas, "The Wireless Craze, the Unlimited Bandwidth Myth, the Spectrum Auction Faux Pas, and the Punchline to Ronald Coase's 'Big Joke': An Essay on Airwave Allocation Policy," Harvard Journal of Law and Technology (Spring 2001).

Ikeda, Nobuo and Lixin Ye, "Spectrum Buyouts: A Mechanism to Open Spectrum," Draft paper, October 17, 2003.

Kolodzy, Paul, *Spectrum Policy Task Force*, Office of Engineering & Technology, Federal Communications Commission, November 2002.

Kwerel, Evan and John Williams, "A Proposal for a Rapid Transition to Market Allocation of Spectrum," OPP Working Paper #38, Federal Communications Commission, November 2002.

Lehr, William, "Economic Case for Dedicated Unlicensed Spectrum Below 3 GHz," paper prepared for New America Foundation Conference, April 2004.

Lehr, William and Lee McKnight, "Wireless Internet Access: 3G vs. WiFi?" *Telecommunications Policy*, 27 (2003) 351–370.

Lehr, William, Sharon Gillett, and Fuencisla Merino, "Software Radio: Implications for Wireless Services, Industry Structure, and Public Policy," *Communications and Strategies*, IDATE, Issue 49 (1st Quarter 2003) 15–42.

Lehr, William, Marvin Sirbu, and Sharon Gillett, "Municipal Wireless Broadband: Policy and Business Implications of Emerging Access Technologies," paper prepared for "Competition in Networking: Wireless and Wireline," London Business School, April 13–14, 2004.

Lessig, Lawrence, The Future of Ideas: The Fate of the Commons in a Connected World, New York: Random House, 2001.

Noam, Eli, "Taking the Next Step Towards Open Spectrum Access," *IEEE Communications Magazine*, 33 (1995) 66.

Ofcom, "Spectrum Framework Review: A consultation on Ofcom's views as to how radio spectrum should be managed," UK Communications Regulatory Authority, November 23, 2004 (available at: http://www.ofcom.org.uk/consultations/current/sfr/sfr.pdf?a=87101).

Reed, David, "How Wireless Networks Scale: The Illusion of Spectrum Scarcity," presentation slides to FCC Technology Advisory Council, Washington, DC, April 26, 2002 (available at: http://www.jacksons.net/tac/Spectrum%20capacity%20myth%20FCC%20TAC.pdf).

Werbach, Kevin, "Radio Revolution: The Coming Age of Unlicensed Wireless," white paper prepared for New America Foundation, Washington, DC, December 2003.

Chapter 12
You Can Lead a Horse to Water but You Can't Make It Drink: The Music Industry and Peer-to-Peer

Alain Bourdeau de Fontenay and Eric Bourdeau de Fontenay

Introduction

It is easy to outline a new strategy. To succeed in its implementation is another matter, especially where there is a large historical baggage. There is no question that the music sector has been facing a major challenge since the 1990s and that it correctly places peer-to-peer as the core issue. It is also obvious that the music industry's strategy has been steadfast in defending today's institutions and the associated "illegality" of peer-to-peer. That has meant that it has marshaled, very successfully, huge resources to ensure that the "illegality" remains unchallenged. That has meant making sure that institutions were preserved if not reinforced to establish the "illegality" of the activities of peer-to-peer networks as well as those of file sharers of copyrighted materials. In its management of peer-to-peer, the music industry has been exceptionally successful in the court, success that can only have reinforced the music industry's instinctual culture of defending the existing nature of copyrights. The same does not hold for the music industry's business performance.

The industry has shown its willingness to use resources to sue those who have been downloading illegal files as to undermine peer-to-peer in other ways, such as hacking peer-to-peer networks as well as poisoning songs (Gibbs, 2002; Koman, 2007). Here also, policies have "unintended consequences, creating incentives to address the hacking and poisoning problem (Christin et al., 2005; Krishnan et al., 2003; Steinmueller, 2008).

The established orthodoxy of a one-to-one link between file sharing and sale of CDs has been the cornerstone of the music industry approach. Peer-to-peer is said to be single-handedly responsible for the industry's crisis. This is a position that has

A. Bourdeau de Fontenay (✉)
Senior Affiliated Researcher with Columbia Institute for Tele-information, Columbia University, New York, NY, USA
email: ad2239@columbia.edu

W.H. Lehr and L.M. Pupillo (eds.), *Internet Policy and Economics*,
DOI 10.1007/978-1-4419-0038-8_12,

been largely accepted by governments as illustrated by the trend in Europe to penalize individuals who download music "illegally" as well as by many court decisions, most visibly the US Supreme Court Decision. We have seen that the economic literature has taken a more nuanced approach to the problem. Steinmueller (2008) raises questions about the legality of the RIAA strategy.

Our central argument is that it is rather for reasons that are internal to RIAA and the labels that the RIAA's strategy is costly and harmful to RIAA and its stated objective to further the growth of the sector. The strategy is inconsistent with a commercial goal built on the sector's growth and it hampers the sector's effectiveness to develop imaginative business cases that are responsive to the new expectations which peer-to-peer has created among customers. With such a frame of mind, it is hard to imagine how those stakeholders will be able to credibly turn toward the future and build a business that takes advantage of a technology that consumers have so wholeheartedly adopted. After all, other firms in other sectors have rarely been able to achieve such a turn around.

Independently, there is now a large econometric literature that looks at the way by which peer-to-peer is supposed to have affected the industry. Those quantitative estimates are ambiguous with many questioning whether peer-to-peer did any harm to the industry, whereas many others concluding that peer-to-peer has contributed to lower the industry's sales of CDs. Even in those situations, the results are far from being as dramatic as argued by the industry and as accepted by governments.

More recently, the music sector has begun, in parallel with its legal strategy, to push a multiobjective strategy that recognizes the technological changes the sector is going through and the need for new approaches (Krishnan et al., 2007). This has been translated by a concerted effort to seek new approaches and new business models that would bring back the sector's high profitability of the late-1980s and early-1990s. But pronouncements and even good intentions are unlikely to act as an effective counterweight to the large sunk costs which the old routines have created. We would like to suggest that this why, "the early potential benefits are outweighed by the destabilization to established profitable ways" (Noam, 2008).

Whatever new products emerge from the transformation of the music industry and whichever way the industry chooses to tackle the peer-to-peer challenge, RIAA recognizes that, like it or not, file sharing is here to stay. The question is whether the industry should continue along today's course or open a new path, integrating peer-to-peer in its business strategy. The complementary concern, one that will be introduced in this chapter, is whether the industry has a chance to succeed in promoting a more commercially oriented strategy. Maintaining the present course means learning to live with a large population of potential customers who choose file sharing as an alternative way to obtain some of their music. The status quo has many characteristics that suggest instability in the long run. Integrating peer-to-peer in the industry's commercial activities by developing new products is a challenge. However, if we look at the experience gained in other industries, it would seem that the music industry's challenge in developing new business strategies is probably even more cultural internal to the industry than technical (Besanko et al., 2007; Nagle and Hogan, 2006). This means nothing less than changing the roots of the firms' culture so as to be able to fit under the new conditions (Tripsas and Gavetti, 2004). The challenge those stakeholders face is the rigidity of their culture and the inertia of routines, dimensions that tend to be those firms' Achilles Heel (Nelson and Winter, 1982). The problem is compounded by the government protection which takes primarily the form of enforcement of copyrights.

The old English saying, "You can lead a horse to water but you can't make it drink" describes well the challenge that RIAA and the industry face when refocusing their business strategy toward online services in light of its legal success. In this chapter, we are interested in the implications of the saying for the music industry's management for its new, pro-online services strategy. We develop what Malerba et al. (2008) have called a "user-friendly" analysis of the music industry, one that is highly simplified and highly stylized but one that highlights important issues that have been largely ignored, reflecting the industry's almost exclusive concern with "illegal file sharing."

Looking at the music industry from that broader perspective shows that there is little that is music-specific in the way the industry has been responding to peer-to-peer. RIAA's response looks very much like the response of many other firms in many other sectors that find themselves face-to-face to a disruptive innovation. This is good news for the music industry since it means that it can learn from the experience gained in those other sectors. Tushman and O'Reilly (1996) have shown how well-run, innovative firms often fail to exploit major technological changes that may have emerged from inventions made in their research facilities as with the Swiss watch industry which invented the quartz motor that Seiko exploited (Tushman and Radov, 2000a, 2000b). Even more significant is Xerox's inability to exploit the inventions that flowed from PARC, Xerox's Palo Alto research laboratory, one of the most prolific research facilities of all time (Chesbrough and Rosenbloom, 2002).

From a methodological perspective, we complement our economic analysis, including the post-neoclassical economic literature, with contributions from the management of innovation literature. While our analysis is heuristic, we chose in many instances to analyze the problems using a post-neoclassical framework, even if in many instances there are results from the mainstream economic literature that could have been used. Our methodological choice is due to the nonfalsifiable, hence unscientific nature of much of today's neoclassical analysis, as applied to the present problem. There is also a pragmatic dimension to our approach, namely that, at least in the present context, it forces one to probe further results that have become established truths; hence, "that much can be learned by uncovering durable economic principles that are applicable to many different strategic situations" (Besanko et al., 2007).

For instance, we argue in this chapter that it is inadequate to study "the optimal copyright law" without studying factors such as the institutional setting, say the behavior of individuals with respect to file sharing, and the market structure considering, for instance, the incentive of the various intermediaries to invest in shaping those laws to their benefit (Liebowitz and Watt, 2006). Whatever the merits of that literature in other contexts, in a dynamic world that is going through discontinuous transformations as a result of innovations such as peer-to-peer and with dimensions such as learning and firms' behaviors that are path dependent, we show that the usefulness of optimal copyright laws is restricted and potentially misleading.

Beyond the legal success, the industry has shown its willingness to put resources to sue those who have been downloading "illegally" copyrighted files as to undermine peer-to-peer in other ways, such as hacking peer-to-peer networks and poisoning songs (Gibbs, 2002; Koman, 2007). Here also, policies have "unintended consequences," creating incentives to address the hacking and poisoning problem (Christin et al., 2005; Krishnan et al., 2003; Malan and Smith, 2005; Steinmueller, 2008). In this chapter, we do not focus on this aspect of RIAA's strategy since its impact not so much on its business case, in spite of comments such as Koman, is not obviously harmful. Those individuals who download "illegally" copyrighted material are unlikely to buy fewer or more CDs and/or commercial online services in response to such actions. It is to say that it is doubtful short of a quantitative study with unambiguous results that it would have a significant impact on today's business case. Liebowitz and Watt (2006) suggest that many would probably not buy CDs in the absence of peer-to-peer. It is doubtful that those who are and/or would buy music would decide to retaliate against the industry by stopping to buy music.

Recently, the music sector has begun, in parallel with its legal strategy, to push a multiobjective strategy that recognizes the technological changes the sector is going through and the need for new approaches (Krishnan et al., 2007). This has been translated by a concerted effort to seek new approaches and new business models that would bring back the sector's high profitability of the late-1980s and early-1990s. This is a necessary step but it is only a small step which in and of itself is inadequate to solve the music industry's business problems.

Although we do not have a magic wand, we observe that firms often falter under such challenges whereas some flourish. In the late-1980s, information service providers, including AOL, were still making their living by charging end-users by the minute when a new entrant, Prodigy, chose to offer a flat rate predicated upon a high-growth strategy. AOL did respond to the challenge and, eventually, became the one which achieved the highest growth rate to eventually dominate the industry.

In the next section, we rapidly discuss some of the data that have been used to assess peer-to-peer's impact on the music industry, and then in the following section, we review briefly the econometric literature. Our objective is to provide some background to basic pitfalls which the industry is facing as it is refocusing on profitability. One of those is the common orthodoxy of whether peer-to-peer might have harmed the sales of CDs.

In the third section, we discuss the role which the majors and others play as intermediaries between the artists and the general public. Then we show that beyond intermediation, the industry contributes to the internalization of the externalities that are inherent, in a world without intermediaries, between artists and consumers. This leads us to argue that one should study the sector on the basis of a two-sided market. We argue that this will have to be incorporated in the economic analysis and that its implications for the intermediaries' strategy are still to be studied. An immediate conclusion is that marginal product-based pricing is not generally economically efficient even in the most formal neoclassical specification.

In the fourth section, we turn toward the industry's highly successful legal strategy, highly successful when assessed in terms of victories in courts. Those victories have all the characteristics of Pyrrhic victories as the majors have not come out of the slump they have been in since the late-1990s and peer-to-peer is now so deeply embedded in today's culture that as RIAA acknowledges, "more than half of the nation's college students frequently download music… 'illegally' from unlicensed peer-to-peer networks." From a business perspective, it is hard to find much more than defeat. Yet, RIAA also states that its mission is to help, "…the music business thrive. Our goal is to foster a business and legal climate that protects the ability of our members – the record companies that create, manufacture, and/or distribute some 90 percent of all legitimate sound recordings produced and sold in the United States – to invest in the next generation of music." This leads us to question whether it is the industry's effort to entrench copyrights in a rigid framework rather than managing the legality more creatively may not still be a factor that hampers the industry's commercial effort.

In the last section, we argue that this industry is not all that different from other industries and that, like many industries, it falters on its inability to transform itself in response to peer-to-peer. Evidently, it is now taking a proactive role toward online business but, again, if we go by what we learn from other industries, this is not even the first step. We would like to suggest that there is a lot of merit in paraphrasing (Nagle and Hogan, 2006): "Transforming your company… is challenging. Interestingly,… [t]he real change comes from changing ingrained behaviors and beliefs that limit the company's ability to proactively manage customers and competitors in a way that maximizes profitability."

What Have They Observed?

Science progresses from observation to theory and from theory to observation. Both theory and observation are limited in their ability to provide reliable support for decision making and it is the responsibility of scientific research to clearly identify the scope of the analysis and the reliability of the conclusions and analysis upon which those conclusions are derived. For instance, economists usually restrict their conclusions to questions of economic efficiency and rarely address issues of social welfare.

The proper function of science is to question established knowledge in order to extend it further. This means identifying and analyzing new dimensions, the economist's "unintended consequences." In the next two sections, our objective is to highlight lacuna in existing data sources in the way that they can be used to address policy questions and in the ways existing theories are being used. We intend to make up for some of those shortcomings through analogies with other sectors of the economy.

There appears at first sight plenty of data to quantify how peer-to-peer has been changing the industry. Hence, it should be easy to establish peer-to-peer's impact on the industry. The US Supreme Court's decision that MGM Studios v. Grokster, Ltd. 545 US 913 illustrates how prevalent the view that peer-to-peer has been harmful has been outside the academic community. Evidently, such a conclusion is highly dependent on certain data sources that highlight the sheer magnitude of file sharing. However, Liebowitz (2006)'s review of the data sources for one shows that the data are not as helpful as one might want. The data problem impacts most dimensions associated with music file sharing. This is illustrated by Supreme Court's decision and the empirical data upon which it primarily relies. The inconsistencies in the data help understand the difference in perspective with the 2004 District Court's decision. The Supreme Court chose to focus on what it saw as the magnitude of file sharing downloads itself based on the source which the court chose to rely on ("billions of files are shared across peer-to-peer networks each month"). In addition, the court associated uncritical downloads with the industry's shortfall. "Billions" convinced it that other factors such as the benefits from innovation were dwarfed by the harm on the sector that it traced to those "billions." Liebowitz (2006) finds an extreme dispersion in the estimates of downloads across different sources. He identifies the largest estimates, IDATE's estimates (that are consistent with the numbers cited by the court 20 time larger than NPD's estimates), as an outlier. Liebowitz's chosen data source appears also to be an outlier, at the other end of the spectrum. He argues that "file sharing activity, instead of surpassing the legitimate music business in size, is actually considerably dwarfed by the legitimate market." Whether one agrees with Liebowitz's assessment of the other sources, there seems to be merit to his contention that "some of IDATE's prognostications appear rather incredible." The court's reaction reminds us of the assertions that were made about the incredible growth of Internet in the late-1990s, factor that led to the dot-com collapse in 2000. At the same time, the data that Liebowitz selects are even more surprising unless one can establish that consumers are indifferent between the various medium, CD versus online, especially peer-to-peer.

What matters here is to highlight how little we know about the scope of peer-to-peer file sharing and how one has to be skeptical in quantifying peer-to-peer's impact without a critical economic analysis of the underlying economic forces. However, while unreliable data leads one to question the econometric estimates of the impact of file sharing on the sales of album, this should not even be the industry's senior management's and the policymakers' primary concern. We argue that the problem is more serious and that even if the data were perfect, whether peer-to-peer can be shown to have caused a fall in the sale of CDs distracts management from the real business questions they have to address and misleads decision makers.

Nevertheless, the kind of numbers the court refers to and the way academics and policymakers have been using them raise additional questions. For instance, one would have to be able to explain how peer-to-peer-based consumption has increased by such a magnitude, that is so unrelated to experience while using marginal-type analyses. If it is nothing more than a response to price, and this seems to be the court's position, then one would have to develop reasonable arguments for such an extreme elasticity. The numbers cited by the Supreme Court were to have a minimum of credibility when combined with the court's analytical framework, and if one could overlook the change in nature in the good would suggest an industry that has been overpricing CDs to its own detriment – evidently, this is based upon the almost universal, implicit assumption that a CD and a peer-to-peer's download are essential undistinguishable. If this were not the case, then the arguments that substantiate the court's decision are even less convincing. To the extent that those data played a central role and to the extent the court's economic analysis fails to recognize the significance of the contributions of many economists, it is realistic to imagine that with time, the decisions will become increasingly marginalized. If it conflicts so much with the actual environment, it is likely that the industry, de facto, will contribute significantly to such marginalization.

There are other dimensions that will further contribute through time to the decision's progressive marginalization. For instance, there is every indication that the peer-to-peer file sharing population is heterogeneous and that the industry as it shifts from a legal focus to a business strategy will increasingly segment the file sharing population, what Nagle and Hogan (2006) stress is a fundamental requirement for a profit-focused strategy (Becker and Clement, 2006; Bhattacharjee et al., 2006 ; Bounie et al., 2005; Einav, 2008).

One of the ways by which this will be achieved is that the institutions will become endogenous, managed and shaped for their contribution to profits. In particular, it is the industry that is likely to contribute the most to that marginalization to the extent that it is hard to reconcile with likely business strategies. In the meantime, the industry's strategy that is focused on reinforcing "illegality" has led to an interpretation that is even more restrictive. Effectively, it is as if the music world, and the CD, and people's tastes had stood still unchanged for 10 years. This means that it relies upon the assumption that there has not been an online revolution nor any business fluctuations and that no other external forces have intervened.

We conclude from Liebowitz's review of the available data that they are too inconsistent with each other to support any sound business and/or policy decisions better than a purely heuristic approach. This reinforces our conclusion that there is no econometric evidence in support of the US Supreme Court's decision, even if many econometric studies, used uncritically, provide some support for the court's decision. The problem is the court's inability to apply simple, common-sense-based economic tool to introduce many considerations that have a significant bearing on how to interpret peer-to-peer. For instance, it overlooks how peer-to-peer has transformed the "music good" as an element in her utility function, that is, how it has transformed the demand for music regardless of price (Bourdeau de Fontenay et al., 2008).

Those are some of the problems that lead us to extend economic analyses by Gayer and Shy (2005) and Hughes et al. (2008), as we fully agree with Liebowitz's emphasis upon the need for sound economic analysis. The question is not one of sophistication but of insuring that analytical results far from being misleading contribute rather to sound decision making. There is a need to assess the industry on the basis of solid economic theory in order to better understand peer-to-peer file sharing problem if we are to provide results that are helpful to all stakeholders.

One of the most important flaws in many of today's economic analyses has been the question they study. They assume that the process which RIAA has identified, even with the insight we have provided above, can harmlessly be carried out without looking at the structure of the music industry and at that industry's decision-making process and at the ways that structure is influencing pricing by the majors.

Is It the Sales of CDs That Matters?

In this section, we consider the music industry's idiosyncrasies that justify a careful use of economic tools to better understand what has been happening since 1990s. From the day Napster appeared, the music industry has blamed peer-to-peer for its predicament, focusing exclusively upon file sharing's free downloads. Peer-to-peer by itself is said to be responsible for the drop in the sale of CDs. One of the hypotheses to most peer-to-peer discussions is the assumption that free downloading, that is, not paying for music, is the only reason for using peer-to-peer for file sharing. For those who have looked at who download music, the picture that emerges is more complex. The simple-minded picture of Homo economicus who focuses on nothing but price does explain well the behavior of a nontrivial fraction of the file sharing population. However, the file sharing is more diverse and more complex. Economists have identified many reasons why peer-to-peer file sharing need not result in lower sales of CDs and we add to that list in this chapter.

The industry's assertion has attracted economists who were quick to point out that the correlation between the two need not mean causality, that is, that third factors, say the need to gather information about the music good to be purchased, what Liebowitz calls the sampling effect, had theoretically the potential to explain what happened to the sales of CDs. They also pointed out that other factors could show that, in fact, peer-to-peer might have been beneficial and that if it were not for peer-to-peer, the industry's business performance might have been even worse. Economists have challenged the RIAA's assertion that, a priori, peer-to-peer file sharing is responsible for the large decrease in the sale of CDs on a one-to-one basis even if most have concluded that it is responsible for some of the fall in the sales of CDs. Economic consideration show that such an assertion could not be taken at face value. They were quick to note that many other factors could have contributed to the fall in the number of CDs sold. They have identified and quantified many of those determinants and they have estimated how they interact with one another. Liebowitz (2007) has reviewed many of those determinants that could have resulted with peer-to-peer file sharing in an increase in the sales of CDs. This has led economists to predict that the adjusted impact of peer-to-peer on CD sales would lead to an outcome that would differ from RIAA's presumption. Oberholzer-Gee and Strumpf (2007) have concluded that lower CD sales could not be attributed to peer-to-peer.

The interpretation of factors such as those listed by Liebowitz is far from being straightforward and there is room for disagreement. For instance, even the most casual observation of the way people listen to music shows that even if time is the constraint on listening to music, a truism, that constraint is fundamentally different in a world of MP3, file sharing, and iPod because, for instance, people now have the ability to listen to music in a much larger set of circumstances (Liebowitz, 2006). Basically, Liebowitz et al. have not regarded peer-to-peer and other approaches to online music downloading, regardless of price, as an essentially dynamic and different good – even if, for instance, Liebowitz introduces such factors as "increased portability." The problem is not the significance of "increased portability" or lack of it but that it can be treated as incremental independent of other factors, static and without learning effect. As one has observed when innovation transformed a sector, say the sector of hard drive Christensen studied, the quantity demanded changes by orders of magnitude and the population of buyers often changed significantly. Thus, Liebowitz and Watt (2006) note that many of those who download "illegal" copyrighted material would not buy it if file sharing were not available. That change may increase the number of works individuals accumulate, ceteris paribus, to such an extent that consumers listen to music in new setting, that is, may spend more time in listening to music. There may be another change in consumer behavior with many people hoarding music to have the option to listen to it in the future whether or not they actually do it (Frank, 2006). To show how this might be happening, one may make an analogy with the restaurant business. In that business, buffets are often offered to patrons as a substitute to conventional menus. In those situations, buffets elicit very different behavior from consumers, with hoarding food in quantities larger than what one would normally eat. Peer-to-peer consumers have accessed to catalogues that are much larger than commercial catalogues that may be one factor that causes hoarding. The impact of catalogue and of the ease of access to catalogue is a dimension that, once again, has been treated as incremental rather than as inframarginal in that literature.

Chiang and Assane (2007) observe, for instance, that many students are willing to take what seems to be unreasonable risk, in the sense that they are not utility-maximizing, to use file sharing. As any evaluation of file sharing, whether peer-to-peer is estimated to be harmful or beneficial have been taken with a grain of salt. The same is true when estimating the impact of the industry's legal actions against individuals, some agreeing with the industry that it did reduce "illegal" file sharing, a conclusion Chiang and Djeto accept, whereas others concluding that it had no measurable impact (Karagiannis et al., 2004).

There has been some attempt at segmenting the file sharing population. Bhattacharjee et al. (2006) have divided it in low and heavy users to show that the RIAA's strategy of suing file sharers had some success. Bounie et al. (2005) divide the population of file sharers into two segments, the "explorers" who sample a lot of music and the "pirates" who do not sample. Whether a cost–benefit analysis justifies going after "pirates," their "explorers" are some of the people who benefited from what the industry never offered them and what the industry is still not offering them. Liebowitz (2006) correctly points out that in a static world, whether explorers diminish their consumption of CDs is a function of the demand elasticity for the kind of music the explorer likes – greater sampling means fewer bad CDs which means lower transaction costs that translates in cheaper good CDs. He assumes implicitly that music is homogeneous even if he suggests elsewhere that this is not the case. If music is heterogeneous, sampling lowers the cost of searching across genres, increasing in turn the willingness to pay for CDs of different genres. As those are imperfect substitutes, this would increase, relative to the absence of genres, the total demand for CDs. The effect is obviously ambiguous except that the impact on transaction costs, hence on the price of CDs, is substantial. However, this discussion neglects the benefit of staying online, given the relative high usage cost of a physical medium such as CDs relative to online music. The latter as well as the structural change in portability makes the CD even more costly relative to online music.

This suggests that the "aggregate" approach which RIAA is pursuing against those who use file sharing, even if there were merits in attacking pirates, is likely to be counterproductive for the explorer segment. The need for a discriminatory marketing strategy is also illustrated by genres such as classical and Latin music and jazz. Liebowitz (2006) observes that the download pattern for jazz and classical music differs from the pattern of many other genres. Moreno (2006) makes an observation that challenges also "one-size-fit-all" when she remarks that Latin music commercialized by the music recording industry continues to grow at an accelerated pace that parallels peer-to-peer's rate of growth.

We would like to suggest that much of the quantitative literature has failed to consider the questions that the industry and the various government bodies need to address if they are to come out of today's slump, hence are short-sighted. It is true that they acknowledge some degree of product differentiation when they recognize that there are factors that make "peer-to-peer music" different from "CD music." However, this is not adequately integrated in existing econometric models. Peer-to-peer file sharing produces a product that is fundamentally different from CDs. This discontinuity imposes an inframarginal analysis even where consumers consumes both, often for the same work (BBC News, 2007b).

It is beyond the scope of this chapter to go in depth in identifying reasons that have not been considered in the econometric literature. To list only a few, we note that starting from the most elementary, the CD is a bundle product that does not give the option to the buyer to demand individual works and yet this is one of the characteristic of the online world where albums are giving way to single song as a result of the flexibility created by peer-to-peer and online music. The indirect cost of downloading online music (i.e., excluding the price paid for the work), including file sharing, is lower by orders of magnitude than the indirect cost of purchasing a CD, and casual information suggests that consumers value highly the ability to download music anywhere, whenever they feel like it. This is like ignoring the significance of e-commerce as an alternative to the way commerce used to be carried out. The significance of low indirect cost is reflected by the "convenient" attribute which Liebowitz associates with online downloads.

The industry's position that peer-to-peer is the factor responsible for the drop in the sales of CDs, conditional upon existing institutions, for example, the "illegality" of file sharing of copyrighted material, might be correct, as suggested by Hong (2007), Liebowitz (2006, 2007), Oberholzer-Gee and Strumpf (2007), Rob and Waldfogel (2004, 2006), and Zentner (2005, 2006). This does not mean that it is necessarily "illegal" and that making it "illegal" inevitably makes good business sense. The present situation can be traced to the industry's decision to block an innovation that, independently of price, continues to be highly valued by consumers. In effect, consumers had no option but to go around the industry to be able to procure the kind of good they were striving to consume. The lynch pin is the way peer-to-peer as a disruptive innovation has been fundamentally changing the market, offering consumers, regardless of price, a product that is so much friendlier than CDs. That new, innovative product, as much and probably more than price, motivated consumers to migrate "en masse."

Those econometric studies take a static view of the subject, neglecting the dynamic and evolutionary dimensions that are so central to the study of innovation, hence of the ways peer-to-peer is inevitably transforming the product that is commercialized by the industry. They ignore the complexity of consumer decisions and their path dependence, dimensions that are so well understood by the advertising industry.

Today's research stresses the need to establish when the "Homo economicus" theoretical framework results in unsatisfactory forecasts, using Friedman (1953)'s criteria. This means that there is an urgent need to identify the kind of problems where it might be an acceptable simplification, that is, the scope of various theories.

Today's studies have not even integrated the work of Becker's on what might be a neoclassically rational response to "illegal" file sharing (Becker, 1968). Yet, a position such as Becker is very sensitive to a mainstream (by opposition to a Chicago-type) rationality, that is, it is in fact an irrational approach where some of the assumptions upon which it is based do not hold (Shermer, 2007; Thaler, 2000). Chiang and Assane (2007)'s work does identify empirically some of the limitation of mainstream economic, that is, the extent to which those quantitative models may be misleading.

Liebowitz (2007) expressed probably the feeling of most econometricians when he concluded that "[c]ommon sense is, or should be, the handmaiden of economic analysis. When given the choice of free and convenient high-quality copies versus purchased originals, is it really a surprise that a significant number of individuals will choose to substitute the free copy for the purchase?" Unfortunately, his conclusion relies on many unstated assumptions that are fundamental to the decision-making process. The failure to identify them makes his conclusion misleading.

We can only be agnostic about the link between peer-to-peer and sales of CDs since our objective is to point out what is required to assess whether there is such an effect and if yes what its magnitude might be. In fact, it is rational to suggest that those econometric studies may have understated the impact of peer-to-peer by failing to take into account the disruptive dimension of peer-to-peer. After all, arguing that peer-to-peer has not had a large impact upon the CD market would be like, by analogy, arguing that the introduction of the automobile at the beginning of the twentieth century had not had a large impact on the horse-buggy sector. We are not suggesting that there had not been a number of people whose sole motivation continues to be getting a free ride, David et al. (2005)'s pirating. We are agnostic since the literature has not looked at those questions in a meaningful manner.

There are other flaws. For instance, the economic literature (in contrast to the engineering literature) has been taking the existence of peer-to-peer as a data ignoring what was required for peer-to-peer to emerge. The emergence of peer-to-peer networks is inconsistent with Homo economicus. A peer-to-peer network can emerge and survive only as long as some members of society act altruistically.[1] It has also ignored the unique role of the industry as an intermediary, hence, through the unique function it fulfills, its ability to largely internalize the externalities that characterize the relationship between artists and consumers in the absence of the labels, that is, the two-sided characteristic of the market structure.

The market framework is fundamental to disentangling the way peer-to-peer impacts the industry from other forces. As such, it challenges what economists have taken as conventional wisdom. We need to point out that the two-sided market dimension of the music industry applies only to the majors. It is reasonable to see them as offering a product that is completely differentiated from what the Indies produce, that is, to look at both markets as almost separate markets (Evans and Schmalensee, 2005). The major labels are effectively able to largely internalize the externalities between artists and consumers (Gordon, 2005).

The industry and some economists have argued that markets were superior to alternatives in bringing about an efficient outcome to the copyright problem. This is Liebowitz (2006)'s conclusion based on the view that markets are normally superior even if he acknowledges that we should know more to be able to establish a superior method. While some question the economic efficiency of any government-mandated trade restrictions, discussions have generally focused on the efficiency of variations in government intervention that highlight implicitly the significance of path dependency (Bastiat, 1862–1864; Bullock, 1901; Nelson and Rosenberg). It is an empty argument even if one limits oneself to a static neoclassical paradigm. This is not to downplay the role that markets can play. In the music industry's copyrights, markets do influence the process as when they contain the copyright owners' control over residual rights where those have been disproportionately allocated in their favor. This situation is illustrated by the industry's debacle in the implementation of DRM. Market responses have shown that consumers do not want DRM-constrained music forcing an industry retreat. There are other ways that markets appear to impose a discipline on the industry. For instance, the entry of players such as Apple and now others, say MySpace, suggests that incumbent and/or new entrants will have to reevaluate the merits of integrating in their business strategies some form of peer-to-peer possibly combined with other elements, say Web 2.0 (Adegoke, 2008).

Nelson and Winter (1982)'s firms avoid the rut of their strategy because they are constantly under pressure to increase their efficiency in order to stay alive. In contrast, RIAA and the majors benefit from government protection and are not threatened by Schumpeter (1942)'s "perennial gale of creative destruction." Radical innovation are a challenge for firms anywhere and even efficient, established firms fall in that kind of Schumpeterian trap (Christensen, 2000; Sull, 2004). There is a divide with the music industry where the factors we have identified above, especially their ability to forestall change, are thus reinforced toward defending the status quo. This may help better appreciate why Garland's statement "They have to demonstrate to the artists and also to Wall Street that they are doing everything that they can to fight piracy" is so representative of the majors' mantra (Koman, 2007).

Between Artists and Consumers: Intermediation and Two-Sided Markets

Studies of peer-to-peer have divided the music sector in two elements, consumers and producers. The music sector is made up, as a first approximation, of two sectors, the artists and the various intermediaries such as the RIAA and the labels. Bourdeau de Fontenay et al. (2008) have argued that one cannot assess properly the impact of peer-to-peer on the industry without treating as distinct sectors artists and the various intermediaries. Clearly, as long as one can presume that working with the aggregate does not have a large impact on the analysis of the peer-to-peer problem, it would be preferable to ignore that differentiation.

We have seen that many have argued that it was necessary to segment the file sharing population. It is a disaggregation that presents few problems, at least as long as we ignore the externalities, for example, how the choices made by Bounie et al. (2005)'s explorers impact and/or are influenced by those of their pirates. The question is not trivial as suggested by the work that is carried out on the role of Internet and especially of Web 2.0 on marketing (Kono, 2008). However, there is another far more serious issue as suggested by Bourdeau de Fontenay et al. (2008) that whether it is appropriate to study peer-to-peer while ignoring the differences between artists and the music industry's intermediaries, that is while treating them as a single decision unit. It is obvious that they are different but the question is whether that difference matters when assessing peer-to-peer. After all, it was Metallica group that was the first to use the legal system to attack peer-to-peer.

What matters here is Friedman (1953)'s warning that, while theories should be based on as simple a set of hypotheses as possible, not all sets of hypotheses are equally good. Thus, while he argues that "the more significant the theory, the more unrealistic the assumptions [in the sense of descriptive detail, a ledger of all entries as it were]," he adds, "The converse of the proposition does not of course hold: assumptions that are unrealistic (in this sense) do not guarantee a significant theory."

The music industry acts as a mediator between the artist and the general public, producing mediation services that enable artists to commercialize their music and that help consumers identify music – quoting RIAA: "RIAA acts as agents for hundreds of thousands of artists." Intermediation is the primary if not exclusive role of the recording industry's primary. That intermediation corresponds to RIAA's members production of services to help artists commercialize their works including using any of a number of retailing channels. It is a contribution of Spulber (1999) to have analyzed the unique role of intermediaries and to identify the unique market structure that is associated with intermediation, say the inherent market power of intermediaries.

However, it is still not evident that, as an approximation, it should not be good enough not to isolate the role of intermediation. There is plenty of circumstantial evidence that many artists have been discouraged by the labels from exploring peer-to-peer's commercial potential. There are artists such as Radiohead who have chosen to use peer-to-peer to commercialize their music (BBC News, 2000a, 2007b, 2000b, 2008). In addition, there is a growing number of independent artists who use peer-to-peer-based services such a www.musicdish.net to gain visibility by making music available to consumers very much the same way Prince seems to have done with "Planet Earth" (BBC News, 2007a). Krishnan et al. (2007) discuss other artists that are exploring and, in some case, adopting that path. What is important in that movement, even if it is still quite small, is that peer-to-peer is a technology that is transforming the way by which artists can access the general public, one of the basic functions of today's intermediation. Bhattacharjee et al. (2008)'s contribution shows also the role and impact of peer-to-peer on intermediation, that is, the extent to which it is used by consumers to learn about new music. In fact, the labels have themselves began to use peer-to-peer as a new, cost-saving instrument in the role of intermediation when they use firms such as BigChampagne not just to monitor the "illegal" copyrighted material but also how new albums are doing. What we have shown is that peer-to-peer is an innovation that is revolutionizing intermediation in ways that make some of the services incumbents offer obsolete. This is not new and it is not specific to peer-to-peer since intermediation is just as sensitive to innovation, especially disruptive innovation, as any other type of economic activities. After all, it was the way the sheet music industry had to give way to recording. We have shown that it is not possible to study peer-to-peer and its impact on the industry without treating separately the intermediaries and the artists.

The music recording industry's intermediation function is complex. For instance, a common way for artists to obtain a label's services has been to barter the ownership of their copyrights (Gordon, 2005). An outcome has been the accumulation of huge libraries of copyrighted material by the majors. Garland's quote: "RIAA acts as agents for hundreds of thousands of artists and for millions of songs." The way intermediation has been functioning means that recording industry is partially vertically integrated, selling services to and, at the same time, competing through its downstream activities with those "hundreds of thousands of artists." To that extent, RIAA's arguments as outlined in its web site is partially disingenuous (Koman, 2007).

Artists need visibility to be able to sell their work to the public and, to be known, they have to expand substantial resources. In the same way, consumers have to learn about artists to know what is available and what they may want to buy.

Both processes are complexes and artists and consumers cannot internalize the resources expanded. The music recording industry's primary function is to identify ways to resolve that problem, that is, to internalize externalities between artists and consumers. The process is complex and the music recording industry has to identify who they consider as talents and find ways to transform them in commercial products. The process through which music recording industry goes to shape the taste and expectation of the public and to transform artists into new and innovative final products is not fundamentally different from the process game consol manufacturers to attract people with the talent to create new and popular games while being entrepreneurs in identifying the features which the consoles must have to attract the public. Economists call such a setting a two-sided market. Here it is a market structure that highlights the majors' complex role in shaping intermediation (Bourdeau de Fontenay et al., 2008). It is not a conventional, passive form of intermediation where the intermediary's function is only to inform both parties of the products that are being traded. In any case and especially in two-sided markets, intermediaries always have market power.

Rochet and Tirole (2004) have consistently stressed that two-sided markets are tricky to specify (and we use our terminology). This means that one cannot jump to the conclusion that because there is an intermediary, the music industry is a two-sided market. Thus, Rochet and Tirole (2004) argue that "Getting the two sides on board' [here, the artist and the consumer] is… not restrictive enough. Indeed, if the analysis just stopped there, pretty much any market would be two-sided, since buyers and sellers need to be brought together for markets to exist and gains from trade to be realized." That dimension is at the heart of Spulber (1999)'s contribution. Two-sided markets are much less common. In fact, Rochet and Tirole point out that "[f]or an increase in the share allocated to the seller, say, to matter, it must be the case that the seller cannot pass the increase in his cost of interacting with the buyer through to the buyer… Such concerns of course do not arise if most of the download is already part of commercial transactions, as in the case of the licensing of a music file."

Jullien (2006) has studied the function of iPod as a platform in a two-sided market. He argues in that study that "[i]n many media industries, firms receive revenues from two sources." However, this is only marginally related to the problem we are studying here; hence, we cannot use it to justify our position that the music industry is best modeled as a two-sided market. The dimension that makes the music industry, with the music recording industry at its center, a two-sided market is the function that the music recording industry plays in identifying artists whose works they feel they can commercialize, the process and the resources they expand to commercialize such artists, and the way they have to distribute and charge for their works. The major labels' profits, at least in an ideal and static world with unchanging technology, depend upon their ability to price their services to both the artists and the consumers in a way that balance each side's interests so as to maximize their own profits. Unhappy consumers do not buy as much music as the labels are slowly learning and, when they buy it, it is because they have found new channels who offer the kinds of product they are looking for, say Apple through iTunes. Unhappy artists have an incentive to look for alternative paths to consumers, including peer-to-peer-based paths (BBC News, 2007b). More significantly, the externalities the music industry internalizes in its function means that profit maximizing is inconsistent with marginal returns.

The Strategic Use of Copyrights: Immutable or Endogenous

The US Constitution, Article I, Section 8, specifies that "[t]he Congress shall have the power… [t]o promote the progress of science and useful arts, by securing for limited times to authors and inventors the exclusive right to their respective writings and discoveries." The US Constitution does not specify what must actually be done. It only provides broad principles. It is the responsibility of Congress to translate those into more concrete policy guidelines on how the Constitution's principles must be implemented. Essentially, Congress has to decide what limitations it should impose on the artist's property rights. Today, this has meant addressing questions such as:

- What is the duration of "limited times"?
- What are "fair use"-type limitations?
- What does "exclusive" actually mean, for example, what are the conditions under which those rights can be traded?
- What is the process or mechanism through which artists receive royalties?

Historically, Congress has chosen to rely to a large extent on market forces to implement the Constitution. In itself, markets must be created and managed and still leave a lot of leeway on its impact on artists and the public. It is easy to talk of markets as discussed in an economics 101 course but this is not helpful here. Markets are all embedded in human societies, all with their own idiosyncrasy and when talking of the use of markets one has to specify the institutions within which they operate and ignoring not only the cost of creating, managing, and using markets is one of the factors that result in an inappropriate analysis (McMillan, 2002). This is particularly relevant in the music industry where markets are so far from the theoretical, abstract markets associated with "perfect competition." In addition, historically, Congress has not considered "unfettered markets." It has interpreted "authors" as including a broad class of artists and individuals and organizations that create original content. It is the function of the Executive to be more specific and provide the necessary details and of the Judicial branch to resolve disagreements. The artists' exclusive right to their works has been interpreted as the artist's option of withholding her works from the commercial process. However, once those are commercialized, then the sector's laws and regulations come into play.

If we look at the use of markets, some agree with Bastiat (1862–1864), seeking an environment where the sole function of government is to minimize market power. They argue that minimizing the period over which artists are granted exclusive rights, that is, setting it at the limit at zero, would maximize the welfare of all, including artists. Bastiat's approach is probably the closest to an "unfettered" market model. Congress has never had that model in mind. Rather it has consistently been of the view that some amount of government regulation is required to meet the Constitution's mandate, rejecting the idea of "unfettered markets." The point is that the use of markets tells us little about how this is to be implemented, the extent to which "unfettered markets" are in fact "fettered," that is, the extent to which they cannot be defined independently of time and place, independently of the social context within which they operate. It also shows that such markets differ only in the way they balance the rights of the buyers from those of the sellers with other compensation mechanisms.

Granovetter (1985) has looked at the requirements for markets to function, studying how markets are embedded within a complex institutional environment that is idiosyncratic to, here, the music sector. This embeddedness is obvious when one considers the narrow scope of the courts' interpretation. Thus, their range of options does not extend to many systems "unfettered markets" and rejects other systems such as that of Netanel (2003).

One may want to argue that one only have to choose the "best" market institutions but even this is hopeless. For instance, the heterogeneity of the artist population as well as of the general public means that even a social welfare-maximizing, benevolent central planner would find it impossible to choose among the various equilibriums (Hayek, 1945). Furthermore, a stakeholder such as the music industry could consider the strategic merits of alternative, nonmarket-based approaches to set and allocate royalties since they could be superior to conventional market solutions under some profit-maximizing situations.

One way to look at the process of selecting the market institutions is to look at it as a compromise that is intended to balance the rights of the artists with those of individuals based on society's ability and willingness to deviate from its existing path. The previous analysis shows that an adequate balancing of those rights is a complex process that cannot hope to ever "maximize" social welfare (Markoff, 2008). The absence of a simple, unambiguous empirical solution is well illustrated by the difference of the respective decisions by the US District Court and the US Supreme Court. While the US District Court focused on innovation, that is, dynamic efficiency, by extending the Betamax precedent to Grokster, the US Supreme Court based its decision on static rather than dynamic efficiency, sharing with the music intermediaries, just like the governments in France and in the UK today, the fear of "the destabilization to established profitable ways," using Noam (2008)'s words, whatever benefits peer-to-peer will be bringing about (Andrews, 2008b).

Copyrights and the institutions that are used to manage them need to be viewed as endogenous, strategic variables that are managed by stakeholders. This is effectively the case since the allocation of the rights associated with them is in the hands of governments who respond to the demands made by various stakeholders. This endogeneity highlights the fact that the constitution itself does not make file sharing "illegal." Its legality depends upon the process selected by Congress to implement the Constitution. One can formulate efficient methods that create the necessary incentives while ensuring the legality of file sharing as an efficient solution. This would mean departing substantially from established practices. One might argue that path dependence may make it costly to deviate substantially from the historical. The experience of former communist countries suggests that this is not the case. Staying on the same, bad path can easily be even more costly. In fact, to better understand the social and business value of this approach, one could use another analogy to describe what is happening, the speed limit. The social value of imposing a speed limit on streets and highways is not the law proper. The law is only a tool to an end not one to create a population of criminals (Bourdeau de Fontenay et al., 2008; Shirky, 2000). Rather, imposing a speed limit can be an effective tool as long as it is enforced in a way that is both responsive to the general public and capable of contributing to safety. The review of the policy's historical enforcement by RIAA brings in mind the wisdom of Aesop's fable, "The Oak and the Reed." RIAA's statement "[i]t's not realistic to wipe out… [piracy on the Internet] entirely but instead to bring it to a level of manageable control" demonstrates an acceptance of that principle.

Rights that are granted by governments are not always tradable and they may be constrained by regulations even where they can be traded. This is illustrated by the radio spectrum where broadcasters could not trade their rights to spectrum. Where spectrum rights can be traded as PCS for the digital, mobile spectrum in Australia, they are still typically constrained to specific classes of applications with constraints upon the levels and types of interferences. Congress has not imposed such restrictions on copyrights and this has meant the emergence of intermediaries such as the majors.

Copyrights provide monopoly power to those to whom they have been granted. In fact, many in the Chicago School have argued that governments are for all practical purposes the sole source of monopoly (George J. Stigler). Governments tend to restrict monopolies because they are considered inefficient. This is done here through such conditions as restricting the duration of the copyrights. However, the artist's monopoly power that results from her work is for most artists and most art works ephemeral with new songs and new genre challenging established songs and established genres. Nevertheless, the issue is important because the pooling of individual monopoly rights transforms those individual rights with little market power when they are taken one-by-one into large libraries that give intermediaries considerable market power. This is reinforced by the inherent market power that intermediation conveys (Spulber, 1999).

At a point in time, the legacy copyrights that have been granted by governments are transformed by technological and institutional innovations that change the nature and the scope of those rights and effectively create residual rights. These new rights are obvious in innovations such as Betamax and peer-to-peer. On paper, the government addresses how those rights must be allocated between the parties involved and the Constitution by imposing (or removing) constraints on copyrights. As the above discussion shows, formula that would specify how this is to be done does not exist. Historically, government institutions have used a trial and error process that gropes toward some outcome that is, hopefully, social welfare-enhancing. The process could be thought as a generalization of Walras' "disequilibrium-production" model (Walker, 1987). To that extent, technology and institutional changes go a long way toward reshaping the industry, often in disruptive ways.

The way the allocation of residual rights affects the earnings of those stakeholders means that those stakeholders have an incentive to invest, that is, allocate resources in the long run to influence governments on what the allocation should be. Over the years, the courts have established boundaries on existing copyrights as when it clarified the concept of fair use and when it expanded it in response to the innovation that led to copy copyrighted content in 1984 (Sony Corp. of America, Inc. v. Universal City Studios, Inc.,464 US 417). Predictably, in those instances, the industry argues that they should control all residual rights as the RIAA has been arguing in its challenge of peer-to-peer. It has been the responsibility of the courts to decide how to arrive at a just and reasonable allocation.

The way the courts have chosen to allocate the residual rights derived from peer-to-peer differs from past approaches to the extent that they have accepted the copyright owners' position expounded by the RIAA. This effectively shifted the burden of proof to those who saw merits in limiting the impact of such disruptive innovations. This asymmetrical position does not follow from the basic premise of copyright protection, namely to balance content creation incentives and the welfare benefits from innovative technologies, here, peer-to-peer. The courts' decision to treat the problem as static, protecting the industry from forces that would be seen as reflecting healthy competition in other segments of the economy, implied setting aside the benefits the necessity to acknowledge the peer-to-peer innovation in terms of service to consumers reflecting its inability to look at peer-to-peer beyond free file sharing. This is illustrated by the question the Pew Foundation asked in a survey that makes it evident how different peer-to-peer is from CDs for consumers, "Do you ever download music files onto your computer so you can play them at any time you want?" (Lee, 2005; Liebowitz, 2006).

Public choice tells us that the music recording industry's return on investment directed to informing and shaping the way government thinks about the sector is likely to be the highest for such players with market power relative to the return to artists and consumers (Buchanan and Tullock, 1962). While the public choice paradigm is useful in better understanding the forces that shape the sector and the course it is on, it has severe limitations. As a theory, it presumes that both private stakeholders and governments are fully informed and that they are able to "optimize" their respective functions. Yet, dimensions such as bounded rationality limit the ability of the various stakeholders to identify "the optimal solution" (Simon, 1957).

Sandulli and Martin-Barnero (2007) have produced a fascinating study of the impact of peer-to-peer on the industry, probably the only one that addresses how peer-to-peer is affecting the sector even if one has to assess their estimates critically. They look at the determinants of the conventional demand for music. Then they look at the determinants of music consumers download through file sharing. This enables them to determine how a song should be priced to be competitive with file sharing. That price, they estimate, is about two-third of what Apple is charging through iTunes. This does not seem an unrealistic price for song once competition begins to impact the retailing of music and Apple looses its quasimonopoly. Their paper is only a first step in that direction and the quantitative approaches have to be evaluated carefully. Nevertheless, it shows how it makes sense for someone who studies RIAA's strategy to conclude that the narrowness of the industry's approach to the peer-to-peer phenomenon, especially its interpretation, is self-defeating. It looks like a lose-lose situation, harmful just as much for the majors as for the artists not withstanding the many court decisions that it won.

If the copyright debate started, tabula rasa, from the Constitution, the range of ways by which music could be promoted would be much greater. Starting from the Constitution is far too radical for most stakeholders since it does not acknowledge the role of Granovetter's embeddedness. Ideally, it should not be true for the industry that would benefit from looking beyond legacy institutions. However, the music industry has historically interpreted its property rights as entitling it to ignore the benefits and risks it could derive from alternative business models. Among those models, one would think of those that address the convergence of communications and digitalization, say to problems associated with peer-to-peer. Neither the political institutions nor the economic academic community have acknowledged this claim to unfettered rights as well as the possibility that their own analyses were restricting the range of options available to the detriment of social welfare and to the music industry. Neither have considered how sensitive their results are to such challenges to the assumption of rationality as those by Alchian (1950), Friedman (1953), Becker (1962), Kahneman and Tversky (1979), and Thaler (2000).

If we focus on the industry's legal approach and ignore the new business strategy, it is reasonable to suggest that the comfort of protecting yesterday's system that was being challenged by peer-to-peer has been preferred to the option of negotiating new licenses with entrepreneurs looking for new ways to commercialize music. Posner (1975)'s analysis would suggest such an outcome which is the antithesis of firms that are focused on profit maximization (Bhidé, 2008).

RIAA's discussion have all been turned toward the status quo, leaving no room for entrepreneurship and the Congress and the courts have de facto acquiesced to ignoring everything but a narrow interpretation of the legacy institutional system. As demonstrated by the single question economists have studied, that has meant ignoring the commercial goal of maximizing profits, what the industry could not have afforded had it had to be competitive.

There are many ways for royalties to be paid to artists and different ways have totally different implications for the music industry and for any profit-based peer-to-peer strategy it chose to pursue. The lack of discussions about the various stakeholders, their objective functions, as well as the institutional setting contribute also to the view that the industry's strategy and, in particular, the strategy of the largest, individual holders of copyrighted content fail to be profit maximizing. For instance, it is possible to create a system of compulsory license as shown by Fisher (2004) and Netanel (2003). The approach consists in some sort of levy, say at the hardware level, a system that has been used for close to a century in the UK and in a number of other countries around the world (Bourdeau de Fontenay and Nakamura, 2006). Liebowitz (2003) recognizes the problem with both the present copyright system and the proposed system of compulsory licenses. Nevertheless he concludes that the value of compulsory licenses needs to be studied more carefully. However, his conclusion that this has to done before its being used to replace the present market system does not follow logically. There is merit to favor a priori markets but as long as one is confident that they are not overly distorted and we have seen that his argument, a priori attractive properties of an unfettered market does not hold here. While he is right that an alternative such as compulsory licenses needs to be studied carefully, today's system may be largely market-based but the lack of competition undermines any efficiency claims that he makes in its favor. The lack of transparency in today's system combined with high transaction costs strongly suggests that objective efficiency criteria need to be developed. Only then will one be able to get a very imperfect sense whether today's "market-based process" is worth preferring to proposals such as Netanel's proposal.

In this section, we have shown that an analysis of peer-to-peer and of its implications for the music industry needs to treat copyrights as endogenous, largely shaped by the industry acting as intermediary between artists and consumers to be useful to the policy and business processes. This means that there is a need to expand the analysis to include options where peer-to-peer file sharing is legal.

What Can the Music Industry Learn from the Swiss Watch Industry?

There is no question that the music sector has been facing a major challenge since 1990s and that it correctly places peer-to-peer as the issue it has to address successfully. The established orthodoxy has been the cornerstone of the music industry approach. Peer-to-peer is said to be single-handedly responsible for the industry's crisis. This is a position that has been largely accepted by governments as illustrated by the fight in Europe regarding how to address "illegal" music file sharing, fight which pitches the music industry against the concern of the impact on civil liberties of the customers' usage monitoring by ISPs (Andrews, 2008a, 2008b). However, Noam (2008) suggests that one must be able to look beyond the immediate and take a historical perspective to understand the process through which such radical innovations tend to transform society. He discusses the emergence of the radio but it is tempting to compare the response of the music industry to the way the canals responded to the railroad in the first half of the nineteenth century.

More recently, the music sector has begun, in parallel with its legal strategy, to push a strategy that recognizes the technological changes the sector is going through and the need for new approaches (Krishnan et al., 2007). This has been translated by a concerted effort to seek new approaches and new business models that would bring back the sector's high profitability of the late-1980s and early-1990s. This is a necessary but only a small step which in and of itself is inadequate to solve the music industry's business problems.

In this section, we argue that the first steps taken by the industry to return to a business focus may not achieve their goals for a number of reasons. First and the more obvious is that it is almost impossible to pursue simultaneously conflicting strategies, especially if one of those has been for so long the industry's cornerstone. Tushman and O'Reilly (1996) have developed a model for firms to pursue simultaneously a policy that would help a firm to simultaneously manage its operational activities efficiently and develop a capability to respond to architectural and radical innovations but that model was not to address the kinds of conflicts that have been inherent in the music industry. Its scope is much more limited and it was not conceived to manage two conflicting business objectives.

There is a large body of knowledge that shows that industries and firms are embedded in complex cultures and that it is a complete and rarely successful task for such organizations to radically change course. In other words, we argue that it is common for firms and industries to incur very high costs and often to fail in this process. There are many reasons for that such as the need and cost of transforming those routines that had contributed to the firm's efficiency (Nelson and Winter, 1982). After all, "we can't teach an old dog new tricks." We could think, as an analogy, of the energy, time, and space that are required for a large cruise ship to overcome its inertia and change direction. In essence, the industry faces hurdles far greater than just acknowledging the age of online music.

The industry has failed to recognize that peer-to-peer was a major innovation. We have seen earlier that peer-to-peer's impact is far more complex. We have argued that peer-to-peer is a major innovation which, using Christensen (2000)'s terminology, is obviously disruptive. We consider that, even if no other factors were to affect the drop in the sales of CDs, the arguments advanced by the industry were misleading. However, what matters for us is not so much the problems with those arguments but that they reflect an approach by the industry that is inconsistent with the industry's presumed profit motive and its recent interest to take a more positive approach. To that extent, it is important to understand what are the factors that cause the industry to deviate from proper business motive to the harm not only of other players but even of its shareholders.

The failure of RIAA's strategy, namely its inability to deliver to its owners, seems to reflect a lack of a business focus, one that translates the ongoing, large of "illegal" file sharing from a burden and, effectively, a potential source of instability, into a strategy that finds way to commercialize those individuals' demand for music (Einav, 2008). It is an empirical question whether the industry's campaign against the "illegal" downloading of copyrighted material harms the industry's sale of music; a priori, one would imagine that it does not (Koman, 2007).

The business that is able to implement a business strategy that has at his core two conflicting objectives, an effective and proactive commercial, profit-maximizing strategy and an abstract "law and order" strategy, is, if it exists at all, exceptional. This is especially true if it were able to implement it, with high visibility both internally and externally. This is what leads us to suggest that it is necessary to study the environment within which the firm operates, not just the formulation and implementation of new business strategies such as those that are found in the literature (Hughes et al., 2008; Krishnan et al., 2007).

In and of itself, the profit-maximizing motive applied to the firm's commercial objective does not automatically mean foregoing a proactive legal strategy. Rather, it suggests to assess carefully its cost, subjecting it, for instance, to a game-theoretical cost–benefit (Bhattacharjee et al., 2006). A closer look at its past strategy helps understand why its stated strategy continues to have a negative effect on itself, on the major labels, on other members, and on artists and most other stakeholders. This is a failure that was predictable from the beginning, looking at way it dealt with Napster. Through its unswerving legal focus, RIAA has demonstrated its ability to increase the cost of "illegal" downloads like a medicine that is conceived around a single goal, even if it has shown itself to be of limited effectiveness. However, the more proper analogy might be Thalidomide, that is, whatever success it might have achieved, this success seems to be swamped by its side effects, here the missed opportunity in understanding the potential of peer-to-peer-like online music products. RIAA focused exclusively on the direct, ex post consequence of the shift ignoring the ex ante dynamic. It effectively acted as if its proper business objective was to decrease the file sharing of copyrighted material rather than helping "the music business thrive."

What is happening to the music industry is not unique to that industry and the management of innovation literature has identified many industries that faltered very much the same way when they were confronted with a disruptive innovation comparable to peer-to-peer to the music industry. The major difference is that the highly regulated nature of the industry and the considerable protection such government intervention gives to the industry have slowed down the adjustment process, making it costlier to all. The benefits of government intervention are well illustrated by the way the telecommunications incumbents were able to use the regulatory process to significantly limit the benefits of new entry (Bourdeau de Fontenay and Liebenau, 2006; Bourdeau de Fontenay et al., 2005). It is also illustrated by what often happens in industries that are less sheltered, say in the transition from the steam to the diesel locomotive engine in the railroad sector (Scranton, 1999). This has effectively given the industry time to correct its initial response to technological changes and to progressively learn to control those innovations so as to make them less threatening (rather than squashing them) and then to learn to manage and integrate in its business practice. The music industry is in the same position. As with sectors such as the telecommunication sector, it has, relative to competitive sectors such as the disk drive industry, more time to correct its initial response, hence a greater chance to formulate a strategy it can implement to adjust successfully to peer-to-peer.

In many industries (but not all), the management of innovation literature has shown how established firms find it very hard to respond successfully to radical innovations. This can be associated with any of a number of factors. There is much in the economic literature that would provide support to such an analysis but that is beyond the scope of this chapter.

While a detailed case study would provide more rigor to this analysis, one can nevertheless observe that the music recording industry's response has nothing unique to peer-to-peer or to the sector but rather that it is like a carbon copy of what has been observed in so many industries. For instance, we find the same kind of concern with sunk investments, legacy, and internal inertia that hinder the firm's ability to properly assess the changes brought about by the innovation at the expense of its own long-term profitability (Christensen, 2000; Tushman and O'Reilly, 1996). For instance, we observe that not only an innovation lowers price or that it provides new functionalities, but what is the norm is for radical innovation to do both what was observed in the Swiss watch industry or in locomotive manufacturing for railroads and what we observe with peer-to-peer (Scranton, 1999; Tushman and Radov, 2000a, 2000b). Firms after firms fail to understand that the new product that was created through the innovation is essentially different from the old one even though they are almost always fully informed. Firms after firms are unable to look beyond their history and conclude that they won't be able to survive their sector's shrinking. This is well illustrated by Liebowitz (2006)'s assessment of the sampling effect analyzed earlier. Time after time, the new product is such that the demand shifts outward, increasing by orders of magnitude. Those models of incumbent firms the management of innovation literature has developed are useful to better understand how to address that problem which is the problem of the music industry. It is a useful model that helps better understand how many firms respond and why so many of them fail to adjust successfully. In this analysis, it is important to incorporate the benefits of regulation as we have done earlier when we argue that such a regulatory process needs to be seen as endogenous, used as an integral part of the business strategy. This is what the telecommunication has successfully done, putting large resources to convince the courts to severely restrict the implementation of the 1996 Communication Act, for instance, to essentially neutralize a key element, unbundling (Bourdeau de Fontenay et al., 2005; Garcia-Murillo and MacInnes, 2001). The music industry has also been successful in using the courts to neutralize peer-to-peer. However, in its case, this has had little impact of file sharing as it itself recognizes. This implies that its strategy has effectively failed, that is, has not furthered its obligations to its shareholders.

The interplay of industry–peer-to-peer threatens to create Hardin (1968)'s tragedy of the commons. The industry's failure to develop creative business models that take advantage of the new technology, or at least incorporate it constructively in its business strategy, deprives consumers of access to commercial music products the new technology entitled them to, motivating them to shift en masse to peer-to-peer. The absence of commercialization makes the works of artists like a commons where the flow of new works run the risk of drying, artists not being provided a viable way to create the kind of music consumers demand. The commons were fields that were commonly shared by English and Scottish farmers from the Middle Ages to the nineteenth century. Hardin argued that such governance gave individual farmers the incentive to maximize the grazing by their own cattle even if this was harmful to them in as much that all farmers overgrazing made the land far less fertile. In the music industry, the equivalent to the land to be grazed is the production of music by artists and the commons' overgrazing corresponds to individuals using file sharing even if, collectively, it had the potential to reduce the contribution of artists. In practice, governance largely in the form of customs limited the ability of individual farmers to overgraze. The literature has also shown that societies are often able to create governance that avoided the tragedy of the commons, something that Hardin finally acknowledged after 30 years (Hardin, 1998). The music industry as an intermediary between artists and consumers is in a unique position to create new governance that respond to the nature of peer-to-peer and avoid its continuous growth outside of the commercial environment. It has failed in that task as, for instance, when it recognizes that a disproportionate number of college students continue to use file sharing in spite of the RIAA's legal strategy. Einav (2008) gives numbers of between 80% and 90% citing the US General Accounting Office and Pew Internet Research.

The digital revolution, through features such as online retailing and peer-to-peer, is a set of innovations, most of which are highly disruptive. The impact of peer-to-peer, one of the most disruptive from the music recording industry's perspective, is multifaceted. For instance, some independent artists use peer-to-peer-based services such a www.musicdish.net to gain visibility by making music available to consumers very much the way Prince seems to have done with "Planet Earth" (BBC News, 2007a). Peer-to-peer as an innovation is transforming intermediation in ways that make some of the services that incumbents offer obsolete. This is not new and it is not specific to peer-to-peer. After all, it is the way the sheet music industry had to give way to recording.

Most incumbents in the music industry were aware early of the emergence of the digital revolution as a disruptive innovation and most appear to be aware of the potential for the digital revolution to bring about the kinds of changes peer-to-peer eventually brought about even if they did not realize the sheer magnitude of the innovation's impact. This applies to the majors which began to study the emerging online technologies in the early-1990s (Tushman and Radov, 2000a, 2000b). The majors had years to prepare for the changes that Internet and more generally ICT were bringing about, hence to the kinds of issues peer-to-peer came to create. However, like many firms in other sectors, they did not focus on the innovation as a tool to expand their business looking at peer-to-peer as nothing more than a new form of piracy in a static world that could be quash by force. They chose to defend the status quo rather than positioning themselves to take advantage of their knowledge to position themselves advantageously as innovations were to reshaped the industry. They did introduce new products such as Napster which on the surface looked as if they were using the new technology but those ignored what consumers had learned they should expect from the new technology. They were so embedded in a pre-peer-to-peer setting that they were complete failures. Shirky (2000) describes that kind of response as the "Clarinet" strategy in reference to the newspapers' failed attempt to introduce online services in the early-1990s. He compares the music industry's strategy to the failed attempt to keep the speed limit at 55 mph: "The people arguing in favor of keeping the 55-MPH limit had almost everything on their side – facts and figures, commonsense concerns about safety and fuel efficiency, even the force of federal law. The only thing they lacked was the willingness of the people to go along. As with the speed limit, Napster shows us a case where millions of people are willing to see the law, understand the law, and violate it anyway on a daily basis. The bad news for the RIAA is not that the law isn't on their side. It plainly is. The bad news for the RIAA is that in a democracy, when the will of the people and the law diverge too strongly for too long, it is the law that changes. Thus are speed limits raised" (Bourdeau de Fontenay et al., 2008).

To illustrate to what extent there is nothing "music-specific" to their response, one could compare the response of the entertainment industry, as reviewed by Liebowitz (2006), to that of the hard drive sector faced with progressively smaller models. As in so many other sectors, that industry found themselves facing new entrants that were not hobbled by old paradigms, firms such as Apple. Without new business strategies built around the new technological world, it is a matter of time before they find themselves marginalized. Duchène and Waelbroeck (2004) describe the broad technology change as a shift from "information-push" to "information-pull" technologies with consumers now allocating resources to searching themselves the kind of music they want. That shift looks very much like the shift in the 1950s when radio became competitive and when new labels like Atlantic were created to discover new talents to meet changes in taste, inviting consumers to play a far more proactive role having to select among a large array of new names (many of which are today's established artists). Duchène and Waelbroeck's categorization might be too sweeping. Thus, many of today's consumers remain "couch potatoes," waiting for intermediaries to tell them what they should like. One might equate in the peer-to-peer world those "couch potatoes" to Bounie et al. (2005)'s "pirates" since pirates appear to have little interest in sampling, concentrating largely on downloading the big hit the majors had selected for mass consumption. Nevertheless, the "information-pull" categorization corresponds probably fairly well to Bounie et al.'s "explorers."

Mainstream economic analysis tells us little about the adjustment process in the presence of a disruptive innovation. What matters here is that disruptive technological changes cannot be analyzed through conventional marginal analyses. One can use an analogy, Zeno's arrow paradox, to appreciate how fundamental it is to introduce the dynamic dimension of the process through which the stakeholders respond to each other. Zeno observed an arrow that is flying in the air (could be in any gas or liquid medium) on its path to its target. Observing the arrow in the air, Zeno wondered why, at every instant, gravity would not make the arrow fall straight down from the point it is in the air the way it makes a satellite or a stone fall. The arrow Zeno conceived of was an object because the concept of motion had not been developed. Zeno could describe in great details the arrow but he could not take into the force of motion, an integral part of the arrow in flight and the reason why it continues on its trajectory.

Zeno's arrow teaches us a lot about the scope of conventional economic analysis. The description of the arrow, abstracting from the force of motion, has some use as long as the problem studied was as if it were in equilibrium, that is, as long as it remains approximately around the point Zeno had in his mind. This is required if we do not consider the environment within which it is moving, say water instead of air or still air as opposed to wind. This helps us understand Williamson (2000)'s argument that neoclassical analysis is useful but only over very short period. Granovetter (1985)'s embeddedness, using Zeno's arrow, is to point out that how the arrow will behave in response to the forces of motion differs if it is flying in, say, water as opposed to the air. Here we have the neoclassical perfect competition and monopoly Friedman considered adequate to study most economic problems.

In the same way as Zeno's static concept of the arrow is unable to tackle the forces of motion, the analysis of the impact of peer-to-peer on the industry, say its impact on the sales of CDs, misses the essential economic, social, and technological dimensions that are reshaping the industry as, for instance, it offers a product of which were unavailable to consumers before as we discussed earlier.

That is why we show how mainstream tools are inappropriate to study a disruptive innovation. This is easily deduced from our earlier discussion on the sampling effect. Whatever economic theory one adopts, it must be dynamic but again one cannot rely on whatever is called dynamic. The dynamic process that is required is one that accounts for such things as learning and routines. This means that it must be specified in historical time where the future is essentially different from the past, hence where it is not possible to return to the past. For instance, it is obvious that individuals who have used online services would consume music the way they did it before ICT; in other words, the demand for music does not return to what it was in a pre-peer-to-peer, pre-1999 world. Consumers' accumulated knowledge and experience translate in a change of their utility function.

There are a number of dynamic models based on historical time. The two best known are those initiated by Young (1928) and Schumpeter (1934) analyzed through frameworks such as the general purpose technologies (Bresnahan and Trajtenberg, 1995; Lipsey et al., 2005).

Mainstream analysis fails for other reasons. Disruptive innovations such as peer-to-peer create discontinuities, something the music industry is very much aware of. Discontinuities are inconsistent with marginal analysis. Rather it requires inframarginal tools (Yang, 2001). The need to shift to an inframarginal analysis does not just apply to consumers. In the same way, the music industry is confronted to changes that invalidate "business-as-usual." Those changes affect numerous dimensions of music incumbents such as the majors.

Evidently, focusing on the transformation of the product in response to a major disruptive technology such as peer-to-peer would seem to reinforce the conclusion that peer-to-peer is having a harmful effect on the sale of CDs. This is similar to Liebowitz's argument that, where there is no sampling, individuals have to buy more CDs in order to find those it likes. Within the conventional framework he uses, this is evidently correct (even though he showed that this was only one of a number of factors, e.g., the lower transaction cost in finding the desired CD resulting in increased demand) is just like arguing that the automobile decreased employment since a horse carriage took almost as much labor to produce as the automobile – Studebaker Brothers Manufacturing Company was one of the horse carriage manufacturers who had introduced mass production; interestingly, this was one of the few horse carriage manufacturers that succeeded in the transition to the automobile (Kinney, 2004). The automobile is one of those innovations which, as noted above, resulted in a discontinuous increase in demand, with Ford selling a million Model T in a short period, which could only be studied using inframarginal tools. The example of the automobile industry points to the challenge the music industry faces, namely using the government to protect the old market or finding new business models that would achieve growth through new products.

Whatever new products emerge from the transformation of the music industry and whichever way the industry chooses to tackle the peer-to-peer challenge, RIAA appears reasonable to recognize that file sharing is here to stay. The question the industry faces is whether the industry, having now acknowledged that peer-to-peer is here to stay, will be able to develop new business models that are centered on the new environment in such a way that they can profitably attract the file sharing population by better meeting their needs. This is a tall order task but it is not essentially different, we believe, from those that have been studied in other industries.

Nevertheless, it is also reasonable to assume that those networks will increasingly face competition with new services such as iTunes and MySpace Music. In other words, even if RIAA is becoming more responsive to the new market environment, one would hope to observe even more creativity in the formulation of new business models that address the peer-to-peer challenge. Apple's success is a strong motivation for the industry to find innovative ways to increase competition and expand the market even with lower and decreasing prices. Through time, it is reasonable to expect newer business models to emerge that incorporate some unstructured peer-to-peer business models in mainstream music commercialization. It is premature to forecast the form those business models will take. The challenge of coming up with new and profitable business models is not limited to RIAA. It is pervasive to much of the Internet. Nevertheless, many forces point to the need for innovation, forces such as competition's impact on prices, the expectation by consumers for new services that make a better use of Internet's capabilities, and the potential of transforming today's two-sided market into a multisided one. This may be helped by a less rigid interpretation of the way residual rights are to be allocated relative to the Grokster decision as well a greater willingness to search for a viable solution on both sides of the peer-to-peer chasm. Bourdeau de Fontenay et al. (2008) look at the institutional and cultural dimension of the legal process to show how it corresponds to a trial and error process. This process might provide a viable solution to those who have chosen peer-to-peer for lack of an adequate commercial product. It is possible to imagine that it could reduce and possibly eliminate the problems with "pirates." This step is fundamental to the extent that the inability to develop a viable commercial product for such a large file sharing population suggests a continued period of instability.

It took a long time for the music recording industry to act upon the fact that peer-to-peer was generating information that was invaluable for a profit-focused strategy. Eventually, the industry realized that there was value beyond showing the world how "illegal" music downloading was ruining them. It is that realization that made firms such as BigChampagne essential by helping monitor more carefully the patterns in peer-to-peer file sharing. To provide a perspective to that dimension, we can observe Amazon's business case that takes into account the value of having a catalogue that is uniquely exhaustive by complementing its listing of new books with that of used books. While the markup on secondhand books is likely lower than that of new books – the markup has to be shared with stores which have specific book in stock and the transaction cost is certainly higher than that of a new book – the greater catalogue means that individuals are much more confident to find the book they are looking for; hence, the average lower transaction cost means that they are more likely to return to Amazon.

It is not for us to suggest how the labels would have found ways to gain access to those sources which Napster created. We only want to point out that there is merit to Schumpeter (1942)'s "perennial gale of creative destruction" as a fundamental forces established firms, here the majors, can only ignore at their perils. This is not to say that incumbents have not been attempting to develop new commercially based peer-to-peer paradigms they could use to compete with existing peer-to-peer networks such as Limewire. However, experience with other businesses suggests that they faced internal roadblocks due to the challenge of thinking outside the box when one has been dominant for so long. In this context, psychologically, the free nature of existing peer-to-peer networks easily appears insurmountable. This is no different from AOL's challenge in reconciling Prodigy's flat rate pricing model with their business models – at first, they could not see how they could do that viably and yet, once they adjusted, they were able to eliminate Prodigy as a competitive threat while thriving. Here again, there is a lesson to be learned. AOL turned around, avoided other mistakes made by Prodigy such as its decision to rescind its free e-mail offering and went to dominate the market. Christensen (1993) has studied how many disk drive manufacturers stumbled when they had to adjust to a new, radically different generations of disk drives. Typically, established firms looked at the industry as they knew it and concluded that there were no business models that justified adopting the innovation (Glasmeier, 1991). The disk drive industry only looked at the market they knew and concluded that the lower cost of the new generation of disk drive would force them to contract to a fraction of their size. Yet, whether the incumbents adjusted or not, at each stage, the industry discovered new markets, first the minicomputer, then the PC, to be followed in the next generation by the laptop, and now MP3 players. It is that growth that led the new entrants to often dominate the sector and achieve high profitability (Tushman and Radov, 2000a). Innovations, especially disruptive innovations, do not always result in products that are more advanced, at least at first. The innovation's typical contribution is a drastic reduction in cost. From the incumbents' perspective, this is perceived as a disaster because a low price means less profit. This is the way incumbents almost always look at radical innovation. What they almost always miss is that the market is not fixed. Such drastic innovations tend to translate in increases in output that are orders of magnitude larger than what established firms are able to conceive. Yet, such innovations tend to lead to increases in profit that benefit the successful entrants as well as those incumbents that are able to transform their internal culture. That dimension is missing from today's econometric papers and its absence contributes to limit their value.

There are many factors that contribute to the poor track records of established firms that are faced with a radical technology. Mainstream economics conventionally assumes rational behavior and very few constraints on information and on the ability to process it efficiently. Players not just the labels but also other intermediaries and artists and consumers are all treated as acting rationally.

This contrasts with some of Chicago School individuals such as Alchian (1950) and Becker (1962) have recognized early on that firms are unlikely to be very rational and that they may be very bad at maximizing profit. They also argue that there is a natural selection process that tends to weed away those that, rationally or not, seem to deviate more systematically from achieving minimum profits. Friedman (1953) did not go as far as Alchian or Becker arguing only that firms effectively act "as if" they were actually maximizing profits the way leaves on a tree position themselves "as if" they intentionally were maximizing their individual exposure to the sun. In practice, in all of these models, they differ fundamentally from mainstream models that assume rationality at the individual agent level as in the principal-agent literature. Aggregation is at the core of Alchian, Friedman, and Becker's solutions; however, others such as Felipe and Fisher (2001) have shown the problems with aggregation. This is a two-way problem since an aggregation of rational agents need not produce a rational aggregate result (Kirman, 1992).

The new institutional literature is not the only one that had to identify another, more satisfactory approach. Behavioral and evolutionary economics are two among many post-neoclassical schools that had to formulate their different approaches to avoid the conventional problems. If we go in some details in the ways different groups of economists, it is to find ways to be able to identify economic tools that can help to understand results from business history and from the management of innovation literature that appear to be applicable to players such as the majors. Such steps would then be useful to the music industry as well as to other stakeholders to find ways to come out of the trap in which the sector fell with the emergence of peer-to-peer.

Economists are fond of referring to the natural selection, the cornerstone of the "perfect" market system, as discussed earlier. There is a large literature that relies on the assumption that only those firms which learn to adjust to disruptive innovation survive (Christensen, 2000; Diamond, 2005). From this perspective, the paper identifies key elements that are likely to shape the music industry as peer-to-peer matures.

In practice, additional factors amplify the forces that bring about a market failure with the majors being the most influential. Kahneman and Tversky (1979)'s prospect theory helps us understand how individuals and organization such as RIAA would invest huge energy on protecting the status quo even if it is not optimal for them. The management of innovation literature has shown that such comportment is common among established firms whatever the sector even if it is not profit maximizing for artists and, apparently, for copyright owners. However, Bion (1989)'s trap where individuals come to act as a group to reject external inputs help us to go even further in understanding the mechanism that seems to have taken the industry so far from its business objective. It provides a solid framework to go beyond the analysis of individual firms and analyze the group, here the interaction among the major labels and with RIAA. Group analysis help us study how the feedback mechanism among group members, here, the majors as well as other intermediaries, reinforces their inherent desire to protect the status quo. This feedback mechanism leads them as a group to move progressively to an entrenched position that is more extreme than the position they would arrive at in isolation.

The problem the music industry has faced in its response to the peer-to-peer challenges can be subdivided into two effects. On the one hand, as one would infer from Bion's and from Kahneman and Tversky's contributions, it is reasonable to assume that the industry chose initially a suboptimal strategy. Bion's model with its reinforcing feedback mechanisms may be a useful way to explain what led the various players to dismiss peer-to-peer as a temporary, aberrant phenomenon that could be crushed and eliminated through the use of the courts. It is reasonable to consider whether that failure to acknowledge the new technological and social environment has contributed to sustaining the poor performance of the industry. Even if RIAA had been able to select a good strategy among those it considers, it may be that, like economists who have studied the impact of peer-to-peer on the sale of CDs, RIAA is still ignoring a large set of strategies. One suspects that what may see as "good" strategic choices are only good in relation to the limited set of options considered. It would be surprising not to find strategies that clearly dominate everything RIAA has considered at this stage through a broader search that is not so constrained by existing paradigms.

The first type of error is the failure to choose a good option among the set of options that are being considered (Roxburgh, 2006; Thaler, 2000). This kind of error is illustrated, in the telephony sector, by the modification of the original proposed settlement between the US Department of Justice and AT&T in 1983 (Temin, 1987). Judge Green chose to add to the local telephone companies' local network a substantial portion of the long distance network through the creation of LATA (local access and transport areas). A number of economists have been studying many characteristics of the human decision process, including its lack of rationality in many circumstances

There is a second type of error because of using a very small set of options when evaluating the course to be pursued. It is the failure to think outside of the box. The need to focus one's attention to the inside of the box is probably necessary and sufficient when an organization is de facto developing routines to foster the efficiency of its decision-making process (Nelson and Winter, 1982). This efficiency precludes the emergence of disruptive forces as with the emergence of peer-to-peer. While we all tend to fall in that kind of trap, it is often a costly problem for incumbents. For instance, Tripsas and Gavetti (2004) have shown how Polaroid's culture was so embedded in the Gillette business model, with which it made fortune that it could not conceive of a different model when developing the digital camera. We would like to understand whether the same kind of error applies to the RIAA.

It seems trivial to argue that wrong decisions are unavoidable and that firms, like individuals, will make them and yet this is rarely acknowledged in economics. As Thaler (2000) observed, "[h]omo economicus... is typically taken to be a quick study" and, yet, failure is seen as a fundamental dimension of entrepreneurship in a place such as Silicon Valley. At the same time, many management economists have shown how common it is to identify poor decision making among well run enterprises in response to a disruptive technology, sometimes leading to their complete demise (Christensen, 1993; Sull, 2004). Such errors are generally costly in efficiently run, well-established firms (Lovallo and Sibony, 2006) and they must be managed by corporations and/or governments carefully (Roxburgh, 2006). However, the problem is not solely making the wrong decision for a decision maker. It is at least as much one of not going beyond the established business models (Tripsas and Gavetti, 2000). Often, especially when being confronted with a disruptive technology, a firm's or an industry's management needs to go beyond the established models when designing business strategies. What might be good and justified in response to an incremental innovation breaks down vis a vis architectural and radical innovations. One would think that the later problem might be the most significant one for the music industry. In this section, we argue that the industry, unable to look outside the path they have confined themselves to, may have significantly contributed to its poor performance independently of Napster and Grokster. A sector would look beyond the copyright paradigms it has lived with for almost a century if it aims to maximize profits. This is particularly important in the present situation when a major, disruptive innovation is radically transforming the industry. This leads us to argue that the industry should look at the copyright paradigm as endogenous, to be shaped to its advantage, rather than as a monopoly right the way it has been doing it.

The market-based natural selection process should be slower where firms are protected by regulation. Their observation appears to apply to the recording industry's response to peer-to-peer when for too long it displayed a tunnel vision, focusing on the short run and ignoring the market as seems to have been the case for too long. Then their effort may not be profit maximizing. Where rules are set that are too much at odds with established practices, they influence the political system in order to make the system more compatible with social norms (Bourdeau de Fontenay et al., 2008; Shirky, 2000). From that perspective, RIAA's rigidity and the very large number of individuals who are downloading file, especially in the younger generations, suggest a conflict that has many of the characteristics of the Prohibition Era in the 1920s. This suggests that a wise strategy is to take peer-to-peer as a technology that is well established and unlikely to disappear until it will be replaced by the next innovation. In other words, we believe that peer-to-peer is here for good where we do not just refer to peer-to-peer's technological characteristics but also to its institutional and legal characteristics.

Technological change does not do away with intermediation as demonstrated by the emergence of new intermediaries as Musicdish and iTunes but at times it may transform it in radical ways, eliminating those functions the innovation, here peer-to-peer, has made obsolete. This step means greater unbundling and new entrants taking advantage of their greater mastery of new technologies so as to develop new approaches to elements of intermediation where they are more efficient. Intermediation is a fundamental process in economics. It is particularly sensitive to technological changes and innovations such as peer-to-peer mean that many things artists had to rely upon the majors can now be more efficiently be done through peer-to-peer and other ICT services. As those functions become gradually obsolete, the music recording industry will find it increasingly hard to sell them to artists. However, this does not mean that intermediation is likely to disappear. In practice, new functions emerge that respond to the new technology and intermediaries have to adjust the way they do things. To wit, intermediation has become a major dimension of Internet where it flourishes. In addition, many of those new intermediation-type services are services that did not yet exist in the recent past.

The situation faced by new entrants can be contrasted to that of the music recording industry's incumbents. New entrants and incumbents face very asymmetrical situations that result in an uncertain outcome (Cabral, 2000). The incumbent has massive investment in legacy technologies and the ability to use them to set low price so as to deter entry – the alternative is to write off those investments. This explains to some extent the response of the music recording industry to peer-to-peer. New entrants have the advantage of not being burdened by legacy investment. This may give them a sufficient advantage to get a foothold in spite of the incumbents' dominance (Christensen, 1993).

Innovations have to overcome more than incumbency and their sunk investments. They have to overcome legacy before they can transform the industry progressively. This is illustrated by Radiohead's Yorke who observed at their last release that, "the band would have been 'mad' to ignore a physical release... And it's really important to have an artifact as well, as they call it, an object." This may still be true for my generation – the artifact for someone of Yorke's generation is a CD – but for my son, a teenager, the artifact is a device, be it a computer and/or an MP3 that hold the song (Leeds, 2008). The only thing he would ever do with the physical CD is to download it immediately on his computer (BBC News, 2008).

Note

1. Axelrod's and Ostrom's analyses have shown years ago that the problem is endemic to neoclassical-inspired paradigms. For instance in repeated games, people are generally able to overcome the curse of the prisoner's dilemma, something they can only do through trust since even in a tit-for-tat, the punishment is less costly, that is, the defector ends up with a net benefit relative to the other player.

References

Adegoke, Yinka. "Myspace Music to Launch in Days: Sources," *Reuters Special Coverage*. Reuters, 2008.

Alchian, Armen A. "Uncertainty, Evolution, and Economic Theory." *Journal of Political Economy*, 1950, 58, pp. 211–221.

Andrews, Robert. "Eu Parliament Warns against Isp Monitoring in Music Piracy Fight," *paidContent:UK*, 2008a.

Andrews, Robert. "France Creates €15 Million Body to Enforce 'Three Strikes' Music Policy," *paidContent:UK*, 2008b.

Bastiat, Frédérique. *"Œuvres Complètes De Frédéric Bastiat, Mis En Ordre, Revues Et Annotées D'après Les Manuscrits De L'auteur,"* P. Paillottet and R. Bourdeau de Fontenay, Paris: Guillaumin, 1862–1864.

BBC News. *"Cd Review: Radiohead," Entertainment*. UK, 2000a.

BBC News. *"Radiohead Take Aimster," Entertainment*. UK: BBC, 2000b.

BBC News. *"Prince Album Set Free on Internet," BBC News*. 2007a.

BBC News. *"Radiohead Album Set Free on Web," BBC News*. 2007b.

BBC News. *"Web-Only Album 'Mad', Says Yorke," BBC News*. 2008.

Becker, Gary S. "Irrational Behavior and Economic Theory." *Journal of Political Economy*, 1962, *70*(1), pp. 1–13.

Becker, Gary S. "Crime and Punishment: An Economic Approach." *Journal of Political Economy*, 1968, *76*(2), pp. 169–217.

Becker, Jan U. and Clement, Michel. "Dynamics of Illegal Participation in Peer-to-Peer Networks – Why Do People Illegally Share Media Files?" *Journal of Media Economics*, 2006, *19*(1), pp. 7–32.

Besanko, David; Dranove, David; Shanley, Mark T. and Schaefer, Scott. *Economics of Strategy*. Hoboken, NJ: Wiley, 2007.

Bhattacharjee, Sudip; Gopal, Ram D.; Lertwachara, Kaveepan and Marsden, James R. "Impact of Legal Threats on Online Music Sharing Activity: An Analysis of Music Industry Legal Actions." *Journal of Law and Economics*, 2006, *49*(1), pp. 91–114.

Bhattacharjee, Sudid; Gopal, Ram D.; Marsden, James R. and Telang, Rahul. "A Survival Analysis of Albums on Ranking Charts," E. M. Noam and L. Pupillo, *Peer-to-Peer Video: The Economics, Policy, and Culture of Today's New Mass Medium.* New York: Springer, 2008, 183–206.

Bhidé, Amarnath V. *The Venturesome Economy: How Innovation Sustains Prosperity in a More Connected World.* Princeton: Princeton University Press, 2008.

Bion, Wilfred Ruprecht. *Experiences in Groups and Other Papers.* London: Routledge, 1989.

Bounie, David; Bourreau, Marc and Waelbroeck, Patrick. *"Pirates or Explorers? Analysis of Music Consumption in French Graduate Schools," Working Paper.* Paris: ENST-Paris, 2005.

Bourdeau de Fontenay, Alain; Bourdeau de Fontenay, Eric C. and Pupillo, Lorenzo. "The Economics of Peer-to-Peer," E. M. Noam and L. Pupillo, *Peer-to-Peer Video: The Economics, Policy, and Culture of Today's New Mass Medium.* New York: Springer, 2008, 37–78.

Bourdeau de Fontenay, Alain and Liebenau, Jonathan M. "Modeling Scale and Scope in Telecommunications Industry." *Communications & Strategies*, 2006, 61, pp. 139–56.

Bourdeau de Fontenay, Alain; Liebenau, Jonathan M. and Savin, A. Brian. "A New View of Scale and Scope in the Telecommunications Industry: Implications for Competition and Innovation." *Communications & Strategies*, 2005, *60*(4), pp. 85–103.

Bourdeau de Fontenay, Alain and Nakamura, Kyoshi. "A Critical Analysis of Public Service Broadcasting in the Digital Environment," *TPRC.* Arlington, VA: CITI, Columbia Business School, 2006.

Bresnahan, Timothy F. and Trajtenberg, Manuel. "General Purpose Technologies – Engines of Growth." *Journal of Econometrics*, 1995, 65(1), pp. 83–108.

Buchanan, James M. and Tullock, Gordon. *The Calculus of Consent: Logical Foundations of Constitutional Democracy.* Ann Arbor: University of Michigan Press, 1962.

Bullock, Charles J. "Trust Literature: A Survey and a Criticism." *Quarterly Journal of Econometrics*, 1901, *15*(2), pp. 167–207.

Cabral, Luis M.B. *Introduction to Industrial Organization.* Cambridge, MA: MIT Press, 2000.

Chesbrough, Henry and Rosenbloom, Richard S. "The Role of Business Model in Capturing Value from Innovation: Evidence from Xerix Corporation's Technology Spin-Off Companies." *Industrial and Corporate Change*, 2002, 11(3), pp. 529–555.

Chiang, Eric P. and Assane, Djeto. "Determinants of Music Copyright Violations on the University Campus." *Journal of Cultural Economics*, 2007, *31*(3).

Christensen, Clayton M. "The Rigid Disk Drive Industry: A History of Commercial and Technological Disturbance." *The Business History Review*, 1993, *67*(4), pp. 531–588.

Christensen, Clayton M. *The Innovator's Dilemma: When New Technologies Cause Great Firm to Fail.* Boston, MA: Harvard Business School Press, 2000.

Christin, Nicolas; Weigend, Andreas S. and Chuang, John. *"Content Availability, Pollution and Poisoning in File Sharing Peer-to-Peer Networks," ACM EC'05.* Vancouver, 2005.

Diamond, Jared M. *Collapse: How Societies Choose to Fail or Succeed.* New York: Penguin, 2005.

Duchène, Anne and Waelbroeck, Patrick. *"Legal and Technological Battle in Music Industry: Information-Push vs. Information-Pull Technologies," Sauder School of Business Working Paper.* Vancouver: University of British Columbia, 2004.

Einav, Gali. "College Students: The Rationale for Peer-to-Peer Video File Sharing," E. M. Noam and L. Pupillo, *Peer-to-Peer Video: The Economics, Policy, and Culture of Today's New Mass Medium.* New York: Springer, 2008,

Evans, David S. and Schmalensee, Richard. *"The Industrial Organization of Markets with Two-Sided Platforms," NBER Working Papers.* Cambridge, MA: NBER, 2005.

Felipe, Jesus and Fisher, Franklin M. "Aggregation in Production Functions: What Applied Economists Should Know," 2001.

Fisher, William W. III. *Promises to Keep: Technology, Law, and the Future of Entertainment.* Palo Alto: Stanford University Press, 2004.

Frank, Robert H. *Microeconomics and behavior*. New York: McGraw-Hill Irwin, 2006.
Friedman, Milton. "The Methodology of Positive Economics," M. Friedman, *Essays in Positive Economics*. Chicago: Chicago University Press, 1953, 3–43.
Garcia-Murillo, Martha A. and MacInnes, Ian. "The Impact of Incentives in the Telecommunications Act of 1996 on Corporate Strategies," 29th TPRC Conference. 2001.
Gayer, Amit and Shy, Oz. "Copyright Enforcement in the Digital Era." *CESifo Economic Studies*, 2005, *51*(2–3), pp. 477–489.
Gibbs, Mark. "Riaa: Licensed to Hack?," *NetworkWorld*. 2002, 62.
Glasmeier, Amy. "Technological Discontinuities and Flexible Production Networks: The Case of Switzerland and the World Watch Industry." *Research Policy*, 1991, 20(5), pp. 469–485.
Gordon, Steve. *The Future of the Music Business: How to Succeed in the New Digital Technologies*. Berkeley, CA: Backbeat Books, 2005.
Granovetter, Mark. "Economic Action and Social Structure: The Problem of Embeddedness." *American Journal of Sociology*, 1985, *91*(3), pp. 481–510.
Hardin, Garrett. "The Tragedy of the Commons." *Science*, 1968, *162*, pp. 1243–1248.
Hardin, Garrett. "Extensions of 'the Tragedy of the Commons'." *Science*, 1998, 280, pp. 682–683.
Hayek, Friedrich A. "The Use of Knowledge in Society." *American Economic Review*, 1945, *35*(4), pp. 519–530.
Hong, Seung-Hyun. "The Recent Growth of the Internet and Changes in Household-Level Demand for Entertainment." *Information Economics and Policy*, 2007, *19*(3–4), pp. 304–318.
Hughes, Jerald; Lang, Karl Reiner and Vragov, Roumen. "An Analytical Framework for Evaluating Peer-to-Peer Business Models." *Electronic Commerce Research and Applications*, 2008, *7*(1), pp. 105–118.
Jullien, Bruno. "Two-Sided Markets and Electronic Intermediaries," G. Illing and M. Peitz, *Industrial Organization and the Digital Economy*. Cambridge, MA: MIT Press, 2006, 273–300.
Kahneman, Daniel and Tversky, Amos. "Prospect Theory: An Analysis of Decision Under Risk." *Econometrica*, 1979, *47*(2), pp. 263–292.
Karagiannis, Thomas; Broida, Andre; Brownlee, Nevil; Claffy, KC and Faloutsos, Michalis. "Is P2p Dying or Just Hiding?," IEEE Globecom. Dallas, 2004.
Kinney, Thomas A. *The Carriage Trade: Making Horse-Drawn Vehicles in America*. Baltimore: John Hopkins University Press, 2004.
Kirman, Alan P. "Whom or What Does the Representative Individual Representative Individual Represent?" *Journal of Economic perspectives*, 1992, *6*(2), pp. 117–136.
Koman, Richard. "RIAA Willing to Take Its Lumps in Filesharing Fight," *ZDNet*. 2007.
Kono, Satoshi. *"Interactive Media in Japan: Update,"* New York: CITI, Columbia University, 2008.
Krishnan, Ramayya; Smith, Michael D. and Telang, Rahul. "The Economics of Peer-to-Peer Networks." *Journal of Information Technology Theory and Applications*, 2003, *5*(3), pp. 31–44.
Krishnan, Ramayya; Smith, Michael D.; Tang, Zhulei and Telang, Rahul. "Digital Business Models for Peer-to-Peer Networks: Analysis and Economic Issue." *Review of Network Economics*, 2007, *6*(2), pp. 194–213.
Lee, Edward. "The Ethics of Innovation: P2p Software Developers and Designing Substantial Noninfringing Uses under the Sony Doctrine." *Journal of Business Ethics*, 2005, *62*, pp. 147–162.
Leeds, Jeff. "Radiohead Finds Sales, Even after Downloads," New York Times. New York, 2008.
Liebowitz, Stan J. *"Alternative Copyright Systems: The Problems with a Compulsory License,"* Dallas: School of Management, University of Texas at Dallas, 2003.
Liebowitz, Stan J. "File-Sharing: Creative Destruction or Just Plain Destruction." *Journal of Law and Economics*, 2006, *49*(1), pp. 1–28.
Liebowitz, Stan J. "File-Sharing: Creative Destruction or Just Plain Destruction." *Journal of Law and Economics*, 2007, *49*(1), pp. 1–28.
Liebowitz, Stan J. and Watt, Richard. "How to Best Ensure Remuneration for Creators in the Market for Music? Copyright and Its Alternatives." *Journal of Economic Surveys*, 2006, *20*(4), pp. 513–545.

Lipsey, Richard G.; Carlaw, Kenneth I. and Bekar, Clifford T. *Economic Transformations: General Purposes Technologies and Long Term Economic Growth*. New York: Oxford University Press, 2005.

Lovallo, Dan P. and Sibony, Olivier. "Distortions and Deceptions in Strategic Decisions." *The McKinsey Quarterly*, 2006.

Malan, David J. and Smith, Michael D. *"Host-Based Detection of Worms through Peer-to-Peer Cooperation," ACM WORM'05*. Fairfax, VA: ACM, 2005.

Malerba, Franco; Nelson, Richard R.; Orsenigo, Luigi and Winter, Sidney G. "Vertical Integration and Disintegration of Computer Firms: A History-Friendly Model of Coevolution of the Computer and Semiconductor." *Industrial and Corporate Change*, 2008, *17*(2), pp. 2197–2231.

Markoff, John. *"Two Views of Innovation, Colliding in Washington,"* New York Times. New York, 2008.

McMillan, John. *Reinventing the Bazaar; a Natural History of Markets*. New York: Norton, 2002.

Moreno, Jenalia. *"Recording/Hispanic Music Staying Upbeat/Producers Say Illegal Downloading a Problem for Genre,"* Houston Chronicle. Houston, 2006.

Nagle, Thomas T. and Hogan, John E. *The Strategy and Tactics of Pricing: A Guide to Growing More Profitably*. Saddle Brook, NJ: Prentice Hall, 2006.

Nelson, Richard R. and Rosenberg, Nathan. "Science, Technological Advance and Economic Growth." In A. D. J. Chandler, P. Hagström and Ö. Sölvell (Eds.), *The Dynamic Firm: The Role of Technology, Strategy, Organization, and Regions*. Oxford: Oxford University Press, 1999.

Nelson, Richard R. and Winter, Sydney S. *An Evolutionary Theory of Economic Change*. Cambridge, MA: Harvard University Press, 1982.

Netanel, Neil Weinstock. "Impose a Non-Commercial Use Levy to Allow Free Peer-to-Peer File Sharing." *Harvard Journal of Law and Technology*, 2003, *17*, pp. 1–84.

Noam, Eli M. "The Economics of User Generated Content and Peer-to-Peer: The Commons as the Enabler of Commerce," E. M. Noam and L. Pupillo, *Peer-to-Peer Video: The Economics, Policy, and Culture of Today's New Mass Medium*. New York: Springer, 2008, 3–13.

Oberholzer-Gee, Felix and Strumpf, Koleman. "The Effect of File Sharing on Record Sales: An Empirical Analysis." *Journal of Political Economy*, 2007, *115*(1).

Posner, Richard A. "The Social Costs of Monopoly and Regulation." *The Journal of Political Economy*, 1975, *83*(4), pp. 807–828.

Rob, Rafael and Waldfogel, Joel. *"Piracy on the High C's: Music Downloading, Sales Displacement, and Social Welfare in a Sample of College Students," NBER Working Paper Series*. Cambridge, MA: NBER, 2004.

Rob, Rafael and Waldfogel, Joel. "Piracy on the High C's: Music Downloading, Sales Displacement, and Social Welfare in a Sample of College Students." *Journal of Law and Economics*, 2006, *49*(1), pp. 29–62.

Rochet, Jean-Charles and Tirole, Jean. *"Defining Two-Sided Markets,"* Toulouse: IDEI, 2004.

Roxburgh, Charles. "The Human Factor in Strategic Decisions: Executives Should Recognize and Compensate for Cognitive Biases and Agency Problems." *The McKinsey Quarterly*, 2006.

Sandulli, Francesco D. and Martin-Barnero. "68 Cents Per Song: A Socio-Economic Survey on the Internet." *Convergence: The International Journal of Research into New Media Technologies*, 2007, *13*(1), pp. 63–78.

Schumpeter, Joseph A. *The Theory of Economic Development*. Cambridge, MA.: Harvard University Press, 1934.

Schumpeter, Joseph A. *Capitalism, Socialism and Democracy*. New York: Harper & Row, 1942.

Scranton, Philip. "Review of Albert Churella, from Steam to Diesel: Managerial Customs and Organizational Capabilities in the Twentieth Century American Locolotive Industry," *EH.Net, H.Net Reviews*. 1999.

Shermer, Michael. "The Prospects of Homo Economicus." *Scientific American*, 2007, *297*(1), pp. 40–42.

Shirky, Clay. "Napster and Music Distribution," C. Shirky, *Clay Shirky's Writings About the Internet: Economics and Culture, Media and Community, Open Source*. shirky-com, 2000.

Simon, Herbert A. *Models of Man*. New York: Wiley, 1957.
Spulber, Daniel F. *Market Microstructure: Intermediaries and the Theory of the Firm*. New York: Cambridge University Press, 1999.
Steinmueller, W. Edward. "Peer-to-Peer Media File Sharing: From Copyright Crisis to Market?," E. M. Noam and L. Pupillo, *Peer-to-Peer Video: The Economics, Policy, and Culture of Today's New Mass Medium*. New York: Springer, 2008,
Stigler, George J. "Monopoly," *The Concise Encyclopedia of Economics*.
Sull, Donald. "The Dynamics of Standing Still: Firestone Tire & Rubber and the Radial Revolution," M. L. Tushman and P. Anderson, *Managing Strategic Innovation and Change: A Collection of Readings*. New York: Oxford University Press, 2004, 108–128.
Temin, Peter. *The Fall of the Bell System*. Cambridge, MA: Cambridge University Press, 1987.
Thaler, Richard H. "From Homo Economicus to Homo Sapiens." *Journal of Economic perspectives*, 2000, *14*(1), pp. 133–141.
Tripsas, Mary and Gavetti, Giovanni. "Capabilities, Cognition, and Inertia," M. L. Tushman and J. C. Anderson, *Managing Strategic Innovation and Change*. New York: Oxford University Press, 2004, 18–32.
Tripsas, Mary and Gavetti, Giovanni. "Capabilities, Cognition, and Inertia: Evidence from Digital Imaging." *Strategic Management Journal*, 2000, *21*(10–11), pp. 1147–1161.
Tushman, Michael L. and O'Reilly, Charles A. III. "The Ambidextrous Organization: Managing Evolutionary and Revolutionary Change." *California Management Review*, 1996, *38*(4), pp. 8–29.
Tushman, Michael L. and Radov, Daniel B. "Rebirth of the Swiss Watch Industry – 1980–1992 (a)," *Harvard Business Online*. 2000a.
Tushman, Michael L. and Radov, Daniel B. "Rebirth of the Swiss Watch Industry – 1980–1992 (B)," *Harvard Business Online*. 2000b.
Walker, Donald A. "Walras' Theory of Tatonnement." *Journal of Political Economy*, 1987, *95*(4), pp. 758–774.
Williamson, Oliver E. "The New Institutional Economics: Taking Stock, Looking Ahead." *Journal of Economic Literature*, 2000, *38*(3), pp. 595–613.
Yang, Xiaokai. *New Classical Versus Neoclassical Frameworks*. Malden, MA: Blackwell, 2001.
Young, Allyn. "Increasing Returns and Economic Progress." *The Economic Journal*, 1928, *38*, pp. 527–542.
Zentner, Alejandro. "File Sharing and International Sales of Copyrighted Music: An Empirical Analysis with a Panel of Countries." *The B.E. Journal of Economic Analysis and Policy*, 2005, *5*(1).
Zentner, Alejandro. "Measuring the Effect of File Sharing on Music Purchases." *Journal of Law and Economics*, 2006, *49*(1), pp. 63–90.

About the Editors and Contributors

Editors

Dr. William H. Lehr is an economist and industry consultant. He is a research associate in the Computer Science and Artificial Intelligence Laboratory (CSAIL) at the Massachusetts Institute of Technology, currently working with the Communications Futures Program (http://cfp.mit.edu), which is an industry-academic multidisciplinary research effort focused on road mapping the communications value chain. Previously, he was the associate director of the MIT Research Program on Internet & Telecoms Convergence (ITC, http://itc.mit.edu/), and was an associate research scholar and assistant professor on the faculty of Columbia University's Graduate School of Business. His research focuses on the economics and regulatory policy of the Internet infrastructure industries. He teaches courses on the economics, business strategy, and public policy issues facing telecommunications, Internet, and eCommerce companies, and is a frequent speaker at international industry and academic conferences. In addition to academic research, he Lehr provides litigation, economic, and business strategy consulting services for firms in the information technology industries. He has prepared expert witness testimony for both private litigation and for regulatory proceedings before the FCC and numerous state commissions. He holds a Ph.D. in Economics from Stanford (1992), an M.B.A. from the Wharton Graduate School (1985), and M.S.E. (1984), B.S. (1979), and B.A. (1979) degrees from the University of Pennsylvania.

Dr. Lorenzo Maria Pupillo is an Executive Director in the Public Affairs Unit of Telecom Italia and Affiliated Researcher at Columbia Institute for Tele-Information. In Telecom Italia, he is working on Geographic Markets, Functional Separation, Next Generation Networks, and ICT Policy. He is an economist by training and has worked in many areas of telecommunications demand and regulatory analysis, publishing papers in applied econometrics and industrial organization. He has also been Advisor to the Global Information and Communication Technologies Department of the World Bank in Washington. He has also been adjunct professor of Economics of ICTs at University of Rome, La Sapienza. Before joining Telecom Italia in 1992, he was a member of technical staff at

AT&T Bell Laboratories in Murray Hill, NJ. He also serves on numerous committees for international organizations and on scientific and advisory boards around the globe. He earned a Ph.D. and an M.A. from University of Pennsylvania, an M.B.A. from Istituto Adriano Olivetti in Ancona, Italy, and an M.S. in Mathematics from University of Rome.

Contributors

Alain Bourdeau de Fontenay is a visiting scholar and Senior Affiliated Researcher with the Columbia Institute for Tele-Information (CITI), Columbia University, as well as cofounder of the International Telecommunications Society (ITS) and Bellcore's (Telcordia). Distinguished member of the Technical Staff, his recent research activities include organizing an international research team on the economics of the "exchange commons" to better account for externalities and other interdependences, a research project on Internet peering in an age of convergence with telephony with applications in areas such as Internet backbone competition, peer-to-peer networks, and vertical integration (www.citi.columbia.edu), and a study on economic growth, information and communications technologies (ICT), and inequality.

Eric Bourdeau de Fontenay is President and CEO of MusicDish as well as manager of the Toronto-based "kaiso" band Kobo Town. Eric has spent his career steeped in what has been called the "digital revolution." In the 1990s, he worked on a variety of policy issues surrounding the communication and broadband sectors for telecommunication carriers and regulators across the world. With the emergence of the Internet, he established MusicDish (formerly Tag It) in 1997 as a new media firm utilizing emerging technologies and models to produce, package, and distribute original web-based content. Making an early bet the music sector, he launched what has grown into some of the leading voices in the growing debates challenging and shaping the industry through its trade e-publications MusicDish and Mi2N. Under his leadership, MusicDish expanded into artist development through saturated marketing and online branding, using innovative strategies such as syndicated and relationship marketing, online street teams, and peer-to-peer viral distribution. He continues to be a frequent speaker at conferences worldwide.

Martin Cave is professor and director of the Centre for Management under Regulation, Warwick Business School. He holds bachelor's, master's, and doctoral degrees from Oxford University. Until 2001 he was professor of Economics at Brunel University. He specializes in regulatory economics. He is coauthor of *Understanding Regulation* (1999) and of *Essentials of Modern Spectrum Management* (2007), coeditor of the *Handbook of Telecommunications Economics*, Vol. 1 (2002) and Vol. 2 (2005), *Digital Broadcasting* (2006) and the *Oxford Handbook of Regulation* (forthcoming), and author of many articles in journals.

As well as his academic work he has also undertaken studies for the European Commission and advised regulatory agencies. He was a member of the UK Competition Commission from 1996 to 2002. He has advised the European Commission on broadband and international roaming issues, and has assisted energy, postal, telecommunications, water, and other regulatory agencies in the UK, Ireland, France, Germany, Greece, Portugal, Cyprus, Singapore, Australia, New Zealand, and elsewhere. He is responsible for two independent reviews of spectrum management carried out for the Chancellor of the Exchequer. In 2006, he was special adviser to the European Commissioner for Information Society and Broadcasting. He has advised the Lord Chancellor's department on regulatory reforms for legal services and in 2007 undertook an independent review of the regulation of social housing for the Secretary of State for Communities and Local Government, entitled Every Tenant Matters. He is currently undertaking a review of competition and innovation in the water industry for DEFRA and HM Treasury.

Brett Frischmann is visiting Cornell Law School during 2007–2008. He is an associate professor at the Loyola University Chicago School of Law, where he teaches courses in intellectual property and Internet law. He graduated Order of the Coif from the Georgetown University Law Center. After law school, he was an associate with Wilmer, Cutler & Pickering in Washington, DC, where his practice focused on communications, e-commerce, and intellectual property law. Prior to joining the Loyola faculty, he clerked for the Honorable Fred I. Parker of the U.S. Court of Appeals for the Second Circuit. He has published articles on a wide variety of topics, ranging from the law and economics of science and technology policy to the role of compliance institutions in international law. His recent work examines the relationships between infrastructural resources, property rights, commons, and spillovers. His scholarship has appeared in leading law journals, including the *Columbia Law Review*, the *University of Chicago Law Review*, and the *Minnesota Law Review*, as well as leading interdisciplinary journals, such as *Science* and the *Review of Law and Economics*. He is currently writing a book on social demand for open infrastructure that will be published by the Yale University Press in 2010.

Austan Goolsbee is a professor of Economics at the University of Chicago, Graduate School of Business, a research associate at the National Bureau of Economic Research, a research fellow of the American Bar Foundation, and an Alfred P. Sloan Research Fellow. His recent research has covered Internet commerce, network externalities, tax policy, and capital investment. He received a B.A. (summa cum laude, 1991) and an M.A. (1991) in Economics from Yale University, and a Ph.D. in Economics (1995) from M.I.T. He is currently editor of the Journal of Law and Economics and serves as a member of the Advisory Committee to the United States Census. In 2001, he was named one of the 100 Global Leaders for Tomorrow by the World Economic Forum. Previously he has served as a special consultant to the Department of Justice for Internet Policy, a member of the Macroeconomic Taskforce for Polish Economic Restructuring, and as a staff member for former Senator David Boren.

Janice Hauge is an assistant professor in the Department of Economics at the University of North Texas. She joined the University of North Texas in 2003 after receiving her doctorate in economics from the University of Florida. Prior to that she earned a B.A. at Hamilton College in New York and an M.Sc. degree from the London School of Economics. Her research focuses on industrial organization, regulation, and sports economics. Most recently she has conducted theoretical and empirical research analyzing the structure of telecommunications markets, telecommunications and energy policy, and the welfare implications of telecommunications policies and regulations. He teaches graduate and undergraduate courses in industrial organization, regulation, microeconomic theory, and the economics of sports.

Mark Jamison is director of the Public Utility Research Center (PURC) at the University of Florida and also serves as its director of Telecommunications Studies. He provides international training and research on business and government policy, focusing primarily on utilities and network industries, and codirects the PURC/World Bank International Training Program on Utility Regulation and Strategy. He received a Ph.D. from the University of Florida and an M.S. and B.S. from Kansas State University. His current research topics include leadership and institutional development in regulation, competition and subsidies in telecommunications, and regulation for next generation networks. He has conducted education programs in numerous countries in Asia, Africa, Europe, the Caribbean, and North, South, and Central America. He is also a research associate with the UF Center for Public Policy Research and with Cambridge Leadership Associates, where he provides consulting and training on adaptive leadership. He is an affiliated scholar with the Communications Media Center at New York Law School. He serves on the editorial board of Utilities Policy and is a referee/reviewer for the International Journal of Industrial Organization, The Information Society, Telecommunications Policy, and Utilities Policy.

Eli Noam is professor of Finance and Economics at the Columbia University Graduate School of Business and Director of the Columbia Institute for Tele-Information. He has also served as Public Service Commissioner engaged in the telecommunications and energy regulation of New York State and on the White House's President's IT Advisory Committee. His publications include 27 books and over 400 articles on U.S. and international telecommunications, television, Internet, and regulation subjects. He served as a board member for the federal government's FTS-2000 telephone network, of the IRS' computer modernization project, and of the National Computer Lab. He is a member of the Council on Foreign Relations. He received an AB (1970, Phi Beta Kappa), a Ph.D. in Economics (1975) and a JD law degree (1975) from Harvard University. He is a member of the New York and Washington D.C. bars, a licensed radio amateur Advanced Class, and a commercially rated pilot.

Bruce Owen is the Gordon Cain Senior Fellow at SIEPR. He is the Morris M. Doyle Professor in Public Policy and director of the Public Policy Program and also a professor, by courtesy, of Economics. He cofounded Economists Inc. in 1981 and was president and chief executive officer until recently. Previously, he was the chief economist of the Antitrust Division of the U.S. Department of Justice and, earlier, of the White House Office of Tele-communications Policy. He was a faculty member in the schools of business and law at Duke University, and before that at Stanford University. He is the author or coauthor of numerous articles and eight books, including *Television Economics* (1974), *Economics and Freedom of Expression* (1975), *The Regulation Game* (1978), *The Political Economy of Deregulation* (1983), *Video Economics* (1992), and *Electric Utility Mergers: Principles of Antitrust Analysis* (1994). He has been an expert witness in a number of antitrust and regulatory proceedings, including United States v. AT&T, United States Football League v. National Football League, and the Federal Energy Regulatory Commission review of Southern California Edison's proposed acquisition of San Diego Gas and Electric Co. In 1992, he headed a World Bank task force that advised the government of Argentina in drafting a new antitrust law. More recently, he has advised government agencies in Mexico and the United States on telecommunications policy and Peru on antitrust policy. He is a consultant to the World Bank in connection with the economic evaluation of legal and judicial reform projects. His latest book, *The Internet Challenge to Television*, was published by Harvard University Press in 1999. His research interests include regulation and antitrust, economic analysis of law, economic development and legal reform, and intellectual property rights. He is a specialist in telecommunications and mass media economics.

Gregory Rosston is a Research Fellow at SIEPR and Visiting Lecturer in Economics at Stanford University. His research has focused on industrial organization, antitrust, and regulation. He has written numerous articles on competition in local telecommunications, implementation of the Telecommunications Act of 1996, auctions, and spectrum policy. He has also coedited two books, including Interconnection and the Internet: Selected Papers from the 1996 Telecommunications Policy Research Conference. At Stanford, he has taught Regulation and Antitrust in the economics department and a seminar for seniors in the Public Policy program. Prior to joining Stanford University, he served as Deputy Chief Economist of the Federal Communications Commission. At the FCC, he helped to implement the Telecommunications Act. In this work, he helped to design and write the rules the Commission adopted as a framework to encourage efficient competition in telecommunications markets. He also helped with the design and implementation of the FCC's spectrum auctions. He received his Ph.D. in Economics from Stanford University and his A.B. in Economics with Honors from the University of California.

Nadine Strossen is professor of Law at New York Law School. She has written, lectured, and practiced extensively in constitutional law, civil liberties, and international human rights. Since 1991, she has served as President of the American Civil Liberties Union, the first woman to head the nation's oldest and largest civil liberties organization. The National Law Journal has named Strossen one of America's "100 Most Influential Lawyers." She makes approximately 200 public presentations per year, before diverse audiences, and she also comments frequently on legal issues in the national media. Her more than 250 published writings have appeared in many scholarly and general interest publications. Her book, *Defending Pornography: Free Speech, Sex, and the Fight for Women's Rights*, was named by the *New York Times* a "notable book" of 1995. Her coauthored book, *Speaking of Race, Speaking of Sex: Hate Speech, Civil Rights, and Civil Liberties*, was named an "outstanding book" by the Gustavus Myers Center for the Study of Human Rights in North America. She graduated Phi Beta Kappa from Harvard College (1972) and magna cum laude from Harvard Law School (1975).

Hal Varian is the chief economist at Google. He started in May 2002 as a consultant and has been involved in many aspects of the company, including auction design, econometric, finance, corporate strategy, and public policy. He also holds academic appointments at the University of California, Berkeley in three departments: business, economics, and information management. He received his SB degree from MIT in 1969 and his MA in Mathematics and Ph.D. in Economics from UC Berkeley in 1973. He has also taught at MIT, Stanford, Oxford, Michigan, and other universities around the world. He is a fellow of the Guggenheim Foundation, the Econometric Society, and the American Academy of Arts and Sciences. He was Coeditor of the American Economic Review from 1987 to 1990 and holds honorary doctorates from the University of Oulu, Finland and the University of Karlsruhe, Germany. He has published numerous papers in economic theory, industrial organization, financial economics, econometrics, and information economics. He is the author of two major economics textbooks which have been translated into 22 languages. He is the coauthor of a bestselling book on business strategy, *Information Rules: A Strategic Guide to the Network Economy*, and wrote a monthly column for the *New York Times* from 2000 to 2007.

Index

GPSR Compliance

The European Union's (EU) General Product Safety Regulation (GPSR) is a set of rules that requires consumer products to be safe and our obligations to ensure this.

If you have any concerns about our products, you can contact us on ProductSafety@springernature.com

In case Publisher is established outside the EU, the EU authorized representative is:

Springer Nature Customer Service Center GmbH
Europaplatz 3
69115 Heidelberg, Germany

Batch number: 10844675

Printed by Printforce, the Netherlands